A Social History of Contemp
Democratic Media

The last few decades have helped dispel the myth that media should remain driven by high-end professionals and market share. This book puts forward the concept of "communications from below" in contrast to the "globalization from above" that characterizes many new developments in international organization and media practices. By examining the social and technological roots that influence current media evolution, Drew allows readers to understand not only the YouTubes and Facebooks of today, but also to anticipate the trajectory of the technologies to come.

Beginning with a look at the inherent weaknesses of the US broadcasting model of mass media, Drew outlines the early 1960s and 1970s experiments in grassroots media, where artists and activists began to reengineer electronic technologies to target local communities and underserved audiences. From these local projects emerged national and international communications projects, creating production models, social networks, and citizen expectations that would challenge traditional means of electronic media and cultural production. Drew's perspective puts the social and cultural use of the user, not the particular media form, at the center. Thus the structure of the book focuses on the local, the national, and the global desire for communications, regardless of the means.

Jesse Drew is Professor of Technocultural Studies at the University of California, Davis, United States.

Routledge Research in Cultural and Media Studies

For a full list of titles in this series, please visit www.routledge.com

A Social History of Contemporary Democratic Media

Jesse Drew

Routledge
Taylor & Francis Group

LONDON AND NEW YORK

First published 2013
by Routledge
711 Third Avenue, New York, NY 10017

Simultaneously published in the UK
by Routledge
2 Park Square, Milton Park, Abingdon, Oxfordshire OX14 4RN

First issued in paperback 2015

*Routledge is an imprint of the Taylor & Francis Group,
an informa business*

Library of Congress Cataloging-in-Publication Data
Drew, Jesse, 1955–
  A social history of contemporary democratic media / by Jesse Drew.
      pages cm. — (Routledge research in cultural and media studies ; 50)
  Includes bibliographical references and index.
  1. Citizen journalism.   2. Social media.   3. Digital media.   4. Local
mass media.   5. Mass media—History.   I. Title.
  PN4784.C615D74 2013
  302.23'1—dc23
  2012047197

ISBN: 978-0-415-65932-1 (hbk)
ISBN: 978-1-138-88825-8 (pbk)
ISBN: 978-0-203-07499-2 (ebk)

Typeset in Sabon
by Apex CoVantage, LLC

Contents

Acknowledgments

I am thrilled to write the acknowledgments for this book, a project that recognizes the many achievements of media makers who have tinkered, invented, advocated, and organized for an invigorated democracy that insists on the rights of all to participate in the public sphere of speech and communications. These rabble-rousers, artists, troublemakers, loudmouths, archivists, alchemists, hackers, performers, soap-boxers, pranksters, exhibitionists, activists, organizers, and musicians have conspired to challenge a monopoly of ideas established by media conglomerates and authoritarian governments. Marginalized and dismissed for decades, the cumulative work of these communications rebels is rebuilding a link between media and democracy that has long been broken. Working in small groups, doing unappreciated and unglamorous work in often impoverished and precarious conditions, these believers in democratic media are finally seeing the ideas they champion embraced by large sectors of the global public. Media activists are cheered that it is no longer necessary to explain why public access to the means of communication is absolutely vital to democracy. I approach these acknowledgments with trepidation, however, knowing I will only begin to touch upon the multitudes of people who have made so many valuable contributions to media and democracy and to whom I owe a great personal debt.

At fifteen years of age I had the good fortune to land in a communal network based in the state of Vermont, where many members had been part of the radical film collective *Newsreel*: Roz Payne, Robert Kramer, John Douglas, Jane Kramer, and many other filmmakers who brought dissenting viewpoints to life in picture and sound. There I was exposed to a plethora of alternative media, for in our house, in addition to an enormous film collection, was an extensive periodicals library where underground newspapers arrived daily—*The Great Speckled Bird*, the *Black Panther*, *Chicago Seed*, *LA Free Press*, *Palante*, *NY Rat*, *Rising Up Angry*, the *Liberated Guardian*, and many others. In Vermont I worked and lived with an incredibly vibrant community of creative, talented and generous people: Peter Huber, co-producer of the multimedia slide show *Vermont Speaks for Itself*, which helped move Vermont into the progressive state it is today; John Peter Phillips, who shared the magic of photographic development in the basement of our rickety old house on North Street; Barry Levine, who I could count on to discuss the implications of media late into the night. I had the privilege of co-launching the Burlington, Vermont, community newspaper *The North Country Star* with the talents and skills of Jon Ment, Mark Furnari, Debbie Gooch, Joyce Bressler, Meri Furnari, Gene Bergman, and many others. This paper, among other things, helped introduce the candidature of Vermont progressive Bernie Sanders. My colleagues in Vermont were instrumental in demonstrating how ideas became valuable by testing them in practice, and much of that practice was how media could organize a community. Thanks to so many others during that Vermont adventure: Sandy Baird, Bob Mueller, David Ross, Caroll Ishee, Paul Glushanok, Greg Guma, Jane Melnick, Tom Phillips, Dee Dee Frazin, Stuart Meacham, Julie Halpern, Ellen Shaffer, Frank Eppich, The Living Theatre, Peter McFarland, Shannon McFarland, Jim Nolfi, Tim Downey, Jennie Ball, Barbara Nolfi, Hilary Woodruff, Joy Catalano, Fletcher Oakes, Barry Flicker, Margaret Boehm, Barry Sofer, Fitz, Tori Osborn, Debbie Bookchin, Michael Parenti, Cathy Snyder, Roby Colodny, Amy Troubh, Murray Bookchin, Larry Rosenstock. In 1975, I was recruited to California by Fred Ross Sr. to work with the United Farm Workers Union, and so I went west, an *El Malcriado* stuck in my back pocket. Active in the labor movement and union reform for years afterward, my work often revolved around producing a myriad of newsletters, flyers, and pamphlets outlining the various viewpoints and strategies of labor activists. Working on assembly lines in traditional factories, I became aware of the immense power of the culture industry over the minds and imaginations of so many of my coworkers. Later, living in France for almost two years opened my eyes to the rich diversity of media options in many other countries. In the library at the Pompidou Center in Paris, I was excited to read in the magazine *After Image* about a new media group that had formed in New York City called Paper Tiger Television. The list of people to thank in the Paper Tiger Television circle would fill all the pages of this book— committed and wonderful people like Dee Dee Halleck, Martha Wallner, Daniel Brooks, Michael Eisenmenger, Mary Feaster, Adriene Jenik, Fiona Boneham, Dan Marcus, Simone Farkhondeh, Nathalie Magnan, Linda Iannacone, Carlos Pareja, Karen Einstein, Shu Lea Cheang, Laura Stein, Maria Byck. My West Coast Paper Tiger colleagues are all too numerous to mention as well: Alan Steinheimer, James Anthony, Luanna Plunkett, Neal Morrison, Christine Cheng, Sarah Lewison, Todd Edelman, Dylan Nolfi, Steve Rhodes, and in particular Carla Leshne, my co-conspirator in the video operation *Mission Creek Video*. I also want to acknowledge the importance of the Mission District media arts community, which helped form the creative and supportive incubator that allowed so much media to flourish: Craig Baldwin, Chris Carlsson, Bill Daniel, Sam Green, Rigo, Greta Snider, Valerie Soe, Scott Williams, Maria Luisa Mendonca, Ted White, Jeff Goldthorpe, Lise Swenson, Daisy Anarchy, Miya Masaoka, and so many others. The community of those committed to media and democracy in the Bay Area is enormous, and their contributions range from legal defense, to filmmaking, to publishing, to performance: Rebecca Solnit, Stoney Burke, Lauren Church, Stephen Parr, Nicole Sawaya, Mona Caron, Steve Hiatt, Iain Boal, Dave "Dog" Swan, Tom Athanasiou, Daniel Del Solar, Steve Hamilton, Alan Korn, Mark Gunson, Gloria La Riva, Tom Hope, William Sievert, Tony Serra, Genny Lim, Adam Cornford, Aviva Grossman, Suzanne Takehara, Rick Longinotti, SRL, Target Video, Linda Pilkin, Mary Liz Thomson, Sasha Lilley, Katie Reifman, Juana Alicia, Terri Massin, Lisa Rudman, Norman Solomon, The SF Mime Troup, Ramsey Kanaan, Keith Hennessy, Natalie Jeremijenko, Erik Davis, Eric Theise, Tetsuo Kogawa, Ben Bagdikian, Herb Schiller, Carol Leigh, Christian Parenti, Pratap Chatterjee, Richard Becker, Denny Smith, David Stern, KPFA, Pam Hitchcock, Joe Berry, Mike Hitchcock, Spain Rodriguez, Barbara Dane, Lonnie Ding, Babette Hogan, Dan Perkins, Lydia Ely, Laura Fraser, Fred Rinne, Utah Phillips, Paul Boden, George Kuchar, Keith Knight, Jackie Summel, Aaron Noble, Med-o, Maxine Gomez, Niki Cousino, Blanche Bebb, Kim Malcheski, Ksiel Sztundel, Caitlin Manning, Robin Balliger, Mike Freeman, Matt Callahan, Osha Neumann, Jello Biafra, Dangerous George, Peter Franck, John Davis, Steve Polta, Marshall Weber, Steve Seid, George Metesky, Aron Ranen, May Ying Welsh, Nathalie Borgers, Hobart Swann, Steve Anker, Jonathan Rosales, Kerry Laitala, Dee Dee Russell, Maggie Morse, Bruce Connor, David Cox, Molly Hankwitz, Mike Alcalay, Gail Silva, Larry Bensky, Toni Lane, Patrick Macias, Michael Couzens, Luke Hiken, Rosa de Anda, Jon Fromer, Tim Yohannon, Julie Mackaman, The Yes Men, Marti Hiken, Jaime Levy, Eric Quezada, David Trend, Chuck Mobley, Rick Prelinger, Lynn Hershman, Christine Tamblyn, Michael Pickman, Megan Pelinger, Roxanne Dunbar-Ortiz, Stephen Dunnifer, Ellison Horne, Steve Zeltzer, Gene Pepi, Steve Lambert, Julio Morales, Keith McHenry. Special thanks must go to Michelle Wolf, who inspired me to become an educator. Much credit to my mentors at the University of Texas in the Radio-Television-Film department, in particular Karin Wilkins, John Downing, Harry Cleaver, and Douglas Kellner. In Texas, I worked with an amazing group of colleagues publishing *(sub)TEX*, a radical alternative monthly, and for that I owe much to Salah Hassan, Sheila Contreras, Polo Rodriguez, Brendan Guilfoyle, Stefan Wray, Natasha Sinutko, and to the many others in my Austin, Texas, crowd: Laura Saponara, Tamara Ford, Doreen Piano, Sheila Ghosh, and Rahdi Taylor.

In Davis, California, I am thrilled to be in cahoots with a vibrant media, art, and DIY scene, which includes Jeff Shaw, Darrick Servis, Autumn Labbe-Renault, Sakura Saunders, Stephen Inness, Melissa Chandon, jesikah maria ross, Wrye Sententia, Richard Boire, John Natsoulas, Andy Jones, Malaquias Montoya, Bob Ostertag, Larry Bogad, Julie Wyman, Blake Stimson, Liz Constable, and Chris Benner, along with a great group of colleagues in Cinema and Technocultural Studies and throughout the UC Davis campus.

Special thanks to Sara Anderson, Anita Grisales, Melissa Strong, John Haffner, and Routledge Press for assisting with this manuscript. Thanks also to Rich Bolecek, lifelong friend and fellow voyager.

Finally, enormous thanks to my family: my wife, principle collaborator, and closest friend, Glenda; my terrific kids, Penelope, Rocket, and Mariko; and my parents, Bob and Joann, who always insisted that everyone has the right to speak.

Introduction

A specter is haunting the boardrooms of media conglomerates—the specter of public intervention into mass media. In a mediascape where once only massive broadcasting and publishing conglomerates dared to tread, an active public has gained ground. Citizens, activists, collectives, artists, musicians, labor organizations, social commentators, and community organizations are contributing their viewpoints, creative energy, and ideas to increasingly larger audiences. Personal communications technologies—including blogs, social networks, online communities, video streaming, and peer-to-peer file sharing networks—have become facets of everyday life. The "blogosphere" has changed from a clever coining of a new word to a concrete entity where opinions are formed, expressed, and argued. A substantial amount of our knowledge of current events now comes from the postings of participants and the video cameras of witnesses, rather than the paid scribes and videographers of mass media institutions. Breaking news is now often revealed via the web of social networks, rather than the broadcast or the special edition newspaper. Media businesses attempt to recoup their once captive audience by adopting, co-opting, or absorbing some of the new media innovations, typically with little success. The proliferation of these various levels of participatory media and the decline of traditional media are acknowledged widely, yet most "experts" provide very little understanding or context for this phenomenon. The accepted wisdom, provided by journalists and corporate public relations, is that new media is powered primarily by the entrepreneurial and technological wizardry at the heart of Silicon Valley, Hollywood, and Wall Street. Such a simplistic and deterministic analysis of these developments provides a one-dimensional model for understanding the radical changes in media and communications that have profound consequences for our social structure, our democracy, and our economy.

A deeper analysis reveals that the stimulus and motivation behind many of these new communication methods came as much from artistic and activist interventions as from entrepreneurial capitalism. A significant part of the democratizing trend in new electronic media can be traced to the video-activism of public access television, subcultural computer bulletin-board hacktivism (BBSs), the clandestine broadcasting of "pirate radio," and the site-specific public art spectacle of micro-cinema. These are all examples of "communications from below" movements that have strongly influenced the growth and direction of the homegrown and DIY (do-it-yourself) technologies currently in vogue. This book seeks to reclaim new media's recent history and explore its origins in order to understand the direction, motivation, and potential of democratic communications.

Blogs, mobile media, podcasts, instant messaging, online communities, miniature video, wireless networking, and the exponentially expanding universe of electronic practices and associated gadgetry multiply daily. Early adopters of technology—the adventurous vanguard of consumers courted by marketing departments everywhere—pride themselves on staying current with these technologies. Other consumers breathlessly try to catch up. Many people, perhaps the majority, are left feeling inadequate and left behind, overwhelmed by media reports and advertising claims about the technological marvels to comprehend and master. Still, there is a general sense of wonder and excitement about the new digital devices and amazement at how quickly they appear, are widely adopted, and are then abandoned. What consumers often do not appreciate, however, is that these commodities are more than toys, electronic distractions, or fetish objects; they are communication devices. Though often presented via the latest marketing campaigns as the entertainment must-have commodity for the young or the glamorous (or both), it must be understood that the principal factor driving their popularity is the promise of an increased ability to communicate: point to point, individual to mass, mass to individual. The desire to create media, express one's opinion, or mark one's social status is irrefutable, despite the culture industry's steady supply of entertainment commodities and the one-hundred-year-old legacy of the broadcasting model of communications.

With the proliferation of cell phones, video cameras, social networks, and iPods/iPads, it is tempting to think the public access to DIY media tools is a recent development, put forth by the good people of Apple, Microsoft, and Sony in a noble attempt to bring the public back into the media equation. Despite ongoing advertising campaigns that champion their products for giving the public control, choice, and freedom over their media environments, these corporations ultimately have no problem with the dominant broadcasting model of communication, conceived as a central commercial hub encircled by the public as consumers. They do not want to topple this model; they want to inherit it. The collapse of the traditional model of media consumption has shaken the foundations of the well-established media corporations tracked and analyzed by media scholar Ben Bagdikian over the last few decades, particularly of the "Big Five": Time Warner, News Corporation (Fox), Viacom, Bertelsmann, and Disney.[1] Their weakness has unleashed ongoing corporate battles for control over the lucrative market for media consumption. The decline of the broadcasting model of media, however, is not a victory for Wall Street; it is a crisis. The centralized model of broadcasting was not felled by the technological achievement of the telecommunications, electronics, and entertainment companies. It was pushed over the edge by generations of innovative media makers, artists, technologists, and activists who understood that media was too precious a commodity to be left solely in the hands of communications conglomerates and media moguls. The media-from-below shift was fostered by many popular movements that strove for media-self-reliance, carried out with a DIY attitude. These creative forces have ranged from video artists and public access advocates to punk and hip-hop artists to radical political and organizational movements. Their work lies behind much of what has helped push us into a new paradigm of media participation. These histories, this past, are too often left out of discussions of contemporary media changes. This book intends to investigate the catalytic influences of social, artistic, and activist groups and their uses of technology, through historical research that also draws on my own personal involvement in these experiments over the last few decades.

THE HOME PAGE AND THE WORLD WIDE WEB

When the World Wide Web reached popular consciousness in the mid-1990s, many media giants' assumptions were turned upside down. What was unique about the early Web experience was the enormous popularity of personal Web sites. The intimacy of homemade sites was a driving impetus for many of the curious media seekers. One of the most popular early sites was Bianca's Smut Shack, an early, primitive by today's standards, Web site that allowed user posts and interactions, which, despite the name, were more banal than indecent. Another was Justin's Links to the Underground, a similar online journey into the personal realm of a young man willing to share his "stuff" and his views with the public. The *New York Times* referred to Justin Hall, the creator of the site, as "the founding father of personal blogging."[2] The ability of almost anyone to master HTML, self-publish such information, and open up their "home" page to others was powerful and exciting. Such activity was a different and refreshing change from the sterile and impersonal sites of mass media. The advertising agencies working on behalf of McDonald's, Coca-Cola, and other corporate enterprises were caught off guard by the new trend, as they poured millions of dollars into Web presences that were not much different from their print publications. Many multinationals found that their corporate names had already been acquired by savvy Web enthusiasts and often had to purchase their trademark domain names back at exorbitant sums. The vast sums of money unleashed by corporations helped drive the "dot-com" boom of the 1990s, a time when many young people who knew a little HTML and some image editing tools could land prestigious jobs in Web startups in San Francisco, New York, Chicago, and other urban centers. Despite this corporate investment, Web users chose, instead, to click on sites such as McSpotlight, an anti-McDonald's site run by Greenpeace members in London, which had over a quarter of a million visitors in its first year of 1996–97.[3]

The Web's ability to present an alternative viewpoint or open up a personal side of one's life, inviting people into a "home" page, was unique and a surprising development in an increasingly depersonalized media landscape. It underscored that something definitely new was developing, something different from the massive, centralized distributors of programs, advertising, and entertainment that broadcasters, cable networks, and satellite delivery systems offered. Before the Web explosion, of course, there were already established online communities, such as The Well or Peacenet, that provided personal, professional, and informal exchange through a UNIX-based text environment. Other text-based electronic bulletin board systems such as Usenet and Fidonet satisfied similar needs. These precursors to today's social networking sites were limited, however, as they required a modicum of technical expertise and, for some, a paid membership. When the Web arrived, it provided images, text, and sound to anyone with a basic browser. It was the Mosaic browser, developed with federal funds provided by the High Performance Computing and Communication Act of 1991,[4] that really opened up the Web to millions of newbie networks surfers. It was the first time on a massive scale that the public was able to experience and appreciate what community and local media advocates such as George Stoney[5] or Dee Dee Halleck[6] had been championing for decades: that ordinary people had something important and unique to say and that millions of people would be interested in it.

The importance of public access to the means of communication had been articulated and advocated in the founding documents of many media activist projects throughout the 1970s and 1980s. As early as 1971, the seminal "Guerilla Television" handbook declared that, "Each citizen of Media-America should be guaranteed as a birthright access to the means of distribution of information."[7] The development of cable television through the 1970s and 1980s energized community media advocates and prompted a grassroots demand for public access television coast-to-coast. The possibility of an infinite number of information channels brought about by cable led to a questioning of who controls and who decides what media and information will be available to the American people. Internationally, pressure for democratizing media coincided with UNESCO's release of the MacBride report in 1980, a document that criticized the existence of a one-sided flow of information from the developed world to the underdeveloped world and spurred calls for building a New World Information and Communication Order.[8] The desire for two-way, democratic mass media has a long historical thread, from Bertolt Brecht's 1932 essay on radio,[9] wherein he challenged the then-new technology of radio to become "a vast network of pipes" that would allow the listener to transmit as well as receive, to Hans Magnus Enzensberger's 1974 essay on communication, where he saw that "for the first time in history, the media are making possible mass participation in a social and socialized productive process."[10] With the maturation of the World Wide Web, it appeared that many of these ideas, once considered radical and utopian, had finally begun to become possible.

Political and corporate elites have often relied on the mass media to isolate, marginalize, and render powerless challengers to the established system of centralized and corporatized mass media.[11] Yet there have always been those who profess a desire to speak truth to power. In the last few decades, these forces have been increasingly active, developing a critique of corporate-controlled media on the one hand, and building alternative systems of independent and autonomous media on the other. *A Social History of Contemporary Democratic Media* investigates the changing nature of participatory communications and media over the last few decades. In particular, it focuses on grassroots media intervention and the purpose-driven communications of civil society. The media message may be aimed from one to one, or one to many, or many to one, or many to many, but it is driven by the desire to impact the neighborhood, the larger community, or the world. It is purpose-driven, by a nonprofessional and not-for-profit individual or group seeking to impact social events. It is based upon the analysis that our mass media institutions have been slowly and steadily deteriorating, as public trust is generally eroding, a tendency noted by polling data over the last few decades.[12]

Television news in particular is marked by the high degree of distrust it generates. A Gallup Poll noted that confidence in broadcast news hit a new low in 2012, registering that a mere twenty-one percent of surveyed adults reported being confident in TV news, down from forty-seven percent eighteen years ago.[13] In its place is an emerging form of communications that gives more credence to public participation and personal experience and less to commercially driven, "objective" news and infotainment. In the aftermath of the first 2012 presidential debate between Barack Obama and Mitt Romney, political analysts noted that the traditional "spin" that erupts from political party spokespeople and television pundits immediately following the debate has lost its impact, as the public analysis has shifted to real-time public discussion as the debate progresses. According to Pew Research Center's Amy Mitchell, this rise of social media in politics "speaks to the degree that other people—not the political advisers or pundits—are helping to shape the narrative."[14] This trend is communications from below. Many previous examinations of alternative media focus primarily on print media, in particular the proliferation of the "underground" press during the 1960s,[15] or the "zine" culture of the 1980s and 1990s.[16] This book expands the focus to electronic media because it has been apparent for decades that the American people receive the bulk of their news and information from electronic, nonprint sources. Chapter One examines how business conglomerates have dominated the media industries in the United States and usurped the fundamental role communications should play in a democratic society. It then describes the evolution and implications of the technical apparatus of broadcast and Internet media. Chapter Two addresses the return of the local and how local alternative media has grown to fulfill a vital need in a commercial media environment that has abandoned the local level. Chapter Three examines how many local projects developed the ability and desire to encompass the global and build ties internationally, bypassing previous restraints that had prohibited such communications. A case in point, and the focus of Chapter Four, is how labor activists began to develop the notion of horizontal communications in response to the global crisis of labor. Chapter Five then considers the content of communications from below and how increasingly restrictive copyright controls threaten the basic communications rights of citizens. *A Social History of Contemporary Democratic Media* concludes in Chapter Six with an analysis of evolving social media trends and considers the future role of professional journalism, new media monopolies, and the blurred borders between surveillance, citizen media, and democracy.

1 The Rise and Fall of the Broadcasting Model

Many economists like to point out that every era has been linked with what is described as a "motor force," a central propellant that drives the social, economic, and cultural development of a society.[1] In the past, such "motors" have included the production of bronze, the introduction of the steam engine, the growth of railroads, and the popularization of the automobile. It is widely accepted that we are currently in an age of "information," a somewhat technical term that implies detached and objective data without specific social context.[2] Perhaps it is time to recognize that it is specifically the social production and processing of this information, the communication of messages between human beings, that is at the heart of the stimulus and the engine of the Information Age.

Emphasizing the central role of communications is not to deny that technological advancements in areas such as medicine, biology, nanotechnology, artificial intelligence, and other spheres of knowledge are also expanding dramatically. It is merely to point out that these advances owe a great debt to the rapid development of accessible communication technologies that accelerate the capacity to share findings, research, and data among engineers, humanities scholars, scientists, and medical professionals, both globally and between disciplines. Such scientific exchange was the primary reason for the construction of the World Wide Web in the first place, "as a place to allow high energy physicists to share data."[3] The rapid growth of international business, of global assembly lines and global markets, is also predicated upon these communications advances. It is the instantaneous transmission of manufacturing specifications, marketing orders, engineering documents, and financial transactions that has created the phenomenon we now call "globalization," a term that was not in use in the early days of the Web, but is now universally recognized. Global communications have fueled many new transportation initiatives that facilitate the routing of raw materials and goods and accelerate the transference of people, cultural practices, beliefs, and knowledge.

Containerization of freight, standardization of packaging, doubling of truck trailers, and other efficiencies are all examples of squeezing greater capacity out of traditional means of hauling goods. Under these circumstances, the wheel, the wagon, the ship, and the jet plane can be understood as communication devices. The explosion of a new global culture is certainly based upon the adaptation of communications devices, in particular by the youth of many nations. The Web and its use of social networks make it easy to share and discover global tastes in music, in humor, in imagery, in literature, and in cultural expression with few boundaries. The importance of communications to the exponential growth of the computer industry and its associated peripherals cannot be underestimated, as its growth did not take off until it was understood that the computer was a communications tool, not just a number cruncher. Indeed, the many computer business leaders who failed to recognize that fact are now immortalized in Web sites devoted to quotes that will live in infamy, such as IBM chairman Thomas Watson, who stated in 1943 that "there is no reason anyone would want a computer in their home."[4]

MEDIA AND DEMOCRACY

Thus, although communications lies at the center of the primary facets of what we refer to as the Age of Information, it is often taken for granted and unrecognized, and it remains invisible to many observers, who oftentimes tend to zoom in on more spectacular technologies and sectors and ignore the communicative glue that binds many sectors together. Though the ability to communicate is taken as a given in most cultures, it would be hard to find a practice more fraught with conflict, repression, reaction, distrust, and intrigue. Communications technology has always been a thorn in the side of the powerful, from the ancient world to modern times. The construction of the written language was a skill closely held to the cloaks of the monks and monastic orders through the centuries of the European medieval period. The printing press, rather than being celebrated as a liberating technology, was feared and monopolized by royalty and clergy who understood the subversive potential it posed. For centuries, the written word was off limits to the masses throughout Europe. As Starr points out, "Control and centralization have a long historical connection. From ancient empires that kept scribes close at hand to the absolutist states of early modern Europe that centralized printing in their capitals, regimes seeking to censor communications have often tried to confine it geographically."[5]

The opinion that keeping written communication out of the hands of the masses was of strategic importance traveled across the Atlantic to the early American colonies, where writing, reading, and publishing were solely the province of the upper classes and political elite. Knowing how to read and write was a serious offense for slaves, and literacy was outlawed throughout many of the slave-holding states, where white people who taught slaves were criminalized. South Carolina, for example, issued the following legislative initiative: "Be it therefore Enacted by the Authority aforesaid, That all and every Person and Persons whatsoever, who shall hereafter teach or cause any Slave to be taught to write, or shall use or employ any slave as a Scribe in any Manner of Writing whatsoever, hereafter taught to write; every such offense forfeit the Sum of One Hundred Pounds current Money."[6] The justification for such laws was often based upon the precedent that "even the Catholic Church denied the scriptures to the ignorant and impressionable."[7] In response, African Americans improvised a broad range of communicatory practices in order to subvert old modes or create new modes of communications, ranging from weaving quilts embedded with maps and escape routes to the north, to incorporating expressions of freedom into tap dancing (one of the few allowable cultural expressions permitted for slaves), and to interpreting the stories and lessons of the Bible in order to show divine support for the struggle of the emancipation of the African American people.[8] Despite countless repressive obstacles to communication, in every nation on Earth, people have always found ways to develop their ability to communicate and to give voice to those who share grievances and desire social change. It is often observed that oppression breeds resistance, and no resistance could have any chance of surviving without communication. Throughout history, all movements for profound social change have in their beginning stages an organ of communication that served as a platform for unity and action. The creation of a media voice is recognized as one of the first tasks for any movement for social change. The early American colonies were rife with printed journals that agitated, inspired, and ultimately led to the War of Independence. Frederick Douglass recognized the importance of an independent media voice when he began publishing the pro-abolitionist *North Star* in 1847. Russian revolutionary V. I. Lenin laid out a central task of media in his polemic "What Is to Be Done," linking the work of the revolutionary newspaper *Iskra* with an overall strategy of building a nationwide revolutionary movement that would eventually result in the Bolshevik Revolution.[9] The Polish insurgent union group Solidarnosc used their newspaper *Robotnik* and other journals to build their revolutionary movement in the 1980s. In the Philippines, Radio Veritas is credited with mobilizing millions of people during the People Power Revolution against the Marcos dictatorship. Many other examples of the crucial role played by independent media spring to mind, such as the Serbian Radio station B92 during the war in Serbia, the audio tape distributors of Iranian opposition to the Shah, and the insurgent communiqués of the Zapatistas; all provided organizational structure and a voice for social change and political action. Arrayed against these grassroots media projects were the established media and communications groups, particularly in the global south, where the connection between the ruling classes and mass media is far more transparent than in the West. In many Latin American countries, for example, the mantle of reaction is often held by the ruling families through their ownership of major newspapers and broadcasting stations.

The United States is rich with many grassroots media projects that seek to amplify dissidents' voices and opinions over the hegemonic media din and seek to speak back to power and privilege, but these communicatory projects rarely show up in history texts, nor are they often given serious consideration in academia. Dispersed and decentralized movements of writers, publishers, artists, designers, photocopiers, silkscreeners, and leafletters conflict with the firmly established and less complex pronouncements that movements are led by charismatic and powerful individuals, not an amoebic and rhizomatic collection of souls. The widely held, one-dimensional "great man" theory of history fails to take account of how new ideas take root, spread like wildflowers, and bloom in the sidewalk cracks, fields, factories, and landscapes of nations, and move great mountains of repression and injustice.

Histories of communications, in the limited texts that exist, typically marginalize alternative and subversive attempts at participatory communication. Everett M. Rogers, author of perhaps the most definitive study of the field of communications in academia, comments that communications research is "mainly empirical, quantitative, and focused on determining the effects of communication."[10] He points out that communication studies are largely funded by media conglomerates, with a particular interest in addressing these research areas. Thus, communications practices that lie outside the commercial arena do not attract the financial incentives for more than cursory investigations. There are few scholars that challenge the established mythologies of heroic inventors and entrepreneurs such as Alexander Graham Bell, Thomas Edison, Samuel Morse, and Guglielmo Marconi, men whose inventions sprang from the work of many other inventors and helped pave the way toward today's communications infrastructure. The framing of these individual success stories helps establish the normative view of media technologies as the fruits of free enterprise that contribute to social progress. James Carey notes that "Edison, Bell, and other wizards were exploited as symbols of the new civilization, used to curry public favor and demonstrate the beneficence of the new technology, while new empires in communications and transportation were created behind the mask of an electrical mystique."[11]

The emergence of large capital involvement in communications began in the mid-1800s as the steel wires of the telegraph crept across the American continent, becoming the primary conduits of regional and international news, and establishing the means for a national stock and commodity market. Despite their often acclaimed role in promoting civilization, democracy, and development of the West, telegraph companies like Western Union were fiercely monopolistic and undemocratic. The early telegraphic enterprises were part and parcel of the holdings of railroad and oil "robber barons," who provoked public outrage among the American people in the late 1800s. Telegraph lines were built alongside railroad lines, where they were used for speeding messages to other towns as well as for electrically switching tracks. The confluence of rail and telegraphy highlights the basis of communications in systems of transportation to electrical messaging, as the mail trains and pony express were replaced by telegraph keys. Though often touted as a symbol of the march of progress, telegraphy is recognized as one of the preconditions for establishing colonialism throughout the underdeveloped world, as it proved essential for governing from afar and alerting the colonial powers to impending insurrection or unrest.

Wireless radio telegraphy, the forerunner of modern radio, was promoted and popularized by groups of amateur tinkers and hobbyists, mostly comprised of young boys who thrilled with the ability to build cheap radio kits and send and receive messages from great distances. Until US business interests came to realize the profit potential of radio, the airwaves in the early 1900s were dominated by these citizen broadcasters. The Radio Act of 1912 claimed the airwaves for US business interests and ensured that the electromagnetic spectrum would be the domain of business and commerce, not citizen communications. As Susan Douglas explains, the radio amateurs were stripped of their rights to broadcast not because of any disruption but because "a very influential business, the press, found their activities a disruptive encroachment on its turf."[12] Early adopters of radio technology included the primary creator of Central American banana republics, the United Fruit Company, which found radio useful in managing its far-flung shipping operations. As wireless telegraphy gave way to voice and music on the airwaves in the 1920s, most of the avid broadcasters were not business interests but community organizations, labor unions, churches, and educational institutions. Subsequent legislative acts pertaining to radio communications further ensured commercial exploitation and eroded public access to the airwaves. As Robert McChesney points out, it was not at all self-evident that the US system of broadcasting would become solely based upon the commercialization of airtime, pointing out that by 1926 only 4.3 percent of US stations were characterized as being "commercial broadcasters."[13] By 1927, the Radio Act of 1927 began to secure the airwaves for large corporations that were beginning to understand the economic potential of radio. The Act established a Federal Radio Commission, which proceeded to allocate the airwaves to large business interests. For example, of the twenty-five frequencies set aside for powerful clear channel stations, twenty-three of them went to the newly formed NBC affiliates. The Communications Act of 1934 and the establishment of the Federal Communications Commission essentially sealed corporate dominance of the airwaves for many years to come and restricted access, experimentation, and development to commercial exploitation, leading the director of Catholic radio station WLWL to note that "the existent set-up of the United States is dominated by two monopolistic networks. They decide the type of educational programs that shall go on the air; what social, political, ethical questions shall be discussed; what point of view will be presented."[14] The commercialization of radio had many detractors, including Lee de Forest, the man credited with the invention of the vacuum tube that helped launch radio broadcasting. He wrote to the National Association of Broadcasters to complain about what the industry has done to his "child." "You have made him a laughing stock to intelligence. . . . [Y]ou have cut time into tiny segments called spots (more rightly stains) herewith the occasional fine program is periodically smeared with impudent insistence to buy and try."[15]

Many communications inventions have faced similar monopolization or thwarted development due to the collusion of manufacturing and entertainment trusts with allies in government. Regulatory agencies such as the FCC, the FDA, and the FTC have become notoriously known as "revolving doors," as they are typically staffed not by "watchdogs" but by a rotating crew of industry representatives. Fax machines, UHF television, FM radio, photocopy technology, Digital Audio Tape (DAT) machines, and video duplicators have all been monopolized, restricted, or delayed by commercial interests or by threatened governments. The extensive repression of communication technologies spans the ages and runs the gamut of activities, ranging from the banning of literacy among slaves to the outlawing of photocopy and mimeograph machines in the former Soviet Union and Eastern Bloc nations. Such communications control is also evident in the imposition of dominant languages upon colonized peoples to ensure central control and weaken cultural resistance. Ireland, noted by some as the first colonized nation in modernity, had its native tongue, the Irish language, suppressed almost to the point of extinction. In Japan, the indigenous Ainu inhabitants also had their language banned in order to weaken resistance to Japanese rule and to retard cultural and national unity.[16] The Japanese strategy for suppressing the Ainu was imported from the US frontier in the 1800s, a strategy based on the removal and concentration of indigenous on reservations and the destruction of indigenous culture and language.

The desire to control speech and cultural communication is not ancient history—it can still be perceived today in attempts by corporations and industry lobbying groups to monopolize common cultural works and ban use of words, phrases, music, literature, and images through predatory and restrictive legal action. Many contemporary trademark fights in the courts would be considered laughable, if not for the fact that they can present serious financial harm to citizens who challenge such absurd control of language. A notorious account of one such battle was Al Franken's fight over the phrase "fair and balanced," which Franken had used in a title of a book he had written. The Murdoch empire of News Corporation/Fox News claimed to own the phrase and insisted that others were prohibited from using it.[17] Franken won that case, but most people would not have had the financial resources to battle such a large corporation. The term "radical media," used for decades by many of the subjects mentioned in this book, was recently acquired by a corporate consortium that now claims to own those words. Soon after this acquisition, a conference in London was threatened by the consortium and subsequently prevented from using the term "radical media" in the name of the very conference where the theme was "radical media."[18] The organizers subsequently changed the name to "rebellious" media.

This ownership of words and phrases extends to all aspects of cultural production. At a certain point, Bart Simpson, Charlie Brown, Wonder Woman, and other cultural icons became integral parts of our social landscape. In a culture where images and sounds are often more important than words and phrases, the ability to refer to or quote a picture of Mickey Mouse or send someone the "Happy Birthday" song without provoking a legal fight is essential to an open and meaningful civic conversation about our current society. Legal precedent for control of intellectual property was instigated by a desire to encourage creativity, not to block speech and ensure corporate profit indefinitely. The Copyright Term Extension Act pushed forth by Congressman Sonny Bono, humorously called by some "the Disney Preservation Act," extends copyright an unprecedented number of years into the future, an act that writer Kembrew McLeod says "means we are allowing much of our cultural history to be locked up and decay only to benefit the very few."[19] Such new provisions in communications law grant increasingly tighter control of intellectual property in a manner spelled out by Lawrence Lessig in the subtitle of his book: "How big media uses technology and the law to lock down culture and control creativity."[20] Claiming restrictive ownership of common words, images, and icons limits the ability to develop conversation around the materiality of our everyday lives, which tend to be heavily media-centric in our modern age.

Repression of free communication becomes more understandable, however, when we see that unlimited communication technologies can represent a serious threat to business interests, to repressive state apparatuses, and to other repressive institutions that depend upon the ignorance or the distraction of the people. The keyboard and the camera can indeed be mightier than the sword.

THE STUDY OF COMMUNICATIONS

Despite the vital position of communications in human and social development, communications as a field of study did not truly come into its own until the mid-twentieth century. It wasn't until the rise of modern urban society, of the "masses," that communications was investigated, provoked by the critical importance of advertising and public relations as well as by the rise of fascism and propaganda. Both of these media models, whether selling products or promoting ideology, rely upon a central creator of messages emanating from a strong central body. This paradigm is the primary model that emerged in the United States, where the private enterprise system was both determined and empowered to be the primary conveyor of news, entertainment, and information. The area of academic study that arose around this phenomenon took for granted this centralized foundation and subsequently ignored communications practices that resided outside of government propaganda or corporate commercial campaigns. This myopia essentially eliminated consideration of cultural and intellectual media exchange developed in the margins of mass media.

Academic investigation of nonmainstream communication would be of great value, but as it has not been deemed as important for the state apparatus or for the purveyors of products, it has not been judged worthy of study. Most study of media is driven by the crucial role of advertising, a multibillion-dollar industry that survives on its ability to deliver data on audience share, demographics, Q score, and other reports on media consumption. Grassroots public communication practices have typically been relegated to the margins of study where they are deemed subcultures, trivialized or dismissed as the foolishness of amateurs. Public communications activities often only come into the limelight when they commit media acts called "out-of-hand" or "irresponsible" by members of the media establishment, such as something considered pornographic, extremist, or conspiratorial. Then these activities have been subjected to control, regulation, censorship, and other forms of curtailment by both the state and businesses, whose interests frequently coincide.

While the power of outsider media, amplified by the new communication technologies, is often dismissed, the drama of communication has never been lost in popular fiction or in cinema. There it is often used as the essential device in building both dramatic and comedic intensity: consider the multiplicity of images ranging from the horror of the handwriting from within the belly of the little girl in *The Exorcist* to the many "messages in a bottle" in lost-at-sea adventure stories such as *Captain Grant's Children* by Jules Verne. Communications and messaging are rife in Biblical lore, from the story of Moses carrying the inscribed tablets down from the mount, to the linguistic chaos that results from the destruction of the Tower of Babel. In humorous contemporary retrocommercial advertisements, we can relive the thrill of young children playing with Walkie-Talkies, decoder rings, Morse code senders, wire radios and tin-can-and-string phones. It is not a great leap ahead to contemporary teenagers and their fascination with instant messaging, texting, cell phones, and smartphones. Language may be basic, but it has always seemed exciting.

MANAGING PUBLIC OPINION

Overt censorship, at least during times of peace, has never been the norm in the United States, primarily because it has not been necessary. Media critics suggest that the United States has historically tended towards a more sophisticated form of media manipulation, a kinder and gentler form of repression: the managing of public opinion and the marginalization of popular forms of grassroots media.[21] This critique of American mass media manipulation is not a recent formulation but has been recognized since the beginnings of US mass media in the early twentieth century.[22] With the emergence of the modern economy and its synergy with mass media and advertising,[23] the democratic potential for communication was sidetracked into its current role, which supports the sale of products and of entertainment commodities. The rampant commercialization of communications was not a foregone conclusion and had many detractors, such as writer Aldous Huxley, for example, who complained that "radio" "has debased the human necessity for speech and has warped human communication into a primarily financial transaction."[24]

The ongoing strategy by governments and corporations has been to promote the idea that only the opinions of the chosen few, the officially anointed, have the right to communicate or, indeed, even have the skills to communicate. US policy has made clear that the primary purpose of communications is for commercial enterprise, not for freedom of expression.[25] For the most part, the right to communicate has been granted to those who both reflect and who advocate for the status quo represented by American business and government. US legislation and regulatory actions thus maintain that commercial entities have the right to monopolize the terrain and to push aside noncommercial, not-for-profit media. According to this pragmatic way of thinking, communication is deemed worthy only if it makes a profit. Facilitating this school of thought are journalism schools that, in a self-preservationist manner, have sought to devalue popular participation, despite their original goals to create a more objective and professional journalistic standard. In this view, the basic right, responsibility, and duty of public citizens to communicate is thus diminished, supplanted by professionals and pundits trained in recognized institutions for commercial purposes. With the commercialization and professionalization of media, outsider viewpoints, ideas, and opinions have easily been marginalized. Over the decades, enthusiasm for popular communications is evidenced by the proliferation of ham radio operators, amateur film clubs, public access producers, AM and FM pirate transmitters, makers of zines, and writers of blogs. Over many decades, millions of such public media producers have been essentially told by mainstream media they have little to offer public life.

Until now.

Despite decades of regulatory restrictions, financially out-of-reach licenses, the privileging of professional journalism, and the marginalization of "amateurs" all calculated to strip the average citizen of their communications rights, abilities, and responsibilities, the public is reinserting itself into communications systems. This invigorated media public can trace part of its roots to an energetic media literacy movement that emerged in the late 1980s and 1990s that encouraged people to see beyond the limited, one-dimensional infotainment offered by mainstream media. The importance of media literacy was highlighted by Len Masterman who wrote that "the democratization of institutions, and the long march towards a truly participatory democracy, will be highly dependent upon the ability of majorities of citizens to take control, become effective change agents, make rational decisions (often on the basis of media evidence), and to communicate effectively perhaps through an active involvement with the media."[26] Media literacy was offered as an inoculation against the perception of lazy and sensationalistic reporting as well as against the self-censorship pervading US mass media, leading to a growing questioning of mainstream news. The sharpening of one's media criticism skills began to become popular as a means of "intellectual self-defense," a term popularized by famed linguist and media critic Noam Chomsky. Chomsky states in an essay entitled "On Staying Informed and Intellectual Self-Defense," "there are many techniques for penetrating the veil of propaganda that should become second nature in dealing with the output of doctrinal institutions (media, journals of opinion, scholarship)."[27] In his landmark book *Manufacturing Consent*, Chomsky illustrates examples of bias and censorship and presents an analysis of the primary "filters" through which corporate media view the world.[28] Such a critical perspective towards mass media became commonplace toward the end of the Reagan years of Iran-Contra and during the first of the Gulf Wars, as the media became particularly reluctant to challenge official viewpoints and information put forth by government. This wariness of war reporting was heightened by the replacement of investigative journalism with pooled footage and "embedded" reporters who were obliged to clear footage with the US military. The complicit and toothless status of mass media came under increasing scrutiny as new alternative sources for news began to be developed, particularly on the early Internet. Early, pre–World Wide Web Internet chatter developed in alt.usenet sites and Bulletin Board Services around interests and events not found in newspapers or television or around subjects and stories seen as perhaps too unsettling, provocative, or counter to the official stance taken by the media establishment. As many scholars have pointed out, mass media institutions rely upon government and politicians for a large percentage of their news sources,[29] and alienating these inside official sources began to be seen as too risky for many news organizations. Media outlets are very aware that independent voices are routinely locked out of press conferences and the news "loop" for not following the understood parameters of questioning and reporting. Controversial subjects are also risky, for advertisers are at the financial heart of media, and alienating them would be detrimental for media companies increasingly driven by their bottom line. Analysis of this economic self-censorship in mainstream media was highlighted in a report that struck a nerve in the growing media literacy movement. In the introduction to the report, the researchers ask, "Who controls the Press? The answer should be apparent—ultimately, those who control the purse. They typically influence it, often shape it, and sometimes openly dictate its content."[30] An increasing awareness of self-censorship and an erosion of the border between news and entertainment provided much of the impetus for finding new communications tools to share information and news.

Oftentimes news items and analysis ignored or dismissed by mainstream media begin circulating around the fringes of alternative media and are then often denigrated as conspiracy theories by political pundits and professional journalists. Humorously, and sometimes tragically, many of these so-called conspiracy theories subsequently turn out to be all too true. One only need review the back-pedaling, public relations spin and too-little, too-late acknowledgments of such former "conspiracy theories" as the Nixon enemy list and botched Watergate burglary, the staged Gulf of Tonkin incident, the Gulf War weapons of mass destruction fabrications, the Iran-Contra denials and subsequent CIA drug smuggling links, not to mention the outlandish, desperate attempts by the CIA to kill, maim, or embarrass Cuba's Fidel Castro. The mainstream media has done a huge disservice to the public interest by too often accepting the official story, instead of asking hard questions of those in power. So-called "conspiracy theories" circulate and develop followers outside of mainstream media because there are often real holes in the official point of view, not because the public is easily misled. By refusing to entertain these real questions, mass media have lost much credibility with the public and are increasingly viewed as propaganda tools rather than investigative journalism. Unexamined facts and remaining questions on vital issues have stimulated large communities of skeptics among many millions of people who rely upon the public discourse provided by the World Wide Web, community radio stations, and micro-cinema venues. Such alternative means of communication have sprouted deep roots across a broad spectrum of people, ranging from those with unpopular political opinions to those who simply want to share thoughts on local events and cultural pleasures. The "technologies of freedom" once described by Ithiel de Sola Pool[31] help provide these new media platforms, and in order to better understand the phenomena, it is worth understanding the technology that underlies them.

THE CONTINUED RELEVANCE OF THE ELECTROMAGNETIC SPECTRUM

Demystifying the technological foundation that lies beneath electronic media is important to understanding the context and the evolution of contemporary communications practices. Though we savor the notion of living in a "wired" society, our data mostly moves through the air in the medium known as "spectrum." The word *spectrum* conjures up an ephemeral, ghostly presence or an intangible, invisible substance, but spectrum is a very real entity, and in today's electronic age, how it is managed has tremendous repercussions for every nation. The spectrum is the medium that connects a nation's central nervous system—its communications network. Police and fire dispatch, aviation air traffic control, radio and television broadcasting, satellite uplinks and downlinks, and microwave and cellular phone communications all depend upon access to different sections of the electromagnetic spectrum. But these transmitted messages do not flow freely through the ether, like ripples in a pond. Rather, these broadcast mechanisms are assigned very specific channels in which to traverse the air, in specific frequencies within their allocated part of the broadcast spectrum. Furthermore, this spectrum of frequencies is not infinite, as there is a limited amount of available spectrum. It is because the spectrum is limited that there is a scarcity of available frequencies, and issues of spectrum management take on vital importance for society. Indeed, the recognition of spectrum scarcity has been one of the fundamental tenets of most of the major communications legislation in the United States.

Electromagnetic radiation is energy waves propagated from oscillations of charged subatomic particles, rapidly switching from positive to negative to positive. These waves are measured in hertz or cycles per second. Thus, 1,000 cycles equals one kilohertz, one million cycles equals one megahertz, and one billion cycles equals one gigahertz. The range of frequencies regarded as the broadcast spectrum generally falls between 3,000 hertz and 300 gigahertz. It is within this range that radiation occurs (hence the word *radio*), whereby electromagnetic waves are transmitted through the air and become useful for communications purposes. A broadcaster who transmits on a particular frequency occupies that particular portion of the spectrum. Interference between two broadcasters operating on that same frequency will occur unless the distance between the broadcasters is sufficient or one operates at less power.

Currently the radio spectrum in the United States is divided into bands of frequencies allocated to certain broadcasting devices. The AM radio, for instance, typically occupies the band between 535 kilohertz and 1605 kilohertz. This band is divided into 107 channels, each with a bandwidth of ten kilohertz. The FM radio occupies the frequencies from 88 to 108 megahertz, divided into 100 channels, 200 kilohertz wide. TV frequencies are at a higher range and occupy much larger portions of the bandwidth. Frequencies useful for microwave and satellite communications are generally found higher up on the spectrum, usually in the gigahertz range. Although the air above us may look like clear sky, it is an essential conduit for communications technologies.

Legal scholars point out that the spectrum is unusual in that "[u]tilization does not use it up or wear it out. It does not require continual maintenance to remain usable. It is subject to pollution (interference), but once the interference is removed the pollution totally disappears. The value of the spectrum lies primarily in its use for conveying a wide variety of information at varying speeds over varying distance: in other words, for communication."[32]

It is important to understand that the concept of what is a usable portion of the electromagnetic spectrum has changed dramatically since its first discovery. Originally only a tiny percentage of frequencies were deemed usable, but as technological improvements developed, increasing amounts of spectrum became available for use. What was considered usable spectrum in the 1920s represents only a small percentage of what we consider usable today. The broadcast spectrum has moved ever higher, as ultra-high-frequency communications via satellites, microwave transmitters, cell phones, and other new technologies have developed. Thus, it is wise to be far-sighted in regards to new frequencies that may not be valuable today but may be of vital importance in the future. That the issue of spectrum is still of utmost importance today is highlighted by a 2010 memorandum issued by President Obama that calls upon federal agencies to look for ways to clear 500 megahertz of spectrum in order to speed development of new wireless services. According to the report, "[T]here would be as many as 50 billion devices transmitting and receiving wireless data by 2020, leading many in the wireless industry to forecast a spectrum crisis."[33] In an interview, coinventor of the cellular telephone Martin Cooper emphasizes the still crucial question of spectrum, saying that "[t]he more we learn about new communications, the more capacity we need, and that is going to keep going on forever. That's been happening since radio was invented, and that's going to keep going. The only way to solve that is by new technology. You can't create new spectrum."[34]

THE INTRODUCTION OF SPECTRUM ALLOCATION

Early radio pioneers such as Guglielmo Marconi and Lee de Forest discovered that when oscillating voltages generated frequencies high enough, radio waves could be generated and could travel long distances through the air. These voltages could then be detected by resonating circuits at a distance. Bursts of such frequencies became useful for wireless telegraphy and led the way to long-distance and transoceanic communications. Further technological improvements allowed voice and music to be broadcast as well. At this early stage of radio, many hobbyists and amateurs took to the air, experimenting with homemade wireless gear. The airwaves were crackling with messages, which often competed with each other within the same frequency range in a somewhat anarchic fashion, as there were no regulatory or allocation policies. The ability of wireless telegraphy to assist in the rescue of survivors from the Titanic helped pave the way toward an understanding of the importance of organization in the spectrum. But formulating the concept of spectrum ownership was a thorny problem. As Susan Douglas points out, the spectrum "was intangible and could not be bought or sold in quite the same way [as traditional property]. Rather, the ether, like the oceans or wilderness areas, was a resource held in common in which all Americans potentially had an interest and in which walls or fences could not be built. This may seem quite obvious to us today, but coming to the realization that the ether was both a resource and one to which Americans had collective rights was just as difficult as thinking of the ether as property at all."[35]

The Radio Act of 1912 was the United States's first attempt to bring some order to radio broadcasting. The act instituted tests for radio operators, assigned frequencies for broadcasters, and generally tried to shut out amateurs from the radio spectrum. Susan Douglas reads the 1912 act as evidence of Americans' struggle to understand an invisible yet communally owned resource. The act "represents a watershed in wireless history, the point after which individual exploration of vast tracts of the ether would diminish and corporate management and exploitation, in close collaboration with the state, would increase."[36] At this point, the "frontier" of the American spectrum became partitioned off and partially closed. The advent of World War I and the increasing importance of electronic communication spurred the US government to take control of the electromagnetic spectrum for its own use, forbidding the public from clogging the broadcast frequencies. On April 7, 1917, as the United States officially entered World War I, the control of the entire radio spectrum was claimed by the US Navy, which did not release it for commercial exploitation until 1919.

After World War I, the government relaxed its control, broadcasting became a popular phenomenon, and voice and music replaced Morse code as the dominant content. Radio policy was further elucidated by the Radio Act of 1927. During this time, many community institutions took to the airwaves to take advantage of radio's unique ability to reach the public. In these early days, most of these radio stations were noncommercial, with the bulk of them being run by community groups, labor unions, churches, and schools.[37] The notion of commercial radio was not yet dominant.

When it soon became apparent that the airwaves could be used as a commercial medium, many large corporations took an aggressive interest in entering the radio-broadcasting field. Groups like RCA and Westinghouse began buying up radio stations and used their clout to push noncommercial stations off the air or to limit them to undesirable frequencies and lower power. The increased competition in the radio field was intensified by the realization that the available frequencies of radio broadcasting were limited and would soon be filled to capacity. The growing power of the commercial radio monopolies was countered by a coalition of noncommercial radio broadcasters, from universities and labor unions to churches and social clubs.[38] Arguing that the spectrum is a natural resource, not unlike waterways, forests, and terrain, they fought to maintain a certain percentage for the public. Advocates for the public interest fought hard to set aside a section of the spectrum for public institutions. This fractious debate ended with the passage of the 1934 Communications Act. Though the economic and political power of the radio trusts in Congress resulted in a Communications Act favorable to the commercial broadcasters, the act also solidified a central tenet of US broadcast policy: the airwaves were a valuable public resource that broadcasters could not own, but could "borrow," as long as the public interest was upheld. Thus, spectrum could be taken back from them if they misused it. This notion has been upheld time and time again in numerous legislative and judicial decisions in the United States. As Carter, Franklin, and Wright observe, while the scarcity of radio frequencies enabled the government to determine whose views received airtime, "the right of the viewers and listeners, not the right of the broadcasters . . . is paramount" due to popular understandings of the First Amendment.[39] This notion of the spectrum as public resource was again recognized within the text of the broadcast section of the Telecommunications Act of 1996, which states that "[n]othing in this section shall be construed as relieving a television broadcasting station from its obligation to serve the public interest, convenience, and necessity."[40]

THE SETTING ASIDE OF THE SPECTRUM FOR PUBLIC USE

Broadcasting monopolies were so powerful at the end of World War II that they were able to develop the early television industry on a solely commercial basis, leaving no space for noncommercial television broadcasters. As late as 1950, for example, there was not a single noncommercial or educational television station. The television industry grew so quickly that the FCC instituted a "freeze" on new channels. As television became almost ubiquitous in American society, an increasingly vocal group of critics began challenging television's lack of educational, local, and relevant programming. Thanks to the concept of the public ownership of the airwaves, many reforms were enacted over the years, such as equal time laws, "fairness" regulations, and increased educational programming. More importantly, sections of the television bandwidth, particularly within the newly developing UHF band, were set aside for educational broadcasters. In April 1952, the FCC suspended its freeze on the licensing of new television stations, hoping to encourage new educational television stations in each of about 1300 communities. As the twelve VHF (very high frequency) channels already in use could not accommodate more channels, the additions were allocated to the UHF (ultra high frequency) band. One channel in each of some 240 communities was reserved for use of noncommercial educational stations.[41] Indisputably, noncommercial television had been established in an educational context. For this reason, state and local governments were its most substantial financial supporters.[42] By 1962, there were seventy-five educational television stations on the air, yet few people were able to access their programs. A special report on the state of public television found that while the FCC reserved the majority of its 650 television frequencies for educational broadcasting, most TVs could not pick up their signals.

To allow for reception of the UHF band, the United States passed legislation mandating that new television sets must be capable of receiving these higher channels. This "set-aside" of noncommercial broadcast spectrum enabled the growth of educational television stations, which soon became a semiformal network of broadcasters that eventually developed into the system of public broadcast stations known as PBS. Indeed, without these "set-asides," there would not be as many educational children's programs, such as *Sesame Street*, nor would there be outlets for many current documentary productions. The dependence on funding from politically controlled institutions, however, has hindered the independence of the public broadcasting system substantially. It is often used as a congressional or senatorial bargaining chip and is frequently threatened with defunding by conservative politicians. Its transition to a corporate-funded system of underwriting support has similarly impacted its independence, as it then became beholden to corporate benefactors. The political implications of the public broadcasting system are nothing new, however. The concept for a national television system was reportedly sold to then-president Johnson in the 1960s as a means by which he could communicate with the public in the event of civil disturbances or martial law.[43]

The development of FM radio occurred in a similar way, though the promise of bandwidth devoted to education and creative experimentation was short-lived, having fallen to the onslaught of media corporations whose AM stations were threatened by the competition. These corporations quickly saw the economic potential of FM's noise-free bandwidth. After World War II, when FM transmission began in many cities, few people had access to FM radios. Ownership of FM stations was held by the same media monopolies that controlled the AM band. Since FM was not yet popular, it remained unexplored territory, except for a handful of adventurous noncommercial enterprises that used the band for the transmission of experimental and innovative programming and to broadcast special genres of music, such as jazz. FM radio, a technology developed in the 1920s, eventually became popular in the 1960s and 1970s as youthful audiences began desiring new forms of music and expression. FM stations, intentionally local operations due to their line-of-sight limitations and their initial experimental nature, began to become extremely popular to new audiences, and increasing numbers of radio listeners switched to the FM band. Unfortunately, the drifting of the AM listeners to FM resulted in renewed interest on the part of their corporate media owners who moved back into FM in force, essentially mimicking the commercial character of the AM band. As a result of public outcry, some sections of the FM band were set aside for noncommercial use. Today, FM is primarily commercial, with a small number of community-based, noncommercial stations on the reserved sections on the lower part of the FM band, including college radio, religious programming, and most National Public Radio stations. Contemporary commercial FM stations have become virtually indistinguishable from their AM counterparts. Satellite radio, such as Sirius and XM, continue the legacy of the broadcast model, beaming centralized radio waves to a national audience. This same centralized model is replicated by the newer Internet radio endeavors Pandora and Spotify.

Through most of the 1960s and 1970s, the public responsibility of television and radio broadcasters was integral to the use of the nation's airwaves. In the late 1970s and early 1980s, a new economic philosophy took hold. The beginnings of the Reagan era were exemplified by widespread deregulation and the dismantling of antimonopoly laws, producing enormous repercussions for the public service requirements of broadcasters. The shift from public service to a "market approach" was primarily the work of Reagan-appointed FCC Chairperson Mark Fowler, who believed that unfettered capitalism in the broadcast market would serve the public best. The takeover of media by corporate conglomerates, so aptly described by Ben Bagdikian in his landmark study *The Media Monopoly*,[44] led to the serious gutting and downsizing of local media. Deregulation removed government guidelines concerning local programming, clearing the way for an increase in syndicated "infotainment" game shows and home shopping. This type of programming represented enormous cost savings and allowed local stations to cut many station personnel, journalists, and news teams. In the radio and television enterprises, a commitment to public service information was tossed aside, and media operations became viewed solely as business ventures with no obligation to serve the public. News operations began to be considered a drag on profits, rather than a necessary public service. News desks were stripped bare while franchised entertainment, such as game shows and Hollywood celebrity programs, took the place of local news, information, and commentary. The few remaining local television programs still in production were quickly replaced by a new breed of "fast food" programs—syndicated reality-based shows vital to today's television lineup. In the gaping time slot left by the once-ubiquitous "Evening Magazine" or by local talk shows that featured people and events from the local community, the public was offered sexual scandal, political punditry, murder, and mayhem, typified especially by the rise of Fox News. These now ubiquitous reality-based "tabloid" or "infotainment" programs pose as conveyors of news and public service information by using the aesthetics and symbolism of news: well-coifed anchors, correspondents, news desks, and picture-in-picture graphics, while delivering entertainment and diversion.

With a paucity of local news production, the production of video news releases (VNRs) soared, as they became a cost-efficient means of delivering a corporate agenda while saving money for news channels operating on a low budget. Corporations produce video news releases to take the traditional press release a step further: they self-produce a news segment and deliver it to the television station ready to air on broadcast-quality media. Essentially highly produced commercials, the Video News Release aided in weakening local community affairs and news production by making local news and information appear low-tech, parochial, and lacking entertainment value. The shift from the local to a more cost-efficient centralization of broadcasting was even more devastating for radio stations, which were increasingly taken over to become mere repeater channels for distant voices and canned music, in some cases even coming from another state. As a result of these changes, community news, city council meetings, neighborhood events, and local commentary, for the most part, have vanished from commercial media in the United States. The culmination of corporate dominance was reached with the passage of the 1996 Telecommunications Act, a legislative action that formalized the monopoly status of the communications and entertainment industries. According to media scholar Robert McChesney, "[T]he corruption in media policy-making culminated in the 1996 Telecommunications Act, arguably one of the most important pieces of US legislation."[45] The act, which passed with very little public review, epitomized the view that the market should decide media policy, with very few regulatory considerations. It did away with many market caps that had previously restricted ownership of multiple broadcast outlets in the same cities, and it freed media corporations from any concrete enforcement of their public responsibility.

Although the notion of "the public interest" may seem a quaint and idealistic anachronism to the media conglomerates currently dominating US media, many sectors of the public still considered it a valid concept. This view holds that the broadcasters have been given a valuable public resource—the airwaves—in exchange for serving the public. This seemingly idealistic formula has been stated time and time again in various FCC statements, although it is rarely enforced by regulators, who often have close ties to the broadcasting industry.

FROM BROADCASTING TO THE WORLD WIDE WEB

The physical world, many social commentators and critical theorists like to say, is an anachronism. Information, they assure us, has replaced the steel and glass of the old industrial age as the new linchpin of a modern age, the Age of Information. The forges, rolling mills, furnaces, and smelters are gone. Today, we process data—extracting it, molding it, combining it, shipping it—adding value to it and extracting profit from it like any other industrial product. In our new century, information is the basic resource, the primary commodity on which the advanced capitalist economy depends.

This transition to an information-based economy has been apparent for many years now, evidenced by the growing number of "knowledge" workers and the declining number of industrial jobs in the last few decades. The greater importance of the information economy has also become evident in another form of activity—the frantic level of financial acquisitions and mergers amongst the media corporations and the creation of mega-monopolies in the media/information sector.

In the early 1990s, it was argued that the continuing growth and development of this new information-based economic model required the construction of a major new type of infrastructure—the "information superhighway." Much as the development of the Interstate Highway System provided the economic stimulus for automobile and suburban home construction in the 1950s, the new superhighway—the National Information Infrastructure—would provide a similar catalyst for new information commodities. The Telecommunications Act of 1996, fought for by the major corporate communications interests such as AT&T, Viacom, and Time Warner, helped to facilitate this economic bonanza.

Nothing symbolizes more powerfully both the potential and the limitations of the new digital age than the rapid growth and popularity of the Internet. A seemingly nebulous web of computer network constellations, it is a popularly held belief that there is no "there" there, that the Internet is a virtual space, with its roots gathered in an endless chain of information nodes. There are two fallacies at work in this belief about the Internet. One is that the Internet is merely virtual, when in fact there is a physical aspect of the Internet that often is ignored. Very much physical, the foundation of the Internet is a core system of switched data lines and computer servers. This tangible property is now overwhelmingly in the hands of large media monopolies, a fact that threatens the very democratic life of the system. The other fallacy concerns the nature of information. Information is frequently thought of as a raw material, as if information were somehow neutral and ubiquitous. Yet information actually is a social product, and it reflects the social conditions under which it was produced. Both the physical properties of the Internet and the nature of information must be understood in order to move beyond the worn paradigm of communications for corporate profit and advertising.

Though American big businesses love to complain about big government, they are the ones to benefit the most from it. The Internet was created by government institutions with the funding of the US taxpaying public. Like many products of public funding, American businesses seek to take advantage of publicly financed research and development, and when given evidence of the clear feasibility of profit-making, they seek to "spin off" the product and take it into their own profit-making enterprise. Although US businesses like to portray their leading figures as risk takers and innovators, business leaders do not like to take risks when those risks can be financed by public dollars. The Internet was publicly financed when it took its first risky steps; it is now overwhelmingly a private domain. This takeover happened at a very rapid pace, and with a minimal amount of debate or publicity. The vast networks of public-funded data lines and supercomputer sites were absorbed for the most part by privatized networks and data services corporations. This corporate incursion turned an initially public, noncommercial space populated by educational, governmental, and organizational sites into a space dominated by the now ubiquitous dot-com.

THE PRIVATIZATION OF THE INTERNET

Our public dollars created the Internet not in the spirit of democratic communication, but rather in the desire for US military command and control centers to communicate in the event of a nuclear war. The basis for the Internet was laid out in a major theoretical research paper by the RAND Corporation in 1962.[46] Suppose, the logic went, the United States was the target of a nuclear attack. As in most bombing attacks, central strategic nerve centers of military communications become prime targets. With its reliance on central computing centers, the United States would be particularly susceptible to a disabling computer attack. The solution suggested by the Request for Proposals required the ability to access these computing systems from anywhere—perhaps, for example, a computer center in an underground bunker in Colorado could be accessed by military authorities from other military outposts in Virginia; Washington, DC; or California. This called for a completely decentralized system. Another suggested problem would be the ability to maintain constant communications with these computers. In the event of a nuclear attack, many transmission lines would be destroyed. The system would need to have the ability to send and receive data in situations of extreme chaos and destruction. The RAND report, "On Distributed Communications Networks," suggested a technique called "packet switching" to bypass this problem. Rather than rely on a continuous stream of data, as in an analog telephone line, a message would be divided up into packets of information, each bearing the address of its final destination. These packets would be sent down the transmission lines, traveling from network to network, in order to reach their eventual destination. It would not matter which transmission route they took; the packets would simply take whatever path was available.[47]

This theoretical concept—a decentralized computer network based on the idea of packet switching—was adopted by the Defense Advanced Research Projects Agency (DARPA), which issued a Request for Proposals to major university computer centers.[48] Researchers at the University of California at Los Angeles (UCLA) responded with a proposal and began work on the project. In 1969, the new system, called ARPANET began construction, with the first "node" (or site) at UCLA, soon thereafter joined by the Stanford Research Institute, the University of California at Santa Barbara, and the University of Utah. The ARPANET allowed researchers on the Net to perform remote computing from the other nodes and allowed for transmission of data from one node to the other. By 1971 there were fifteen other nodes on the Net, mostly located in university research centers. In 1973, the first international connections were made to England and Norway.

As the ARPANET grew, researchers began to look at the problem posed by the diverse amount of computing hardware and software in use. The success of the system required the ability for messages, the packets, to be sent and received, regardless of the underlying hardware or software of the individual machine. A standard form of packeting and addressing was required. In 1974, the original transmission format, known as Network Control Protocol (NCP), was superseded by the more sophisticated standard known as TCP/IP or Transmission Control Protocol/Internet Protocol. TCP is responsible for converting data into packets and then reconverting them at the receiving end. IP is responsible for addressing each packet and sending them across whatever transmission paths are available.

Many more universities became nodes on the system. Several other factors began to impact the Net as well. Computers became increasingly available due to major advances in microprocessors and software engineering. The fact that the internet protocol system, TCP/IP, was in the public domain, allowed other computer users to also link up with the growing Net. Electronic mail, originally set up for scientific and military exchange, began to be used by civilians for social purposes. Discussion boards, with the ability to "broadcast" to lists of subscribers, came into creation, with regular postings on such things as science fiction and computer games. Such electronic spaces were still primarily the domain of the technically literate, however, because the interface to these tools was not yet user-friendly.

The public discussion network known as USENET, essentially a conglomeration of electronic bulletin boards, was created in 1979, followed by BITNET in 1981. In 1983, the military component of the Net split off ARPANET to become MILNET, which merged into the Defense Data Network. In 1984, the National Science Foundation created NSFNET, which dramatically upgraded the networking and computing power of the system. Other government agencies joined up soon thereafter, including groups like NASA, the National Institute of Health, and the Department of Energy. The number of Net users proliferated towards the end of the 1980s, with the growth of public nets like the Cleveland Freenet and Fidonet and the creation of commercial systems like MCI Mail and CompuServe. In 1989, ARPANET was disbanded, leaving behind a rapidly growing, decentralized, and packet-switched network known as the Internet, with the NSFNET as the primary backbone of the system.

During the George H.W. Bush administration, the decision was made to privatize the Internet entirely. To facilitate this transfer of public assets to private corporations, Advanced Network & Services (ANS) was created by MERIT, a group of administrators from the University of Michigan, IBM, and MCI. ANS was empowered to manage the NSFNET and prepare for its eventual replacement. ANS began operating the NSFNET in 1990. Though ANS was ostensibly set up to operate as a nonprofit that received public funds, the organization devoted much of its time to building a for-profit entity called ANS CO-RE, a communications data network that could handle commercial accounts. The MCI/IBM-run NSFNET also awarded lucrative contracts to MCI for use of its data networks to carry NSFNET, provoking conflict of interest charges from other private carriers.[49] In fact, almost the entire NSFNET was carried over lines leased from MCI. Alongside the growing NSFNET, managed by ANS, came other networks built by other carriers, such as Sprint and AT&T. These corporate networks began to carry an increasingly greater percentage of the national data traffic. At the end of 1994, the America Online company (AOL) spent $30 million to buy all ANS CO-RE assets, which included more than 12,000 miles of leased 45 Mbps fiber-optic circuits, mostly from MCI. On April 30, 1995, NSFNET was completely retired, and all national data lines were assumed by the private sector.

What does this privatization and concentrated ownership of the Internet infrastructure mean? Despite the fanfare about the competition and diversity benefits promised by deregulation and privatization in the new Telecommunications Act of 1996, these changes have meant less competition and more monopolization. During the privatization shift, the Internet oper-ated on three different levels: among local providers, regional providers, and national providers. Historically, the national provider was the federally funded portion of the Net that served as the major backbone of the commu-nications system. Other federally funded regional providers acted as the link between the national backbone and local providers, which were primarily universities and small organizations. The new monopolization resulted in greater pressure on the regional providers, while large organizations such as MCI, AT&T, Pacific Telesis, and Sprint consolidated market control with their deep financial pockets and large regional and national infrastructures. The original regional providers were subsidized for their services, but with privatization, these government subsidies were cut off, forcing the regional providers to go private and compete in the monopoly-friendly environment.

At the time, the Regional Bells, like Ameritech and Pacific Telesis, picked up most of the traffic from these regional Nets. Not having the kind of national infrastructure in place that groups like MCI and AT&T had, the Regional Bells found themselves flush with cash from their lucrative posi-tions as local telephone monopolies. The national long-distance providers and the Regional Bells were faced with the prospect of corporate takeover, merger with another large conglomerate, or bankruptcy. Shortly after the new Telecommunications Bill passed on February 1, 1996, Pacific Telesis announced its merger with SBC Corporation, bringing together two regional Bells into one organization. Several days later, two more regional Bells announced their merger—Bell Atlantic and NYNEX—resulting in a tele-phone service provider second only to AT&T. This set the stage for a flurry of ongoing mergers and takeovers that continues today.

That the Internet is monopolized by a small handful of multinational corporations should come as no surprise to any observer of current media. While the culture of the Internet was once ostensibly proud of its noncom-mercial and noble imperative, that principle rapidly become a quaint idea of the past. Commercial messages invaded the Net, popping up on indi-vidual Web sites and on Usenet discussion groups. Services such as America Online—once based on the walled-off village metaphor—began developing more as a giant shopping mall in cyberspace. This commercialization was portrayed by the corporate world and mass media as an indication of the maturation and natural evolution of the Internet. The decentered, individu-alistic nature of the Internet began to be viewed as ideal for new marketing strategies based on the extreme segmentation of a market into lifestyles. What had appeared to be an ideal form of democratic participation and communication now appeared as a very sophisticated tool for reaching a geographically dispersed, high-income consumer market.

The transition to an information-based economy has resulted in enormous amounts of corporate monopolization of broadcasting, cablecasting, print-ing, entertainment, film production, and other information products, and the Internet is seen as just another sector of this economy. Although much of the discussion of new media dwells on the new technology, the ongoing corporate consolidation of media bears a strong resemblance to early decades of corporate media activity. The takeover of the Internet resembles the early days of radio technology, as elucidated by Robert McChesney.[50] Similar to the radio stations that had been set up by public institutions during the 1920s and 1930s and then pushed out by corporations, computer networks had been built primarily by nonprofit organizations, public institutions, individual volunteers, and universities before being shoved aside by large corporations with the help of their allies in Congress. In an historical deja vu, many of the corporations active in new media networks are the same corporations that were active in taking over the early broadcasting industry. RCA (the founder of the first radio network) was absorbed by parent company GE, (which currently is a major supplier of global satellite delivery systems) and owns 49 percent of the NBC network. AT&T, a player in broadcasting from the very beginning with its long-lines links between broadcasting stations, plays a major role in providing telecommunications support, high-speed data lines, and fiber optic links for global networks. Westinghouse, an original manufacturer of radio and consumer electronics, had owned the CBS network before being folded into the Viacom Corporation. These industrial interests, whether or not they function under their old names or their new ones, want the Internet to follow in the footprints of other media technologies, such as radio and television, and to become primarily a delivery system for commercialism, consumerism, and entertainment, not to mention a powerful medium to promote corporate ideology.

In the 1990s, the reality of media conglomeration began to be widely recognized, with many people agreeing that mass media and communications are under the control of just a handful of corporations. As media conglomeration intensified in the 1990s, Gerald Taylor, president of MCI, went so far as to say, "There's probably going to be only four to six global gangs emerge over the next five years as all of this sorts out."[51] These "gangs" came to control an enormous amount of the world's mass media and communications systems. The 1989 merger of Time, Inc. and Warner Communications created the world's largest media complex, combining an extraordinary level of media, including print publications, cable television, and movies. Media giant Viacom bought Paramount Communications in 1994 and Blockbuster Video in 1995. NBC entered into a joint venture with Microsoft and created MSNBC in 1996. Disney bought Cap Cities/ABC in 1996, followed by the Westinghouse purchase of CBS. General Electric continued ownership of NBC, while absorbing Universal/Vivendi. Telephone giants Southwestern Bell and Pacific Telesis merged, as did NYNEX and Bell Atlantic and British Telecom and MCI. MCI, the telecommunications giant that helped break up the national AT&T monopoly into regional Bells, was later absorbed by the failed WorldCom Company in 1998 and was eventually taken over by Verizon in 2006. This corporate media consolidation, whether by hostile takeover, or strategic partnering, still continues at a rapid pace today.

Toward the end of the 1990s, with the rapid expansion of the Internet and computer-based media, many of the previously held assumptions about the power of media corporations began to be questioned. A widespread belief that the Internet was going to change the balance of corporate power was spread by futurists and techno-libertarians, particularly those in the orbit around *Wired* magazine. There was a widely held opinion that the power of new media groups would diminish the power of pure economic might held by established multinationals, who were often portrayed as "dinosaurs." The wildly popular Internet boom spurred the major media corporations into heightened acquisition mode, as they struggled to remain relevant in the rapidly changing media environment. The primary threat from the Internet was the perception that younger audiences were abandoning television screens and would be lost forever from the reaches of the networks and cable television. New startups and dot-coms were capturing the imaginations of many, causing business observers to believe that the traditional names of the industry would be eclipsed by the likes of Google, Yahoo!, Amazon, YouTube, MySpace, Facebook, and other upstarts, fundamentally changing the centralized nature of the media business model. At the pinnacle of the expected absorption of old media by new media shone the symbolic value of the merger of AOL and Time Warner in 2000. What astonished the media world was the fact that it was AOL that acquired Time Warner, not the other way around. Media corporations quickly sought to seal alliances and mergers with technology sector media groups. Within a few years, however, the dot-com bubble burst, and venture capital began to dry up. Although thousands of Web-based businesses employed many thousands of creative and tech-savvy young people, many of these dot-coms were unable to earn any income. Many high-profile dot-coms—including Pets.com, Webvan, and eToys—vanished in a very short period of time, leaving many people out of work and weakening the blind enthusiasm inspired by Internet business models. By the end of the dot-com bubble, a more familiar terrain began to reemerge, where the established corporate players either built an online component of their brand or absorbed smaller Internet innovators. A case in point is popular Internet star MySpace.com, which was acquired by the News Corporation Group (owner of Fox) in 2005 and quickly lost its popularity among its users. Other entities that were enveloped by the traditional media giants include MapQuest, Netscape, CompuServe, and other now-faded stars of the Internet. Often these acquisitions had more to do with eliminating the competition than with nurturing a new media format. More telling perhaps is that the new powers on the block, rather than representing a different approach towards media monopoly, are driven instead by the same imperatives as traditional media monopolies. Google, Facebook, Yahoo!, and others are driven by the intense desire for merger and acquisition. Witness Google's takeover of YouTube in 2006, eBay's purchase of PayPal in 2002, Microsoft's purchase of Skype in 2011, and Google's purchase of Instagram in 2012. Though not paid much attention to, the rate of acquisition of new technology groups by larger groups has been phenomenal. These acquisitions and strategic partnerships are by no means a sure bet, however. In 2009, AOL was peeled off of Time Warner, valued at a fraction of its original worth. In 2011, Comcast took majority control over NBC from General Electric. In 2012, NBC ended its partnership with Microsoft, so that MSNBC became just NBC once again. Facebook's highly anticipated entry in public trading in 2012 proved to be a huge flop, even though it is recognized as one of the most popular online sites in the world. The uncertainty of Facebook has also threatened leading gaming company Zynga, as long-term Internet business models become increasingly perceived as short-term fads.

Even more telling about the behavior of the newly stabilized Internet businesses is their need to maintain, not challenge, the fundamental approach of the broadcasting model created by the original media monopolies. Facebook, Amazon, eBay, Google, Apple, Microsoft—all these groups seek to build a self-contained, centralized environment that can create a closed market of consumers for their products. They pursue a vertically and horizontally integrated monopoly in the purest sense of the word. Google believes its users should not have to leave Google for any aspect of online life, be it email, social media, or information services. Google+, their version of Facebook, was an attempt at plugging the primary leak their environment had, as many Google users would also spend much time on Facebook. Similarly, Apple users should stay entirely within the domain of the Apple brand for hardware, music, and telephone products. The Apple operating system and their app creation process for the iPhone, iPad, and iPod are neatly designed to keep customers within the confines of the Apple fence. Humorously, in order to leave that environment behind, users must "jailbreak" their product. Amazon, which began by only selling books, will now sell anything a consumer wants. It has also entered the electronic market with the Kindle reader, a tool to read the same ebooks it sells. Facebook has engineered its environment to force users to use the email tool built into the system, discouraging users from leaving the environment to check email. Facebook's incorporation of the games made by leading Internet gaming company Zynga is a proven mechanism for keeping users within the Facebook environment, as Zynga's popular games are primarily accessed via Facebook. Ingeniously, in many cases, the product a new media business offers is produced by the same consumers who then buy it back, as in the case of the audience for YouTube videos and Facebook posts. All of these media technology companies are enthralled by the idea of "the cloud," whereby the content of digital media is held on the proprietary server farms of the companies, which the user will then depend upon for retrieval and use, initiating a permanent cycle of production for, and dependency on, the corporation. In any event, the relationship remains the same between the centralized provider of media products, content, and services and the media consumer—whether we analyze new media or old, Facebook, Fox News, or

Viacom Cable. The broadcast model is a center-to-periphery, one-way flow in which the public remains the consumer.

The power of today's media monopolies is unprecedented. As this book is written, six major conglomerates still control the lion's share of the media and information we need to function as a democratic society. These companies and some of their respective operations are the News Corporation (Fox, *Wall Street Journal, NY Post*), General Electric (NBC, Comcast, Universal), Disney (ABC, ESPN), CBS (Showtime), Viacom (MTV, BET, Paramount), and Time Warner (CNN, HBO). Media consolidation is a constantly changing field, as evidenced by a daily perusal of the business sections of the media. Acquisitions and takeovers are a constant in the business, as witnessed by Comcast's merger with NBC in 2011, or the recently failed takeover of T-Mobile by AT&T. It used to be that tracking the ownership of major media corporations was a slow and predictable process, but today it more resembles the speed of the rapidly fluctuating stock market. In order to have a grasp on current media ownership, one must pay attention to groups such as Fairness and Accuracy in Reporting[52] or Free Press[53] to keep up-to-the-minute on media acquisition, partnership, and mergers.

Such a massive amount of financial clout and monopoly control should put these companies in a stable and strategic position. Yet despite their power, they have much to worry about. In the past, technical and financial limitations have played a major role in restricting the tools of media within institutions of power. Not long ago, television cameras were bulky, expensive machines requiring enormous amounts of light and power. Typesetting machines were large, heavy, expensive, and difficult to operate. The ability to disseminate sound, picture, or text required cumbersome and expensive equipment. Communications technology was easily within reach of a multinational conglomerate, but not everyday people. Today the sophistication, mass production, and miniaturization of integrated circuits and microprocessors, coupled with the development of powerful computer languages and algorithms, have created a class of media tools that are easily within reach of small organizations and even individuals. To a greater and greater extent, these tools allow independent voices to bypass the corporate-owned media.

Most remarkably, these new communications practices are being adopted by sectors of society who have historically been shut out of mass media, either by government regulatory restrictions, corporate monopoly, discouragement, apathy, corruption, or lack of resources. Community activists, working-class people, ethnic and cultural minorities, gay and lesbian people, political dissidents, and just plain, fed-up citizens are revolting against media apathy, cultural restrictions, and the overcommercialization of mainstream media. Many media consumers today desire and expect authentic and real communications, not those mediated by distant and homogenized sellers of entertainment commodities. These DIY media makers have become increasingly active in challenging the traditional domain of the mass media. It is clear, as many social observers have pointed out, that recent technological developments have given a tremendous boost to these developments. As this book intends to elucidate, it is also clear that these democratic media practices have been building for decades and have as much to do with the behavior of social activism as with the development of new electronic devices. Though media conglomerates seem stronger than ever, and fewer and fewer corporations own greater and greater shares of mass media, inroads made by democratic media have slowly encroached on the traditional portion of their once-stable mass audience. Like the once-mighty Soviet superpower, the outward strength of the multinational media conglomerates belies the hollowing out of their structure, the weakening of their sinews, the overextension of their reach, and the disillusionment of their audiences. The seeds of their own decline lie within their very embodiment.

2   The DIY Aesthetic and Local Media

LOCAL COMMUNICATIONS IN A GLOBAL SOCIETY

In our superheated age of high technology, the glory often goes to the global, the transborder, and the massive and far-reaching scale of media. Communications satellites hover above the Earth in geostationary orbit, fiber optic cables straddle the globe, microwave links bounce their data from terrestrial dish to dish, e-mail messages penetrate national borders with impunity, and Web sites serve millions of pages a day to a global media audience. With all the emphasis on "mass" and global media, it seems a quaint anachronism to entertain the notion of local, communal, or micromedia. Yet this type of communication plays a pivotal role in driving new technological and media choices in our present age. American media consumers often know more about what's going on around the world than what may be happening down the street. A recurring observation made by many researchers into the foundations of human civilization is that a principal imperative of human-to-human communication is the desire for self-defense, for territorialism, and self-preservation.[1] Anthropological and sociological evidence increasingly suggest the reason the human race has been so successful, at least up until now, has been our ability to cooperate, which of course begins with communication. Language and communications are not merely social practices; they become political as well. The ability to keep a watchful eye and ear and to discuss strategies and responses to events affecting one's community, tribe, or geographical proximity has been paramount to humanity's collective survival. If all politics is local, as social commentators have observed, then local communications would appear to be vitally important. Yet despite such obvious importance, economic and technological developments in communications and media have historically and consistently led away from the local and community development and implementation of media and communication resources. As political economists have noted over many decades, the very structure of the modern corporate economy works against such small-scale development, as larger conglomerates are compelled to absorb local and regional small-scale enterprises in search of an economy of scale.[2]

It stands to reason that media should be able to connect neighbors, communities, precincts, municipalities, counties, or other local entities in a manner that not only serves as a two-way informational warning system, but that also extends the reach of social, cultural, and educational knowledge among those who share geographical, linguistic, or cultural ties. The off-the-radar media projects that, despite the odds, serve these functions are perhaps the most invisible, underappreciated, and misunderstood aspects of the US mediascape. Today's corporate-led mass media conglomerates do not pay mind to the stubborn revolt of the local because their economic interests drive them to follow the big and sensational mass-audience angle. And the less local media that exists, the fewer sources there are to inform the public about it. Local media is not high profile; it is not the domain of corporate giants and kingmakers; yet it profoundly affects how people communicate, how they gather news and information, and how they keep in touch with their friends, families, and neighbors. The trend toward ever-increasing levels of centralization and depersonalization in mass media has left a void in an important area of social interaction. This alienating effect of mass media is a process that began not recently, but decades ago. The void left behind by the erosion of local media has been the terrain of many experimental and activist practitioners, gaining particular momentum in the 1960s.

ART, ACTIVISM, AND DIY TELEVISION IN THE 1960S

As the 1960s began, the electronic media empire of television and radio seemed monolithic, dominated by the three major broadcasting networks: ABC, NBC, and CBS. Challenging this dominance appeared to be a formidable task. The physical and technical infrastructure alone, required by such media production, seemed insurmountable. Ponderous studio cameras weighing hundreds of pounds and run by heavy-equipment operators were a common sight in the studios of the networks. The intense lighting demands of television production often required their own electrical power grid. Radio transmission entailed a specialized team of engineers and technicians to ensure that the thousands of watts of emanated power were stable and drift-free. This was not a media for mere mortals. Yet it was in the 1960s that the first real challenges were mounted against the electronic media monopoly. These seminal projects were begun not on a national or mass scale, but on the community, local, and micro levels. Though small and fragile in scope, these media ventures would have a catalytic and enduring impact on the future of electronic media.

As myth has it, in the midst of the televised beatings of protesters against the Vietnam War by the Chicago Police Department at the 1968 Democratic convention, the chant arose, "The whole world's watching."[3] This vocal response to the frenzied beating of demonstrators has been described as a manifestation of the collective realization of the centrality of television, and of the prophesied global electronic village, as proclaimed by media scholar Marshall McLuhan.[4] That same year the Sony Corporation's consumer-level video camera, the self-contained, battery-powered, quarter-inch, reel-to-reel Portapak machine, became widely available.[5] The camera was affordably priced, and it did not require the technical proficiency normally necessary for television production. The serendipitous concurrence of these two developments resonated with a new generation of artists and activists eager to experiment with the world's most powerful medium.

The Portapak delivered instant image reproduction; it was a technological holy grail that encouraged practitioners to enter the public realm through the medium of television. Previously, this had been the exclusive domain of the Big Three networks. The ability to work on an expanded public stage encouraged a loose movement of artists and activists to experiment with electronic media, and the traditional boundary between fine art and media began to blur, a distinction that continues to confound people today. This fusion of art, activism, and technological experimentation helped create a democratizing trend in both the media world and the art world; it also provoked the imaginations of technicians and engineers. With increasing access to television, many artist and activist groups began working in the video medium, exploring the creative potential of the video image, subverting televisual representations, and tinkering, collaging, and contributing to a growing body of video cultural work.

Armed with the technical apparatus of the day, many of these media artists sought to expose the crises of class and race, deliver a critique of daily life, deconstruct the mechanisms of cultural control, and contribute to the subversion of authority. They also believed passionately in working to produce and present new creative ideas and work to an expanded public by harnessing technology. Scanning the graveyard of video archival material from the 1960s and early 1970s, one sees a plethora of titles shot by collectives and groups of video artists during these early years, groups such as the Alternate Media Center, People's Video Theatre, TVTV, Videofreex, Downtown Community Television Center, Portable Channel, Marin Community Video, Broadside TV, Headwaters TV, University Community Video, and Videopolis. New York State alone had over a dozen functioning video collectives in the late 1960s and early 1970s.

It is this kind of praxis that informs much of the early Portapak work that is gathering dust in archives around the United States, including tapes of the first Woman's Liberation March up New York City's 5th Avenue, images of a family picnic inside the walls of a New York State Prison, early gay liberation activity, anti–Vietnam War demonstrations, and numerous countercultural happenings such as conversations with artists, intellectuals, and activists. In early black-and-white Portapak footage, whether the work of socially conscious video collectives or of individual artists' video studio experiments, one sees a similar self-conscious playfulness onscreen: murky and grainy images appearing to be shot through cheesecloth, with primitive single-tube cameras comet-tailing or blooming across the screen. One can peruse many of these early artists' tapes thanks to the Video Data Bank, based in Chicago, that houses perhaps the largest body of video work in the United States. Bruce Nauman's 1968 work, *Stamping in the Studio*, shows the artist stamping his feet in his studio, circling the perimeter of the TV tube on which the viewer is watching him. Vito Aconci's 1971 work, *Pryings*, depicts a man's hands trying to pry open a woman's eyes as she struggles to keep them closed. Whether we find an overtly political tape, such as *Mayday Realtime* on the enormous 1971 antiwar attempt to shut down Washington, DC, or a more personal tape such as Martha Rosler's *Semiotics of the Kitchen*, the nascent video movement was seen within an overtly political context. The primary publication that rallied these early video pioneers was *Radical Software*, published by a collective of artists and alternative media practitioners. Their collective statement in the first issue stated that "[u]nless we design and implement alternate information structures which transcend and reconfigure the existing ones, other alternate systems and life styles will be no more than products of the existing process."[6]

ELECTRONIC MEDIA AS COLLECTIVE AND SOCIAL PRACTICE

While painting and writing tend to be highly solitary, video production is often collective, tied as it is to practicalities like feeding tape stock, wrangling electricity, and tweaking machines. I would argue that perhaps no other artistic medium has such an integration of craft and art, providing a kind of vitality intrinsic to video productions. For many of these early video makers, the rising of the little Portapak against the major studio cameras presented an electronic David-versus-Goliath conflict. This analogy fed into the articulation of guerilla video through images of a world inflamed by the rebellion of oppressed people against modern imperialism and neocolonialism. Vivid pictures of Watts in flames, the self-immolation of the monks in Saigon, the riotous crowds in Latin America on the eve of David Rockefeller's visit in 1969, the mass mobilization of red guards in China during the Cultural Revolution, and other inflammatory images captured the imaginations of many activists and artists. Che Guevara, the Vietnamese revolution, the uprisings in Africa against Apartheid in the South and against the Portuguese colonies in the North, and a myriad of armed rebellions against the "gorillas" in Latin America played a major role in shaping the mindset of a generation of video artists. Media prankster and Yippie!-organizer Abbie Hoffman urged American revolutionaries to seize the television studios and pointed out the importance of television by noting that there were more television sets in America than toilets. Media production was seen as a social act, and a collective form of organization became part and parcel of this ideology. The transition towards creating audiovisual media within a political context helped launch the Newsreel Collective, a national organization of New Left filmmakers, who particularly exemplified this new style of work and life. Newsreel was comprised of filmmaker collectives in cities around the United States that made films on political struggles ranging from Oakland's Black Panther Party to the Columbia student takeover in New York City.

Guerilla tactics were seen as essential in an environment where television was rigidly controlled by just CBS, NBC, and ABC. And guerilla tactics required a collective style of work. A collective approach to video production was also necessary due to the cost of the essential equipment, the steep prices of which encouraged many artists to collaborate for economic reasons. One of the primary funders of early video art, the New York State Council of the Arts, solely funded groups and collectives for these reasons of economic efficiency. This is radically different than today's practices, in which most funders stipulate that only individual artists can apply for support.

What constitutes a collective is clearly something open to interpretation. Collectives run the gamut from loose associations of like-minded individuals working towards a common goal to rigid, cadrelike, single-minded organizations with a vanguard's democratic centralism at their hearts. A collective running a food co-op is different than an underground newspaper collective. It is safe to say at least that collectives generally seek some kind of consensus around work priorities, be it a film production or a potato harvest. Egalitarian concerns are high on the list of priorities so that rank is downplayed, at least official rank, and the division of labor seeks to be nonhierarchical and rotating so that everyone can do everything. These ideals spring from utopian elements of communalism and are influenced and tempered by political imperatives often derived from clandestine liberation movements. Guerilla manuals often reflect on the necessity for egalitarianism, not only for building the "new society," but also for sustaining a more fungible political movement. In centralized organizations, if the head is cut off, the organism dies, but in a decentralized movement, many more heads just spring back up. Or in more pragmatic terms, if the character generator operator does not show up in time for the shoot, the cameraperson can take over.

There are many reasons, besides technological or financial imperatives, for the collective production of video in the early years of its development. An essential element of late 1960s activism was the desire to incorporate daily life into one's beliefs so that personal and social convictions become one with everyday life. This "lifestyle" ideology was mostly absent from the views of pre–World War II radicals, whose domestic lives often were untouched by their politics. But many in the 1960s and 1970s countercultural milieu could not justify spending the day being an activist or artist only to go home to a routine living arrangement in mainstream culture. The belief in making personal life as important as political or cultural life propelled the movement to build communal living situations throughout the United States.[7] These living arrangements encompassed many thousands of people and established collectives of all kinds, from filmmaking and organizing, to bread baking and newspaper publishing. The growth of feminism and the gay rights movement in the early 1970s helped to spread these concerns to all parts of daily life, throughout the home and into the bedroom and the kitchen. Many of today's video collectives share their predecessors' egalitarian and antihierarchical ideals. As art critic Martha Rosler points out, the early video movement was infused with this kind of "utopian" ideal. Video was going to change the world and collapse the art world into itself by posing a challenge "to the sites of art production in society, to the forms and 'channels' of delivery, and to the passivity of reception built into them."[8] Thus, implicit in early video was "[n]ot only a systemic but also a utopian critique . . . for the effort was not to enter the system but to transform every aspect of it . . . by merging art with social life and making audience and producer interchangeable." This understanding and appreciation of integrating communication and media into everyone's daily life is a strong part of today's media revolution.

As the insurgent period of the 1960s and 1970s ended, as the United States was pushed out of Vietnam, as Nixon was reelected and then forced from office, and as the Carter presidency began, much of the urgency and resolve of activism waned. With this slow decay of the idealism and energy of the 1960s, much of the video art world devolved into a bland narcissism, wrapped up in the solitary gesture or the gimmickry and gadgetry of the medium. Provoked by a culture of ironic detachment, many video artists played around with the form, experimenting with the equipment while sidestepping the medium's roots in television. In the depoliticized climate, eschewing social consciousness provoked a better response from patrons of the arts, and what was good for the patrons was good for the galleries and mainstream cultural institutions.

ART OR MEDIA?

During this period of independent video and film, tension arose between art and media, and perhaps an identity crisis concerning which category such productions fit into. This was not just a rhetorical question: resources such as funding, screening venues, publicity, audience, and recognition depended upon it. The division between "art" and socially conscious media work did not rigidify until the later "museumization" of video work. Marita Sturken, in her essay on early video art, explains that "[t]he standard subcategories that are commonly used to describe video today—such as documentary, media-concerned, image-processing, and narrative—while glaringly inadequate now, had no relevant meaning in the late 1960s and early 1970s."[9]

Early on, the video movement began to attract attention in the art world and mass media establishments, which chose to either co-opt or disparage its practitioners. In peculiarly American fashion, video that had strong social content was often dismissed as "activist" and rejected as amateurish and one-sided, while video that focused more on formal considerations could be given "art" status. Thus began the early division between "artists" and activists within the field of grassroots television, between those whose "primary focus was to use portable video to effect social change, not to experiment with a new medium."[10]

With a fixed base of venues and better cash flow, the art world became important for such media production. Many art critics, gallery curators, and other arbiters of the art world fixated on form, often devaluing work based on content. Likewise, they tended to dismiss such work as "political" art or not art at all, somehow reasoning that art that focused on larger social issues or art situated in the public sphere was too depersonalized, less individualistic, and thus less intrinsic to the approved and marketable stereotype of the sensitive and creative artist. As Martha Rosler explained it, "It is the self-imposed mission of the art world to tie video into its boundaries and cut out more than passing reference to film, photography, and broadcast television, as the art world's competition, and to quash questions of reception, praxis and meaning in favor of the ordinary questions of originality and 'touch.'"[11] Such work was also not welcome to the mass media world, which dismissed it as "amateurish" and "biased." Many of the works denigrated as "activist" were produced by video collectives that naturally tended to focus more on larger, social concerns relevant to the public, the marginalized, and the dispossessed. Contrary to those who dismissed such work as being too "social," proponents of video collectives countered that the seemingly "spontaneous" generation of art, as lionized in the art world, typically manifests the internalization of social norms and culture, absorbed from the artists' social, economic, and political position, and is thus ultimately a collective product as well. Nevertheless, the individual reigned supreme in our self-centered cultural consciousness.

A central question emerged: is independent video production only concerned with new forms and the self-conscious use of the medium? Or can it work to reintegrate media practice with daily life, challenge complacency and cultural passivity, and confront the public's expectations and prejudices? Arts movements such as Surrealism and Dadaism, which are now enshrined within the art establishment, emerged as similar antiestablishment movements. As Rosler puts it, "The disruptive efforts of Expressionism, Dada, and Surrealism intended to transgress against not just the art world but conventional social reality and thereby become an instrument of liberation."[12] Many other oppositional cultural movements that sought to fuse daily life with artistic expression and communication, such as the Situationists, Beats, Diggers, and Hippies continue to influence video and artist collectives today.

Members of video collectives well understand that the art world does not validate the collective role in art production. Contemporary art production is intimately connected to the art market, and thus financial considerations often take precedence over many aesthetic concerns. Thus, the questions of ownership and authorship become crucial if an art product is to have value. However, collective art production is often antithetical to authorship and ownership or is at least ambiguous about these issues, although authorship is strongly tied to the financial value of the work. Authorship also is integral to modern Western ideas of the genius of the individual as the prime mover of history. Prevailing conceptions of individual art production and creativity have been ingrained for so long that they have become nothing less than "common sense." This is the case despite the transformation by mechanization, industrialization, and the recognition of intertextuality that lies at the core of modern cultural production. Even cinema, the most industrially organized of the creative arts, succumbed decades ago to the cult of the individual, with the adoption of the notion of *auteurship*, the theory that creative recognition of a film should be awarded to its director, as opposed to the writer, director of photography, set designer, actors, or other principal collaborators.

NEIGHBORHOOD CINEMA

While technical and logistical barriers to grassroots film and video production fell in the last decades of the twentieth century, barriers to the channels and venues of distribution and exhibition did not. The problem of access to distribution was heightened with the increased monopolization of the media industry, particularly as the vertical integration of the industry stressed least-common-denominator blockbuster hits and took fewer risks with unproven, less-commercial material. As many video and filmmakers can attest, access to an audience is an integral aspect of media making. The primary point of media-making endeavors is to reach people with the images and audio the artist has arranged, a function vital to those who identify as video/film artists and media makers. Organizing independent local video or film playback, exhibition, and distribution became an essential part of the film and video movement. For decades it was typically the only way such work could be seen by an audience. The practice of film and video projection "happenings" in living rooms, backyards, storefronts, and other alternative forms of public space is not new, of course. In the United States, there is a long tradition of pinning a sheet on a wall and projecting work that is kept from the commercial venues. Early African-American cinema has its roots in this tradition, as work created by Black artists that portrayed the Black community in a positive light was not accepted into normal distribution chains. In Black neighborhoods around the United States, viewers could come into the backyards, barns, churches, and other public spaces to see work directed by Black directors with Black casts.

Other historical roots of neighborhood and mobile cinema can be found in the activities of the Film and Photo Leagues of the 1930s,[13] as well as numerous amateur film clubs that proliferated in the mid-twentieth century.

The Film and Photo League was a group of filmmakers who were determined to provide independent media to working people who would not ordinarily be exposed to alternative views. Operating primarily during the years of the Great Depression, the League took their influences from similar groups operating in Europe as part of the great upheavals of labor worldwide. The Film and Photo League was a loose affiliation of local film collectives based in New York City, Detroit, Chicago, San Francisco, Los Angeles, and other regions. Following in the tradition of other social realist photographers of the era, they sought to document the trials and tribulations of workers and poor people during dire economic times. Reflecting their commitment to radical social change, they also showed how working people were fighting back, not wanting just to generate sympathy, but action as well. With this in mind, getting their films to their audience was just as important as filming the strikes, trials, and demonstrations they covered. Carla Leshne's account of the Film and Photo League is instructive in pointing out the importance of local screenings. In one such account of League members Balog and Royce, she writes, "Balog and Royce showed their films to an audience of 1000 at the Fillmore Workers Center, which Balog described as 'very enthusiastic.' They continued to Carmel for a showing the next night, where he observed that the audience in this sort of 'artist colony' was not as enthusiastic as at other showings." "Balog spent 9 October preparing for the continuing tour down the California coast, by helping to print 15,000 publicity leaflets. Over the next two months, they showed the films throughout California."[14] The Film and Photo League also developed "mobile" theatre, whereby trucks were outfitted with screens and projectors to bring independent cinema to outlying neighborhoods.

The link between the Film and Photo League of the 1930s and the US New Left filmmakers collective Newsreel is more than just inspirational; it is somewhat direct, as some past members of the League participated in the beginnings of Newsreel. Newsreel developed at a time when film was still the dominant form of news footage, on the cusp of the adoption of portable video for covering current events.

BLACK PANTHERS AND THE NEWSREEL COLLECTIVE

The insurgent movements of the 1960s demanded new institutions, new ways of doing things, and new outlets for creative expression. The counterculture that "The Movement" spawned created underground newspapers, freeform radio stations, alternative music venues, and radical film and video collectives. The "film at 11" newscast that the Big Three broadcasting empires of CBS, NBC, and ABC piped into US living rooms nightly was often scorned as establishment propaganda or diversion from the real issues of the day. In 1967, the Newsreel Collective was formed in New York City by a diverse group of filmmakers, ranging from experimental artists to commercial producers to military photographers, who all wanted to confront the conservative hegemony of film and television. Traditionally, a newsreel was a short, informational film about important current events projected for audiences at public venues such as movie theaters. The newsreel became popular during World War II as a means of keeping Americans informed about the war effort and to keep the public vigilant and alert. The Newsreel Collective of the 1960s wanted to provide a similar informational wakeup call to the US public.

In the San Francisco Bay Area, one of the most profound and influential political movements in US history—the Black Panther Party—was moving to the forefront of current events. Started as the Black Panther Party for Self-Defense in Oakland, California, in 1966, the group emerged into a full-fledged revolutionary movement that soon found itself face to face with extreme repression from local, state, and federal authorities. Panther offices were frequently raided by police, and Panther members were often physically threatened, abused, and even killed by law enforcement officers. Bay Area radical filmmakers were determined to counter what they saw as the ignorant and fearful mass media representation of the Panthers with their own more sympathetic point of view of the Panther movement. A collaboration arose between Newsreel members in New York City and a group of Bay Area filmmakers and activists, and thus San Francisco Newsreel was born. SF Newsreel's first task was to film the growing power of the Black Panther Party. The group produced two films on the Black Panther movement. Today these films are often called *Black Panther* but were produced as two separate films. *Off the Pig* was shot in 1967 and focused on the goals of the Black Panther Party. The film is a collage of images of police violence, political protest, and scenes of life in Oakland's Black community woven around interviews with leading figures in the Party. *Mayday* was shot in 1969 and centers around a Free Huey Newton rally the Panthers held on May 1 in front of the San Francisco Federal Building. Both films display the power and discipline of the Panthers as well as the concrete steps the Party was taking to help their community survive, from fighting police brutality to providing breakfast for poor children. There was also a third film with the Black Panthers that was produced by Los Angeles Newsreel, entitled *Repression*.

Off the Pig (total run time [TRT]: 14:34) opens with a montage of shattered plate-glass windows with Black Panther posters torn by police bullets. The film reflects the immediacy of low-budget filmmaking—black and white, high contrast, grainy, tattered with wear, frames missing—and the vestiges of a cinema of poverty. African drums keep the beat over handheld scenes of Panthers marching in military formation, carrying their flags and symbols. Scenes of the Oakland ghetto are cut together with the poster art of Panther artist Emory Douglas, whose artwork once kept the streets of Oakland covered with slogans and wheatpaste. Candid, spontaneous, and uncensored interviews with Huey Newton, Eldridge Cleaver, and other leaders bring out the heart and soul of the Black Panther Party's ten-point program, in contrast to the mass media's depiction of the Panthers as violent Black nationalists. *Mayday* (TRT: 13:30) provides footage of a large Free Huey rally, interspersed with footage of police brutality in the Black community and set to a jazz soundtrack. One scene captures the Panthers passing out boxes of Mao Tse Tung's "Little Red Book," while the speaker on bullhorn advocates revolution.

These films, though by now ragged, faded, and perhaps crude, are striking in contrast to today's packaged and commercialized rebellion, a time-worn, clichéd marketing gimmick that seeks to capitalize on consumers' desire to be perceived as rugged individualists. The histrionics of gangsta rap and bad-boy rock seem almost comical next to the Black Panther films, which capture real rebellion in dangerous times, not a public image strategy. The vérité "style" of much of the footage, and the simplicity of the films' structure still gives these films an honest quality, despite their unequivocal stance in favor of the Panther movement.

The organizational mission of the Newsreel Collective was not just to make and distribute films; it was also to actively exhibit them as well. Newsreel members would set up their projectors in community centers, backyards, churches, and even off the backs of trucks onto public walls, in an effort to get their vision out into the public. A Newsreel screening would often include other revolutionary cinema as well, such as work by Cuban director Santiago Alvarez, or films from Vietnam or Africa. Newsreel screenings typically involved a collective member showing up in person in order to stimulate a conversation about the films and to promote an active audience.

Newsreel films were created to urge people to action. The rat-a-tat-tat of the Newsreel logo, as the letters machine-gunned in rapid staccato on the screen, was testament to that desire. The Black Panther films and other Newsreel films were created to be participatory, advocacy media, not detached observations with the classic omniscient voice of authority. Thus, they had more in common with cinéma vérité, the work of Emile de Antonio or the contemporary Cuban cinema, than with traditional US newsreels. In *Black Panther*, the audience is given a privileged position among the Panthers, as part of the movement, rather than situated as lurking from behind police lines, where most establishment media positioned themselves. In taking such a stand, Newsreel was an important contributor to contemporary advocacy and participatory film and video making.

REDISCOVERING MICROCINEMA

The innovative alternative screenings and film events initiated by such groups as the Film and Photo League and the Newsreel Collective helped to build a new cultural alternative that celebrated the gatherings and social space of collective viewing. With the introduction of portable video, the rarity of playback equipment made collective screenings even more important. This was in sharp contrast to the typically solitary activity of modern television viewing of commercial content that originated from the urban studios far away. The necessity for gathering in storefronts, galleries, and other public spaces to watch portable video screenings regenerated the popularity, or rather the rediscovery, of what many refer to as "microcinema," a phenomenon that continues to this day in many communities across the United States. In the "Guerilla Television" handbook by Michael Shamberg and Raindance, the primary manifesto of the Portapak video movement, the importance of group screening and group production is highlighted in this manner. "Videotaping with friends is like having a collective consciousness both for the real-time experience, and the potential of stored (i.e., recorded) experience." "Making a tape with friends is similar to a jam session by a rock group. In a sense, it's an informational jam session: improvised behavior within the parameters of a certain skill."[15]

Microcinema refers to a gathering of video and filmmakers, music video producers, amateurs, and semiprofessionals, to publicly project, exhibit, and share their creations among groups of friends and neighbors. Microcinema events are often comprised of many media makers, who relish the chance to meet with other makers, share experiences and ideas, and get direct feedback on work, either finished or "in-progress." Throughout the early video period, public screenings brought an audience to the wielders of camcorders and home media equipment and built a creative bond among DIY media enthusiasts. Microcinema represents a participatory form of entertainment and discourse that reconnects people and brings together bodies, as well as thoughts and ideas, images and sound. Screenings are typically collective endeavors involving a division of labor in procuring and setting up equipment and assembling an audience in order to culminate in the collective experience of a video screening. The ephemeral nature of microcinema, as well as its reliance upon low-rent brick and mortar sites, means that venues often come and go very quickly; groups combine with other groups, deconstructing, reconvening, and moving from venue to venue. Screening sites have included living rooms, storefronts, classrooms, churches, bars, bowling alleys, parking lots, and other public, low-to-no-rent zones. Some microcinemas have had staying power and have become legendary within the imaginations of alternative film and video communities. Craig Baldwin's Other Cinema, for example, has been instrumental in developing the alternative media scene in the San Francisco Bay Area for many decades. Audiences gather in the funky storefront that Other Cinema shares with Artists Television Access in the city's Mission District and are often filled with media artists eager to engage in the conversations around DIY media. As James Encinas, cofounder of the Los Angeles microcinema group, Access, points out, microcinema may have the power to reconnect communities: "Not only is microcinema bringing audience members together from various walks of life, it's often putting together into a single hour-long show the work of filmmakers with widely different styles, intentions and experience."[16]

The current popularity of microcinema was motivated by the demolition and partition of art house and retro movie theatres that began in the 1970s, transforming eclectic community theatres that understood local taste into multiplex malls programmed around multiple screenings of Hollywood blockbusters. Though alternative screening venues have been around for many decades, they seemed to multiply rapidly in conjunction with the rise of independent media being produced by a new generation of film and video makers, with subjects ranging from radical documentary to fine art and from off-beat narratives to experimental cinema. In particular, microcinemas gave impetus to an increasingly popular genre of media—the personal essay, a style ubiquitous on YouTube today. Microcinema helped tremendously to reconnect local community and spur two-way DIY media communication among artists, youth, activists, and other groups of citizens. The ability to develop microcinemas was greatly accelerated due to the proliferation of relatively inexpensive video projectors that allowed people to raise a white sheet, dim the lights, and enjoy the show. In the Bay Area alone, these sites have numbered in the hundreds, as pointed out by Steve Anker: "Storefronts, lofts, and basements are for a time transformed into gathering spots of small and committed, lively audiences. Hundreds have been used as locations for punk media spaces (Club Generic, Club Foot), a video and performance art gallery-theater (La Mamelle), grassroots centers for underground screenings and workshops (Video Free America, Artist's Television Access), a small basement home theater (Total Mobile Home, the original micro-CINEMA), and an enduring series mixing all kinds of discarded and intriguing films (Oddball Film and Video)."[17] Some of these microcinema spaces have included Artist's Television Access in San Francisco, Orgone Cinema in Pittsburgh, Midnight Special in Los Angeles, and Fun House Cinema in Austin, Texas. Microcinema was a concrete, positive answer to the solitary and isolated viewing practices that surrounded the television set in the living room. Practitioners and promoters of microcinema recognized that media making and media viewing are symbiotic and should be considered as social practice, as a collective, participatory act. Microcinema serves as a powerful catalyst for encouraging regular people to make media and for reminding makers that communities desire such media. Current video sharing sites such as YouTube or Vimeo duplicate the same opportunity to enjoy work made by video makers, as in a similar fashion these venues offer the possibility for your work to be seen by your peers, get feedback, and become part of a community of like-minded souls. An active community of new media makers encourages others to participate as well, and the desire to create one's own media becomes viral. As one of the more famous experimental media artists put it, "Language is a virus."[18]

A NEW LOCAL ELECTRONIC VIDEO NETWORK

In a time of instantaneous global communications, "old" technologies like local radio and community television may not seem important or relevant. It is important to realize, though, that the current allure of many new technologies has depended upon mimicking the social space created by local media. The environment of local media is not just a smaller version of mass media, but also a warmer, more personal, partisan, and passionate space concerned with individual, neighborhood, and communitarian issues. Local, community-based media can provide for a freer exchange of views, with a less hierarchical structure and a more accessible feedback loop. A contemporary notion of community is not necessarily based solely on geographic locality, but on a shared experience of places, languages, cultures, creeds, beliefs, religions, ethnicities, interests, and other ideas that create a social bond. Ideally, such media sites function as an electronic community for like-minded souls, who can develop the ability to interact with each other, whether with voice, text, video, or other mediated means. It is the capacity for multidirectional communication between participants in communities of geographic locale or like minds that has caught the imaginations of so many. It is also what traditional large-scale centralized media cannot deliver. The return of the local is an integral part of why the dominant media model is dissolving. This realization explains why large media corporations are now studying the success of local blogs, social media, and wiki sites, in the hopes they can learn how to maintain local audiences.[19]

Certainly, traditional text-based media such as newspapers, newsletters, and journals have their origins in local geographies. Centuries ago, local print media expanded by taking advantage of national postal systems to extend their reach to other regions and nations, and then by tapping into long-distance telegraphy and, later, by utilizing facsimile photo distribution, to internationalize their coverage. The once-great strength of the newspaper was firmly rooted in its local allegiances and connections, as many newspapers today are rediscovering. Historically, cities and towns have had an abundance of local print journals to choose from, reflecting the various perspectives and allegiances of their citizens. As Ben Bagdikian points out, "[E]very American city of any size had half a dozen papers or more, and their politics both in editorials and news emphasis ranged from far left to far right and everything in between."[20] As mass media grew in the last century, the local newspaper was established as a feature of town life. Through the decades, traditional print media was increasingly supplanted by newer electronic media like radio and television, which similarly attempted to satisfy the demand for local news and events. Local media organizations have been considered vital to public service and community involvement, following the FCC critiques voiced by Newton Minow in the 1960s, who complained of television as "the vast wasteland"[21] with its emphasis on game shows and base entertainment.[22]

Business models for mass media have consistently pulled away from such locality. The early thrill of electronic media was its ability to bring stories, images, sounds, and pictures from great distances into the lives of citizens far-removed from the events. Even so, the spectacle of such events was brought to the attention of people via a local media source and through a local lens and interpretation. Historically, what drove such technologies as the telegraph and radio were business models geared towards centralization and consolidation, the tendency of most industrial models seeking economies of scale. Through the decades, the technological research invested in the film, radio, television, and cable industries has been centered on a profit-based model, developing a centralized model of entertainment and information to be delivered as a commodity wrapped around advertising content.

As we saw in the previous chapter, while newspapers and print have historically been locally and community based, radio and television have been dependent upon a technological infrastructure that not only favors centralization, but that also relies upon a trained base of technicians and skilled professionals. Up until perhaps the 1980s, electronic media have attempted to maintain a local flavor, despite the great distance with which broadcasters must contend. For decades it was not unusual to hear radio stations with regional accents, local personalities, community tie-ins, and ethnic and cultural diversity. Radio powerhouses like WWVA, once known as the "Voice of the American Trucker" boomed out of Wheeling, West Virginia, with a mix of local talent and talk. Station WSM, the "Air Castle of the South," radiated the Grand Ol' Opry out of Nashville, Tennessee, with its eclectic sound of Southern folk and country.[23] Border radio from the Mexico/US divide showered a regional mix of eclecticism upon the hinterlands of the United States. Such diversity is now a thing of the past.

As far back as 1946, the FCC laid out some ground rules for community service programming, specifying that broadcasting stations must provide "'balance' in programming," as laid out in its report known as the "blue book."[24] This recommendation included airing sufficient live, local programs as well as educational programming, news, airtime for nonprofit groups, and discussion of local issues. Most Americans would likely agree that television and radio have failed to provide this kind of local programming. In an increasingly centralized media environment, the least common denominator still drives a large part of the content decisions of media corporations. Even recognizing the atomization of lifestyle markets in today's Web-driven world, the number of total "hits" a Web site receives is still an important financial indicator. Pandering to the widest demographic is the reason behind the historic unwillingness of the entertainment industry to portray people who reflect the diverse nature of the contemporary United States. It also explains the tendency to pander to the least common denominator of their marketing demographic.

It is easy now to take for granted that almost all citizens can gain access to a digital video device, camcorder, or cell phone to record their children, the dog, or summer vacation. The video camera plays a role once occupied by Super 8 and Regular 8 film decades before. But video has some important distinctions from film. With a different approach and intent, video can be broadcast, cablecast, and electronically duplicated and disseminated to millions of people. In short, it can create an impact far beyond the living room and the local screening venue. Early video explorers understood that the ability to exploit the wide reach of their video productions was hindered by the absence of the power to broadcast, a weakness well understood by the activist and artist founders of public access television in the late 1970s and early 1980s. Though there were a few extraordinary experiments done in mainstream and public television with reel-to-reel and Portapak productions (the Videofreex CBS project *Subject to*

Change,[25] or the *National Center for Experiments in Television*[26] at KQED, San Francisco, for example), the access to television sets of the average American viewer lay tantalizingly out of reach until the mid-1970s.

The introduction of cable television presented an important opportunity to reclaim a stake in electronic communications media and find a larger audience while the new forms of alternative and participatory media were gaining popularity. The roots of cable television go much further back than most people realize, to the 1940s, when communities in valley and rural areas shared a community antenna to pick up far-off broadcast television signals. It is for that reason that cable television is referred to as "CATV," which stands for "Community Antenna Television." It wasn't until the 1970s, however, that the modern cable industry began, in particular the Home Box Office services, by competing with the type of programming the major networks offered. In order to compete in urban areas, the cable companies sought permission to rip up streets and lay cable, much like other utilities. The growth of the cable industry happened at a time when there was a still a strong base of community organization from the 1960s, a nascent video arts movement, and a strong desire of the cable companies to appease the demands of the cities in order to sell cable services. The growth of cable was fought by both the motion picture industry and the broadcast networks, who depicted the industry with images of coin-slot boxes that would sit on top of television sets, calling it in one notorious commercial, "the monster" in your living room. Franchise agreements were drawn up to give local municipalities rights to collect a portion of cable profits for community communications. Included in these agreements was certain language brought to the negotiations by community access advocates, which stipulated that the cable companies must provide studios and playback facilities for public use. These public channels eventually became known as the "PEG" channels for their public, educational, and governmental uses, and are still operational today in many cities. Thus, public access came about through the intervention of activists (not the benevolence of the cable companies), and it is generally enforced in the legal language of the contract between the company and the city. Cable television shifted away from local community systems into national systems beginning in 1975, when programming services took advantage of satellite transmission to feed programming to a growing network of local cable systems. In particular, pay-for-show sports events and softcore pornography were the main drivers of cable in the late 1970s, as the industry was not subject to the same FCC rules as over-the-air broadcasters. Over the years, many legislative and legal acts have impacted the public access obligations of cable, but community activism has helped defend it in many places. The cable industry has faced many demands for regulation from the public due to numerous complaints about the industry from consumers. At the same time, the cable industry has been absorbed into the empires of the major media corporations and has enormous political power to fight back against regulation. HBO, for example, is part of the Time Warner conglomerate, as is Cinemax. Depending on the extent of local community organizing, public access stations vary in quality and size from a mere playback deck to state-of-the-art multicamera studios, remote vans, and elaborate postproduction facilities. Through PEG channels, many millions of people have participated in the more than 3000 public access stations that can be found in major cities as well as rural towns. Through the years, access centers have evolved from bare-bones, black-and-white CCTV cameras to sophisticated postproduction centers. As video technology dropped in price while taking great leaps in technological ability, community producers acquired a wide range of media skills through access to cameras, special effects boxes, switchers, computer graphics, remote packages, and audio mixers. But perhaps more importantly, public access producers have had full freedom to develop their own original productions and realize their creative ideas without regard to corporate sponsorship, art gallery recognition, or appeal to a mass audience. Though there is little funding for market share research for public access channels, the few viewing analyses that have been conducted have demonstrated support for community television. More importantly, as Aufderheide points out, "the most useful measure is not, and should not be, numbers of viewers or positive poll results, but the ability of access to make a difference in community life. Access cable should not function like American public television does." "Access needs to be a site for communication among members of the public as the public, about issues of public importance."[27] Indeed, many access activists insist that producing a program is more important than actually watching one, as the experience of media production is reason enough for access. The notion of "narrowcasting" became an important concept because public access programs grow from and serve a local, niche audience, in contrast with "broadcasting," which must attract a wide and homogenous audience. The availability of accessible video technology and the infrastructure of the public access channels put the power of television into the hands of people who have historically been excluded and marginalized by the mass media. In our information age, television means power. After observing their own inaccurate, stereotypical, or shallow representation on the small screen for most of their lives, the people who discover public access often gain a great sense of empowerment by being able to create and define their own media representation. African Americans, Asian Americans, Latino/as, Native Americans, gay and lesbian citizens, foreign-language ethnicities, union members, and political radicals were among the first proponents of public access because it gave them access to a media that was seen as the *sine qua non* of one's existence. The belief that "if you didn't see it on television, it didn't exist" was very real for many people. Out of their own pockets, through countless hours of volunteer labor, public access producers have changed the conventions of television and brought radically new representations of culture, people, and ideas to television. According to the Alliance for Community Media, a national membership organization that represents public, educational, and governmental channels, local producer-programmers produce some 20,000 hours of new programs each week, serving more than a quarter of a million organizations annually through the efforts of 1.2 million citizen producers.[28] Despite often relentless scorn and sarcasm from the mainstream media, and hostility and neglect from the cable companies, public access thrived in the 1980s and 1990s and helped proclaim the elusive goals of serving the public and broadening the cultural diversity of the medium.

Uninvited public interventions into mass media, outside of the gimmicky ways that have been neatly formulated for public input—like call-in shows, contests, games—have historically been frowned upon by the conglomerations of communications corporations whose interest it is to command and control the eyes and ears of the public to deliver their mission of serving audiences to advertisers. To combat popular communications activity, attempts by the public to enter mass media have been marginalized, ridiculed, and labeled as fringe; they are the domain of troublemakers, amateurs, and idealists. Public access frequently offered more local programming, community information, diversity, and, often, more originality than many mainstream stations within a locality. Public access television offered minorities and ethnicities, workers, lesbians and gays, non-English speakers, who are often excluded or caricatured on the screen in our living rooms, a chance to communicate on their own terms. For example, despite decades of activism demanding more roles for African Americans, Asian Americans, Latino/as, workers, gays and lesbians, it was public access television that began to deliver this reform, not mainstream broadcast television.[29] The absence of nonwhite positive role models is still pervasive, as noted recently by Greg Braxton in the Los Angeles Times: "More than two decades after 'The Cosby Show' broke new ground with its portrayal of a loving two-parent black family into the pop culture mainstream, shows featuring nuclear black families or families of color have all but vanished."[30] Braxton notes that this paucity of positive nonwhite representation has kept alive the African-American tradition of providing alternative venues for media. He notes that on a recent Sunday at the First African Methodist Episcopal Church, an overflow crowd gathered after services to see a screening of TV Land's *The Soul Man*. "We're excited about seeing role models for our community and for America," the Reverend John J. Hunter told his congregation.[31]

DEVELOPING A DIY MEDIA MOVEMENT

Public access television succeeded in training many thousands of people in television production and popularized the notion of DIY electronic media throughout the 1980s and 1990s. In doing so, it helped to demystify a key component of the hold broadcasting media had on the public: that only an elite, "professional" few could produce it. The proliferation of public access TV programs from coast to coast created a strong sense of community amongst many sectors of the public, particularly those underserved by media, be it racially, ethnically, linguistically, or culturally. From the origins of public access to today, a steady stream of citizens has taken advantage of the training, production, and distribution resources of this institution. As veteran video activist Dee Dee Halleck puts it, "[T]he most significant development of the public access movement has been the informed practice of thousands of individuals who have taken an activist role in not only the production of their own television, but in the implementation, the nurturing, and the defending of local telecommunications structures. The process of organizing public access in the United States has created a diverse and significant group of media activists who are now knowledgeable and vigilant on issues of technology and communication policy."[32] Many of the same people who cut their teeth on public access have become involved in other interventions into grassroots media such as pirate radio, microcinema, community computing, social networking, and community wifi. The culture of public access has been grafted onto the many diverse movements of new media, especially when it seeks to demystify media technologies and advocate for the right to community media. The spirit of public access can be found all over the globe, from the "guerilla media" of the Indy Media Centers, which I detail in the following chapter, to the many countries around the globe where the US public access model has been emulated. The recent proliferation of socially relevant video podcasting and media activist peer-to-peer networking are often simplistically assumed to represent a new type of aesthetic and form, based entirely on technological evolution. The attributes of today's video-sharing social media were clearly visible in the decades past, however, from the development of the portable video movement based upon the Portapak to the shared cultural efforts of the public access media movement.

PAPER TIGER TELEVISION

The convergence of these new political, cultural, social, technological, artistic, and economic developments provided the impetus for the establishment of Paper Tiger Television in 1981 (PTTV); still active, it is one of the longest-running video collectives in the United States. While the instigators of PTTV had roots in the art and politics scene of the 1960s and 1970s, the raw energy came from a new generation of artists and activists—hungry, angry, and ready to tear into the US dominant culture. The early Paper Tiger collective was an amalgam of artists, activists, critics, cultural theorists, and academics, eager to seize control of the medium of television and reinject it into the American psyche.

According to Dee Dee Halleck, one of the founders of the group, Paper Tiger Television came out of a group of students, artists, and activists in New York City, emerging from a group project called "Communication Update."[33] The first Paper Tiger program was based upon the analysis and personality of Herbert Schiller, then media scholar at Hunter College in New York City. Schiller, with his biting critique of the culture industry and his prophetic take on the consolidation of media by corporate giants (not to mention his heavy New York accent), was the perfect person to begin the series. Shot entirely live-to-tape in the studio, the backdrop consists of Schiller sitting in a funkily arranged New York City subway, while he deconstructs the paper of record, the *New York Times*, which he characterizes as "the steering mechanism of the ruling class."[34] In one scene, he analyzes an image in the paper of an astronaut, a NASA space photo, and reinterprets the framing, perspective, and intent of the photo and accompanying text. He questions whether the image is of a brave and heroic astronaut, or part of a military operation. The production was produced entirely by the newly formed collective and launched the first of many programs.

The Paper Tiger Television collective created over sixty other tapes of this genre in their first few years of its existence, featuring a broad spectrum of scholars, artists, and activists. Some of these early studio productions include "Joan Does Dynasty," Joan Braderman's take on the "Dynasty" TV program; "Renee Tajima Reads Asian Images in American Film: Charlie Chan Go Home"; "Donna Haraway Reads *National Geographic*"; "Artist's Call to Central America: Lucy Lippard and Art for a Cause"; "Eva Cockcroft Reads *Art Forum*: Art and Language and Money"; "Martha Rosler Reads *Vogue*"; "Michele Mattelart Reads the Chilean Press Avant-Coup: Every Day It Gets Harder To Be a Good Housewife"; "The Trial of the Tilted Arc" with Richard Serra; and "Tuli Kupferberg Reads *Rolling Stone*." The idea of the show was based upon a cultural jujitsu, whereby the power of television was harnessed to deliver a critique of television or to highlight those who have been shut out of television. Paper Tiger Television continues to produce alternative media from their base in the lower east side of New York City. The video collectives' entire archive of videotape production, photography, props, and papers was acquired by the Fales Library of New York University in 2011[35] and was noted by a national conference at the New School for Social Research celebrating their thirtieth anniversary, entitled "Being the Media: Designing a Rrradical New Media."[36]

Originally limited to New York City cable systems, Paper Tiger grew on the developing network provided by public access television, the electronic commons fought for by media activists and artists in the 1970s. As Paper Tiger tapes began to be distributed and cablecast through access centers in other cities, it became apparent that an awareness of the creative possibilities of home-grown television was growing among many members of the public.

Through the 1980s and 1990s, the involvement of hundreds and then thousands of community TV producers began to swell the ranks of access stations nationwide as TV programs—ranging from talk shows to documentary, from music programs to news shows—bloomed across the nation's TVs. Such activity stimulated the creation of the National Federation of Local Cable Programmers, an organization that served as the central locus of public access television constituents (now called the Alliance for Community Media). Relying upon this nascent network of public access producers for local cablecast,

Paper Tiger Television began mailing tapes around the country to reach viewers in other locales, provoking the idea of a national distribution network. It became apparent that there were many local video groups producing tapes, and the idea for a national public access television network emerged. Such a network could tie together many of these local groupings into one national network. Observing that the burgeoning commercial cable networks were essentially held together by satellite uplinking and downlinking, Paper Tiger members adopted the same strategy and, with other video activists nationwide, initiated the Deep Dish TV (DDTV) Network to distribute video work. They released a call for submissions of videos based on predetermined themes, such as the housing crisis and military intervention in Central America, and received an enthusiastic response from video makers around the country.

A glance at the booklets and directories produced by DDTV after their first two broadcast seasons conveys a picture of the growing movement of video collectives in the mid-1980s, and of the globalization that I will describe in the next chapter. They created the Deep Dish Directory, publishing contact information on the groups that had submitted tapes to the Deep Dish series, in order to establish lines of communication between newly organized video groups around the country. The booklets contained the work of many collective and group efforts, reflecting a wide range of interests and backgrounds. Groups that had submitted video for the series included Alternative Views from Austin, Texas (a group that had been in existence as long as Paper Tiger); Somerville Producers Group; Southwest Reports; The Committee to Intervene Anywhere; Xchange TV; Madre Video Project; Mill Hunk Herald; Labor Information Committee from Toronto, Canada; The Cambridge Women's Video Collective; Mon Valley Media; Ladies Against Women; Video Band; The Alternative Media Project, based in New Haven, CT; The Atlanta Media Project; Artists TV Network; Subterranean Video; Squeaky Wheel from Buffalo, New York; the Labor Video Project, based in San Francisco; The Coalition to Save General Motors/Van Nuys; The Committee for Labor Access from Chicago; The Labor Media Group from Ann Arbor; The New York City Labor Film Club; The Not For Profit TV, based in Harlem, New York; Video For Kids from Mt. View, California; and Third World News Review.

The proliferation of these groups and collectives shows the growth of the cooperative approach to video work in the 1980s and early 1990s. Groups often came together as video arms of both broad-based and single-focus organizations such as gay and lesbian groups, nuclear freeze groups, Central American activist groups, labor groups, and many more. Some groups focused on issues of race and class, such as Not Channel Zero, which produced work from the perspective of Black and Latino youth in New York City. Among the most active video collectives was DIVA (Damn Interfering Video Artists), allied with the group Act-Up, which became an important and effective catalyst for fighting AIDS and for challenging public perceptions of the disease. This group produced many tapes detailing the fighting spirit of HIV-positive people and helped foster a culture of optimism in a community devastated by sorrow. As Jim Hubbard wrote in an essay for "Fever in the Archives," the 2000 Guggenheim show on archived AIDS videos, while many of the tapes were "made solely as timely responses to the crisis, [they] retain an extraordinary vitality. The video makers clearly positioned themselves in opposition to an unresponsive and often antagonistic government and mainstream media." We see this in their rejection of "the authoritative voice-over, the removed, dispassionate expert, and the media's tendency to scapegoat" as well as their embrace of "a vibrant sexuality and righteous anger."[37]

THE RISE OF CAMCORDER POLITICS

The election of Ronald Reagan and the rise of the Moral Majority in the early 1980s inspired a younger generation of artists, particularly those not part of the art or media establishments, to become politically active. The impending culture wars and the attack on the morals and aesthetics of artists led many to search for the causes of the disconnection between cultural creators and the public. Reaganite defunding of the arts led to major soul-searching and an effort to reconnect community arts with the broader public and reestablish a connection between cultural workers and community. Much culpability was placed on the role of the mass media and the culture industry that had been forming the pictures in people's minds while video artists were busy playing with their own images on the screen. The new political and economic realities of the 1980s led to an investigation into how media artists could reconnect with the public while challenging the views of the religious right and other groups hostile to artists. For many video collectives, public access television was one way that allowed artists' work to enter into the homes of people not accustomed to visiting galleries and museums. The establishment of Media and Neighborhood Art Centers was another way to get such work out of the galleries and into the streets and neighborhoods. As a result, many alternative venues were cultivated across the nation, particularly for film and video. The National Association of Media Art Centers (NAMAC) was one national organization that served as a focal point of exchange and communication for such efforts.

Despite the often-heralded independent video work of the 1960s and 1970s, the early 1980s should really be considered the coalescing moment at the heart of the guerilla television movement. It was then that many of the more utopian ideas of the movement reached some fruition, with greater participation of women and people of color, and with less fetishism and awe invested in the technological gadgetry. This cultural groundswell was not just part of the art scene, however; it was intricately bound up in the burgeoning subcultures of punk and hip-hop, with their funky, homegrown DIY ethos and aesthetics. The endeavors within these subcultures were frequently collective in nature. The punk scene, often deprived of venues for its music, had to organize its own alternative spaces in warehouses, abandoned storefronts and squats, relying on a system of alternative zines to spread the word. Bands, fans, zines, and spaces were part of a collective apparatus that went along with the territory of insurgent punk rock. Do-it-yourself became the clarion call for many active in the punk scene. Hip-hop culture, homegrown in the ghettos and barrios, was often organized around "crews" whose cultural work collectively ranged from spinning vinyl and organizing block parties to holding dance competitions and throwing up spray-can art on trains and public walls. All of these activities contributed to a new type of collective cultural production that privileged group activity over individual activity. These vital and dynamic subcultures grew exponentially without the help of either mass media or the arts establishment, right in the heart of right-wing Reaganite repression. Only after punk and hip-hop had achieved safety in numbers did the culture industries proceed in its hostile takeover of both subcultures.

In the early 1980s, the increasing corporate stranglehold over commercial television and mass media was evermore apparent. For the most part, established video artists showed no great concern because the "professionalism" of the video art genre grew, as galleries and the art world learned to incorporate video art into their venues. In the process, the stakes got higher and higher for experimenting with new high-tech video tools. Artists and galleries wanting to play in this game grew increasingly dependent on corporate sponsorship, frequently from the same corporations benefiting from the new drive toward media conglomeration. Video artists were usually eager to distance themselves from television anyway, which they saw as the hillbilly cousin of aristocracy. Younger video artists, however, who were surrounded by and steeped in popular culture, were eager to critique, comment on, deconstruct, and defeat the message of commercial television and media. Much artwork generated by this younger generation increasingly focused on challenging commercial media by creating spoofs, subverting messages, and implementing the slogan "copyright infringement—your best entertainment value." This approach was very much in tune with bohemian art movements as funk, pop art, collage, and Dadaism, and stood in stark contrast with much of the cold and bleak technoart beeping and flashing in galleries. This upsurge in media activity emerged simultaneously with a heightened interest in cultural studies, mass media studies, and cultural criticism. Television is, after all, at the heart of our popular culture, the culture of the everyday, and it dominates the media landscape. Video ultimately was a form of television, an electronic media device that conveys information. It was natural that video artists would cross the boundaries of art and activism, and would frequently choose to subvert the message rather than simply exploit the form of television. This artistic jujitsu, urging the weight of television to fall upon itself, emerged as a popular strategy among media artists. Increasingly, video artists in the 1980s and 1990s embraced the necessity to reflect on, intervene in, and challenge the contested terrain of television, mass media, and popular culture, and to leave the art-video aesthetic behind. As B. Ruby Rich points out, this approach blurred further the distinction between "art" and "activism": she notes that the dual avant-gardes of the 1970s, form and content, no longer existed as a binary. According to Rich, "Such a construct is irrelevant to a nineties video/film praxis that locates its politic instead within a renegotiated subject position, for both artist and audience. . . . It's no longer possible to speak of aesthetics in a vacuum, to speak of intentionality without the counterbalance of reception, to speak arrogantly of the individual without speaking humbly of the collective, not as something abstract but as a quality within us."[38]

THE MATURATION OF DEMOCRATIC ELECTRONIC MEDIA

By the early 1990s, the culture wars became more pronounced as right-wing politicians hacked away at the funding base for the arts. New video technology freed citizen-producers from the studio and allowed them to get into the streets, particularly with the range of "pro-sumer" formats such as Hi-8 and S-VHS, formats that came close to a professional level of video without the high cost. Mobile video operators proliferated at public events, rallies, protests, and happenings. Video programs began to be produced entirely in postproduction suites, with a new range of special effects technologies. Slow motion, fades, wipes, and text—once only affordable for major broadcasters and posthouses—now allowed DIY video producers a more polished, professional look. All this is not to imply that public access was without problems or that it was the only thing worth watching on television. Such work is often perceived as boring, slow, or amateurish by an audience increasingly accustomed to fast cuts, blinding speed, and gratuitous sexual imagery and violence. It should be noted that network producers have recognized the creative qualities of public access, and they have sought to exploit the look and freshness of access for their own productions. Copious amounts of jittery consumer camcorder shots, grainy pictures, and jump cuts are now used frequently in many productions, often to enhance the "realism" in both reality television and high-end commercials.

Amidst the climate of fear and conservatism in the broadcasting and entertainment industries, demands for representation of people of color, of working people, and of gay and lesbian people fueled the production of independent artistic production of video, television, and film. Many new independent media groups were created, and already-established cultural groups—such as Film Arts Foundation, Cine Accion, Frameline, National Association of Asian Television Artists, Association of Independent Video and Filmmakers, Bay Area Video Coalition, Artist's Television Access, Third World Newsreel, and California Newsreel—swelled with eager younger members. A collaborative effort resulted in the creation of the Independent Television Service in 1991, an important funding resource for independent video makers that was also committed to getting work on the Public Broadcasting System. These efforts were attempts by artists to create or influence television, not to perpetuate the videotape as art object. The people involved in these efforts recognized television as a stream of electronic images and recognized the benefits of some kind of industrial organization in creating an audience for such work.

Many artists welcomed the electoral defeat of the Reagan-Bush dynasty in the early 1990s as a respite from many years of the conservative scapegoating of artists for moral decline and social turmoil. During the last month of the 1992 electoral contest, Paper Tiger TV built a large-scale installation at the McBean Gallery in the San Francisco Art Institute. Modeled as an enormous television, the public walked through the cracked screen of an enormous cathode ray tube and along the electronic copper traces past giant capacitors and resistors to view the "myth" circuits embedded in our electronic culture, such as the myth of High Art and the myth of Freedom of Choice. On election night in 1992, the gallery was standing room only with hundreds of artists and activists as PTTV members performed a live mix of election returns and found footage and sound. The art critic for the Hearst San Francisco Examiner described the event as "[t]he most dramatic demonstration of the beginning of the end, the end of the Reagan/Bush era." Bush's concession speech resulted in "a storm of curses, imprecations and threats that was as terrifying as it was liberating" because it "underscored the widespread hatred felt for Bush and the Republican Party he led into a fatal flirtation with far-right extremism."[39]

THE GREAT "TELECOM" WARS AND THE ATTACK ON ACCESS

By the late 1990s, it was obvious that all was not quiet on the technological front, as a new wave of digital camcorders was weakening the "not broadcast quality" excuse both commercial and public broadcasters often used to reject independent production. The Internet, then referred to as the "information superhighway," was expanding exponentially, multiplying the communications reach of video makers, whose tactics ranged from building listservs of potential viewers to marketing tapes online to streaming postage-stamp–sized real-time video clips. Hypertext, the CD-ROM, DVD, and other formats promised nonlinearity and instantaneous deliverability, and the possibility of including extensive background material inspired many video activists. Yet despite the growing popularity of public access and a large base of video producers, video activists found themselves increasingly threatened as the communications conglomerates fought for market hegemony. Independent media producers were squeezed within an ongoing battle between some of the most powerful corporate sectors in the world for production of, delivery of, and profit from the vast amount of data that speeds across the world every microsecond. As the battle for supremacy among the broadcasters, cable companies, and telephone and cellular companies took on an increasingly global scale, local enterprises such as public, educational, and government access were threatened. The cable companies, fighting the threat of competition from the enormous telecommunication corporations and their fiber optic networks, increasingly found themselves coveting the access channels to run more lucrative commercial and pay-per-view programming. Ironically, the kind of local programming that public access provides is the only real marketing advantage cable has over the national telephone companies' fiber optic networks and the Direct Broadcast Satellite services. Such large-scale monolithic systems deliver standard commercial broadcasts, Hollywood movies, pay-per-view, and home shopping; yet they have little local programming and no accountability to local communities. Despite public demand for local programming initiatives, the total dismantling of local programming became a real threat. New legislation that strips local communities of regulating and establishing franchise agreements has spread coast to coast. Once again, the machinations of the market are working to decay local communications to favor large-scale, centralized media hubs. Public, educational, and government access television systems still represent one of the last spheres of local television in the electronic media "village," a truly unique area of free speech.

The rapid popularity and feasibility of streaming and downloadable video available on the Internet has certainly eclipsed much of the uniqueness of public access. Many of the complaints now made about Internet video sites like YouTube are the same complaints made about public access—that amateurs and misfits use the venue to disseminate vanity programs, controversial viewpoints, and other foolishness. Public access producers would counter these claims by pointing out that the same could easily be said of current network fare.

The sophistication of popular video and the growing acceptance and excitement for it caused the video movement to move beyond the shadow of mainstream media even more. By the mid-1990s there were many venues and channels for such video and an appreciative audience that went along with it. Two notable trends emerged with this maturation: the notion of the video as "witness" and the development of "horizontal" communications. This "utopian" moment of video, seemingly lost in the early 1970s, was growing invisibly under everyone's feet.

THE VIDEO WITNESS

With cameras in the hands of many activist groups, video began to be noted as a "witness" to events that normally would remain invisible and kept from public view. Clearly the most illustrative is the video of Rodney King's beating by the LAPD in 1991, which sparked one of the largest urban rebellions in US history. The Rodney King video-capture was spontaneous and haphazard, but it emphasized to many the power of local, organized video teams. Community groups nationwide had already begun to regularly use video as a counter-surveillance tool; for example, the Cop-Watch collective began video surveillance of rogue police operating in the San Francisco Bay Area. Police brutality has always been a major issue in the ghettos and barrios of the United States, and activists with cameras became the new heroes in many such situations. From its inception, the Black Panther Party demonstrated concern with police brutality in poor black neighborhoods: the original Oakland group followed squad cars of police officers thought to be abusive in order to provide witnesses in the event that police used excessive force. By the end of the 1990s there were many instances of video witnessing circulating on public access television, from depictions of police beatings of white teenagers in Los Angeles,[40] to Federal Bureau of Land Management officers roughing up elderly Native American women. In the Los Angeles riots that followed the Rodney King verdict in 1992, the most relevant footage was shot by community video activists with camcorders, such as producer Matt McDaniel, host of a South-Central Los Angeles-based public access television show. LA-based professional television crews remained safely behind police lines or high in the air in helicopters during the King riots, as they had been attacked by angry community members who felt the media establishment helped perpetuate racism against African Americans. A compilation of the riots from the street view was edited by Matt McDaniel and distributed throughout Los Angeles, under the name "Birth of a Nation."[41] Shortly after the LA uprising, in a remote section of the high desert of Nevada, activists captured the physical abuse of an elderly Native American woman, Carrie Dann, who was trying to stop the Bureau of Land Management from capturing Western-Shoshone livestock.[42] The snippet of video was quickly edited and released to CNN, which broadcast the shocking evidence of abuse. The video was edited into a larger tape that outlined the injustices faced by the Western-Shoshone. The videotape, *Newe Sogobia is Not For Sale*, was sent to over 100 members of Congress and leaders of Indian Nations. It was also played on hundreds of public access and local origination television stations, thanks to the Deep Dish Satellite Network and the Free Speech TV Network. Audio portions were broadcast nationally on an alternative radio network, Making Contact, and it was played in dozens of microcinema venues and video festivals nationwide.[43] Most of these "video witness" tapes circulated among communities and subcultures directly affected by such actions. Informal media activist activity built a growing consensus that broadcast media were becoming not as essential anymore, as relevant news and information could still reach its intended audience—the audience that mattered the most. The practice of building a communications link among peers takes on a much larger role as the ubiquity of video cameras grows. The proliferation of camera phones accentuates this trend even further. Such video witnessing continues to be a major focus of video-sharing sites like YouTube, with many recent examples of abuse circulating. Images of students being struck with tasers, animals being abused, and even people being murdered at the hands of transit police are now standard facets of our grassroots communications system.

Labor and union activists have been in the forefront of popular video and were one of the earlier constituents to work with public access. Long accustomed to hostility and neglect from mainstream media, labor activists have often taken initiatives for developing worker-friendly channels of communications. Labor video groups have been active in Chicago, New York, Pittsburgh, San Francisco, and other cities in order to articulate labor's point of view and to give voice to the creative expression of workers. The growth of these labor video collectives was propelled by the enthusiastic response of audiences and constituents, who were thrilled when their own stories, identities, and representations appeared on monitors and screens in public spaces including storefronts, community centers, and alternative spaces. The fact that these videos were often made by those directly affected by labor struggles, and not by outside professionals, made them all the more powerful. A Paper Tiger Television production produced in conjunction with striking miners in Pittston, Virginia, illustrated such enthusiasm. "Drawing the Line at Pittston"[44] screened at a conference of labor representatives following a screening of a "professional" tape on the same subject, yet the audience reaction to each was drastically different. The "professional" production generated a polite, tepid response, while the PTTV tape played to wild and tumultuous endorsement, as the self-shot viewpoints of the miners themselves came across in the face of police repression, shaky cameras and all. Other memorable self-shot tapes involving workers are the "FlashDance" takeoff videos by Pittsburgh steelworkers[45] and "Desperately Sliming Salmon,"[46] a tape shot by two fisher-workers on an Alaskan salmon canning factory ship. Audience enthusiasm for these kinds of self-shot videotapes helped fuel the creation of a collective movement of grassroots labor video. Labor video activism participated in a general move to develop a system of "horizontal" communications, where the communications is peer-to-peer instead of a traditional top-down broadcasting approach. Such peer-to-peer communications have of course now become foundational in our current Internet culture.

The Paper Tiger collective, along with a multitude of video organizations, began moving beyond media criticism, away from reacting to the culture industry and toward determining its own agenda, its own aesthetics, and its own relationship to technology. By the 1990s, the Paper Tiger collective had made some several hundred video programs on a wide range of both social and artistic subjects that illuminated what was ignored by the culture industry. It did so with the now standard PTTV approach: a sense of humor and a decidedly low-tech, DIY sensibility.

WE WANT THE AIRWAVES: LOW-POWER FM RADIO ACTIVISM

Just as the public imagination was being swept away by a multitude of new high-tech media platforms in the 1990s, media activists embraced one that was over 100 years old: the radio. Activists can claim victory for opening up hundreds of new low-power FM frequencies for community use, despite desperate attempts by both media corporations and federal government to maintain control over the public spectrum. Despite much futuristic technology hyperbole about the electronically networked world, many people still rely upon the 100-year-old broadcasting technology of radio for a large percentage of daily information. In fact, while commercial television channels wring their hands over audience-share lost to other media, radio has had some very consistent audiences. According to researchers, even through the growth of the Internet, traditional radio listenership remained very stable between 1998 and 2004, dropping a mere 1.1%, from 95.3% to 94.2% of the total American population.[47]

Despite the achievements and satisfaction derived from the microcinema and grassroots video and public access movements, there has always been remorse that access to those forms is limited to those who live in cities or to those who can afford cable, that many important sectors of society are not reached, and that the medium does not extend into the disenfranchised audience to the extent that it should. These concerns led many media activists to reconsider the possibilities of the radio medium, a signal that reaches a multitude of teenagers, commuters in automobiles, and the working class and the poor through parks, streets, and public spaces. It is still evident that the power of radio—famed media theorist Marshall McCluhan's favorite hot medium—still reigns supreme among a great proportion of the people of the world. In the urban areas, millions tune in to the voice-with-no-picture during the mass civil ritual of the daily commute. In rural areas, radio is often the only link to the distant centers of power and commerce. It may not be as glamorous as many of the new technologies, but radio is still a powerful medium.

The early days of radio held out many of the same hopes as cable television did in the 1970s and as is promised today by the Internet. Radio, it was promised, would provide a voice for the common person, would offer a multiplicity of views, and would benefit the public good. The first radio stations seemed to fulfill this promise. Radio technology was cheap enough that universities, churches, labor unions, and community groups could raise an antenna and go on the air.[48] The radio spectrum was legally classified as belonging to the public, and radio became a vibrant voice by which to communicate with neighborhoods, constituents, and the general population.

Those days were short-lived, however, after major corporations like AT&T, Westinghouse, and General Electric realized the enormous profits to be generated by harnessing radio as a tool for advertisers and business promotion. Through their powerful lobbying efforts, and the "revolving" door known as the FCC,[49] the corporations conquered the air waves via the Communications Act of 1934, upon which radio became primarily a vehicle to sell soap and breakfast cereals, rather than a unique medium to permit the free flow of ideas amongst the citizenry.

Through the decades, radio, like television, has remained the private domain of the business interests deemed worthy by the FCC and those with the financial ability to maintain an extensive network of radio stations and the engineers, lawyers, and marketers necessary for such enterprise. There are, of course, some exceptions to the rule of radio conformity, most notably the Pacifica stations with their flagship station KPFA in Berkeley, California. Also important are the scattered community radio stations within the National Federation of Community Broadcasters, as well as independently managed college radio stations. Tied as they are to direct government subsidy and corporate underwriting, the public broadcasting stations of National Public Radio are oftentimes less likely than commercial broadcasters to rock the boat. Though there have been some illicit attempts at breaking the blockade of the radio monopoly, most notably by a handful of offshore AM radio tinkerers, radio has primarily been surrendered to the machinations of the corporate media world. One of the first US contemporary "pirate" broadcast station was known as WKOV, an AM station based in Yonkers, New York, by a teenager who thought Yonkers should have its own station. The station operated from December 1969 until mid-1971, when it was shut down. The operator, Alan Weiner, said about his station, "My friends and I believed that Yonkers needed its own station and didn't have one. To this day it doesn't. We felt there were not stations on the air that were open to listeners. They were very orchestrated and tightly controlled. It was out of civil disobedience that we went on the air."[50] Another station was started in a housing project in Brooklyn, also by teenagers who thought radio was "boring." They used a low-power FM transmitter at first, but later switched to a more powerful AM transmitter. Says one of the operators, "Radio had become so huge. It was a multimillion dollar business, and Brooklyn, which is bigger than most cities, had no local programming."[51] There were other attempts in the 1960s and 1970s to commandeer radio frequencies in order to program local voices, but by and large, most of those energies went into video and then computer-based formats. It was in the early 1990s, however, that interest in radio once again began to proliferate, inspired by the same interest in democratic and pluralistic media stimulated by public access television and grassroots video. A nascent DIY tech culture coupled with radical political ideas about media and democracy encouraged DJs, musicians, artists, and activists to reinvestigate the potential of radio, and to take back a modicum of public access to the airwaves. The interest in revitalizing radio was also due to a demographic of radio listeners becoming disillusioned by the extremely commercial nature of music on the air, as well as the proliferation of right-wing talk shows in heavy syndication, in particular Rush Limbaugh's. The primary complaint of radio listeners was that of "boredom." An increase in artists working with technology and an early trend towards DIY electronics led toward experimentation with broadcasting circuits. Techno-artists noticed that advances in electronic technologies had occurred not only with computer networking and audiovisual production but also in the design and operation of basic electronic components such as transistors and integrated circuits. As many low-power FM radio explorers discovered, with a mere handful of components a person could solder together a radio transmitter powerful enough to reach a neighborhood or a city, operating on the very popular and accessible FM band. Experimenting with components, antennas, and transmitters, mini-FM radio operators discovered there was plenty of room on the bandwidth to accommodate new stations. Not only are these new components inexpensive and modular, they are also much more accurate and drift-free than their tube-based ancestors, allowing them to squeeze their frequencies in between the large interference zones allocated decades ago to accommodate the inaccurate radio signals of the first generations of radio. With a typical transmitter design, the turn of one component permits the transmitter to tune its output to any frequency on the FM band, and it is thus able to avoid interference with other channels.[52]

The contemporary mini-FM proliferation has its roots in the 1970s radio rebellions in France, Italy, and Japan, and has direct connections to groups of activists working in guerilla video and public access television. Tetsuo Kogowa, a veteran of the European experiments in pirate radio, and a leader of the mini-FM movement in Japan, had several meetings with guerilla video practitioners in the United States in the early 1990s. As Luke Hiken wrote in the preface to Soley's book on free radio, "In 1993, I attended a meeting at the home of Jesse Drew, one of the producer-directors active with Paper Tiger Television. His guest that evening was Japanese engineer and activist, Tetsuo Kogawa. . . . While he [Kogawa] was giving his talk about the social and political uses of microradio technology, he was simultaneously soldering and scotch-taping a series of Radio Shack parts, worth about fifteen dollars, to a paper plate. Within fifteen minutes, he had completed his soldering and announced that he had finished 'building' his transmitter. . . . Within three more minutes, he announced that we were 'on the air.'"[53] The night was described in an article in the *San Francisco Bay Guardian*:

> On an unusually warm San Francisco night several weeks ago, a new radio station went on the air in the Mission District, at least for a few hours. "This is KXXX, Mission District Radio! Broadcasting from . . . somewhere in the neighborhood."
>
> The first evening's program ranged from excited talk about the possibilities of pirate radio to tapes of music by local groups to a live clarinet performance by an 11-year-old.[54]

This article generated an enthusiastic response by many others who had also been intrigued by the mini-FM idea. One such person was Stephen Dunnifer, an electronics tinkerer and activist who went on to establish Free Radio Berkeley (FRB) in Berkeley, California. FRB is acknowledged by many media activists as being the obstinate radio trailblazer that provoked the FCC into shutting the station down, initiating the legal response that developed much of the current LPFM language, rules, and regulations that legitimate versions of now-legal LPFM. Dunnifer's Free Radio Berkeley, which could be heard in many parts of the Bay Area twenty-four hours a day, was visited by the FCC on a Sunday evening and served with a lawsuit of $20,000 for broadcasting a mix of music and political discussion without FCC approval. Rather than lower the antenna, Dunnifer enlisted the aid of the Committee on Democratic

Communications, a project of the National Lawyers Guild. In a thirteen-page brief contesting the claims of the FCC, Luke Hiken, Dunnifer's counsel, put forth the claim that this form of broadcasting is first and foremost a free-speech right. Claiming that in our current electronic age, the ability to broadcast is akin to the right to print a pamphlet or distribute a leaflet to the public, the defense claimed the FCC action is one of "prior restraint" and therefore unconstitutional. In this way, they hoped to show that "this means of licensing a means of communication is as outrageous as the attempts to license the printing press in the Middle Ages."[55] This argument seemed to make an impact on the courts, and news of the battle between Dunnifer and the FCC helped fan the flames of popularity for this kind of "free" radio.

DIY FM RADIO

According to its practitioners, the excitement generated by mini-FM broadcasting is quite contagious. Typically, a transmitter is plugged into a regular electrical outlet and hooked to a small antenna strung up somewhere on a roof, porch, or deck. A tape deck, CD player, microphone, MP3 player, or other input device is plugged in, and the radio enthusiast is on the air. By turning on an FM radio as a monitor, operators find a dead spot on the FM band, and then tune the frequency output of the transmitter until it is audible on the radio. The new station operators make note of the new frequency of the station and alert their community and friends. To build an audience, standard procedure is to post notices about the new station, with reference to the time and day it is on the air and the frequency. There is no reason to disclose the actual location of the operation, as the station is often moved to a different location every broadcast to avoid detection by the FCC.[56]

It should be noted that low-power radio operators generally reject the term "pirate radio," and regard the large radio monopolies as being the real "pirates" who have absconded with the public airwaves. "Free radio" or "microradio" is the preferred term for these mini-FM station operators, who, having tired of complaining about the state of radio, decided to make some of their own. Perhaps the most famous LPFM station, and possibly the most inspirational, was Human Rights Radio, started by African-American activist Mbanna Kantako in Springfield, Illinois. His station, which operated in the heart of a central housing project for many years, reached a large percentage of the city's Black population with only a few watts of power. Human Rights Radio delivered a voice previously absent in Springfield, a voice from and for the Black community. Besides music and commentary, Kantako's station also offered readings of African-American literature because, as Mbanna points out, many in the Black community cannot read.[57] For his radio work, Mbanna faced many legal challenges by the FCC and relentless police harassment. As of this printing, Mbanna's radio station is still on the air.

Following trailblazers such as Human Rights Radio, Black Liberation Radio, and Free Radio Berkeley, grassroots radio stations sprang up in diverse areas across the United States, including in San Francisco, Phoenix, Detroit, Orlando, the Blue Ridge Mountains, and the Lower East Side of Manhattan. Examples include the San Francisco Mission District's Radio Libre, which offered a diverse, multicultural programming mix in both Spanish and English; San Francisco Liberation Radio (93.7 FM), which provided unlicensed call-in talk shows broadcast along with documentaries on local and national issues; and Food Not Bombs Radio Network, the voice of the influential advocacy group for the homeless. A Paper Tiger Television–produced videotape that aired on hundreds of access channels highlighted Human Rights Radio and included instructions on how to build one's own mini-FM radio station. The same tape included a visit with an Irish women's radio station that showed how women in Galway, Ireland, operate a "pirate" channel right out of their living room and invite women of the neighborhood to participate in ongoing discussion of issues affecting their lives. Such local initiatives that take advantage of advanced technologies but unite, rather than atomize, a neighborhood exemplify the desire for maintaining the local in our networked world.[58] Much like the venues for microcinema described within this chapter, the channels of mini-FM radio are constantly changing, often disappearing and reappearing, due to the ephemeral and illegal status of their operations.

FCC objections to microradio operators frequently rely upon their claim that microbroadcasting endangers aircraft communications, a claim microbroadcasters dismiss as unfounded because mini-FM frequencies are far removed from the range of public service frequencies. Furthermore, the range of mini-FM stations is usually a few miles, which is only enough to cover a neighborhood or perhaps a voting precinct. Microbroadcasters state that the real opposition comes from the commercial stations' fear that such grassroots radio broadcasters will steal audiences away from their pay-to-advertise enterprises. After the FCC agreed with certain arguments upheld by the courts in reference to Free Radio Berkeley, the National Association of Broadcasters, the trade arm of the commercial radio stations, stepped in to quell the growing LPFM movement. The lobbying organization applied tremendous pressure to Congress to circumvent the FCC opinion and greatly watered down the much-needed reforms. While commercial radio networks complain that businesses spend millions of dollars to purchase stations for the right to use their particular spectrum allocation, these arguments don't find much support among proponents of the right to free speech, who maintain that the first amendment rights of the public take priority over such commercial considerations. They further point out that the airwaves are a public resource.

Before the reforms initiated by low-power FM activists, a low-wattage station that chose to legally enter the licensing procedure would find that the FCC did not offer any licensing procedure to stations under 100 watts. To further exclude noncommercial broadcasters from having legal access to the airwaves, the legal fees and engineering support necessary to meet

FCC regulations would cost tens of thousands of dollars, blocking the public enthusiast. These restrictions would be on top of the primary obstacle, which is the contrived scarcity of broadcast frequencies. Faced with these legal and financial obstacles, the microradio option appeared an attractive one to those underserved by present radio stations. The splitting up of analog broadcasting bandwidth into smaller digital slices, combined with the exodus of commercial radio onto satellite systems, has resulted in less and less apparent reason to restrict public access to the airwaves, and the government and business restrictions on the radio waves seem increasingly archaic. Currently, low-power FM activists have won several important battles, clearing the way for hundreds of new stations, typically in more rural and poorer areas. Groups such as Prometheus have tracked and advocated for many of these new stations.[59] The Local Community Radio Act, passed in 2011 and signed by President Obama, will bring substantially greater numbers of community radio stations nationwide. Pete Tridish, one of the low-power radio advocates from the Prometheus Radio Project notes, "A town without a community radio station is like a town without a library."[60]

Although radio doesn't get as much attention as more high-tech media, the advantages offered by homegrown radio are still alluring to many who want to communicate with a local audience. With radio stations in increasingly fewer corporate hands with little record of interest in the public good or local, community concerns, "free radio" stations can be expected to raise their antennas, legal or not. These radio stations complement a number of more established small community and college stations and form a cellular network of progressive FM, the so-called left end of the dial. While these stations play a valuable public service role in serving their communities, they also act as transponders for national programs such as *Democracy Now!* and *Free Speech Radio News*. This contestation of the airwaves waged by media activists has resulted in an achievement many said would never happen: the opening of new frequencies on the bandwidth and the legalization of hundreds of new low-power FM radio stations in the United States.

THE COMPUTER AND A NEW ELECTRONIC LOCALE

Local electronic media generated by mini-FM radio programmers, microcinema organizers, and public access television producers extends well beyond the confines of these long-established mediums. It is well understood by community media makers that efforts to build media democracy are not technology-based but that they spring from social and communitarian goals, a point often missed by technology boosters who position the technology itself at the heart of the phenomenon. Grassroots media practitioners have been intimately involved in many of the digital and new media developments from the beginning. Much of the impetus behind community social networks, open source programming, community wifi, and other socially conscious computer-based practices stem from and are greatly influenced by the philosophy and language of guerilla television, public access, and media activism. The primary communications hub of the early video movement was the journal *Radical Software*, printed in the early 1970s. The term "software" at that point did not refer to computer programs but to a more general sense of the intelligence and information that would be necessary to put hardware electronics to good use. In an introduction to the legacy of the *Radical Software* journal, David Ross says of the Raindance Collective, the journal's founders, that, "[t]hey imagined a world in which the contest of ideas and values could take place freely and openly, outside of the existing institutional framework and in active opposition to the worldview constructed and maintained by broadcast commercial TV. They proposed not only a reordered power structure, but also a new information order in which the very idea of hierarchical power structure might be transformed or even eliminated."[61] From the first issue of the journal in the spring of 1970, references to computers were interspersed throughout, including descriptions of videotapes about computer technology, how to use computers for video art, an explanation of the beginning stages of the DARPA network (the precursor to the Internet), and a warning about the use of computers by police.[62] Many early computer-based experiments came from similar desires to build community and create radical media. The idea for a community computer network was realized with the first incarnation of the Community Memory Project, originating in San Francisco as early as 1973. This project was one of the earliest attempts at creating a community-centered computer social network for public use. Based in kiosks at a music store, a hardware store, and a public library, it predated in many ways what Craigslist and Facebook would build many years later. Another version of Community Memory was established in Berkeley, California, going live in 1984. One of the builders of the system described the value of such computer sites: "They could provide for the elimination of the distinction between producers and consumers of information, encourage public conversations, and, by virtue of being embedded within community social institutions, empower rather than pacify their users."[63] The Community Memory Project described itself thusly:

> Community Memory is a system for the public management of public information. It is an open channel for community communications and information exchange, and a way for people with common interests to find each other. All of the information in the Community Memory is put in directly by the people who use the system: anyone can post messages, read any of the other communications that are there, and add comments or suggestions at any time.[64]

Community Memory was one of the first of many social networks built on the computer, including The Well, established in 1985, and Peacenet, which also started in 1985.[65] It was increasingly obvious to media activists of the time that offering access to computer networks was increasingly obligatory for citizens to participate in civil society. With the rise of popularity of early Internet tools—for example, telnet (1969), Usenet (1979), BITNET (1981), WAIS (late 1980s), Veronica (1992), and gopher (1991)—many community media centers started to offer computers for public use. Often computer access was implemented by public access centers themselves, or through another vitally important US public media institution, the public library. The Cleveland Freenet was created in 1986 and became an important model for community computer users. Originally created as a resource for medical information, it grew to be a major resource for residents of Cleveland. Basically a Bulletin Board Service, it offered users free access to electronic mail, chat, and information in health, government, law, and other areas. Because it was so successful, it began to attract users nationwide who could log in via telnet. According to its founder, "We can not imagine a 21st century which does NOT have free public-access community computer systems, just as our century had the free public library."[66] Benefits for public participation were clearly evident in these early experiments: public documents could be uploaded for inspection, online discussion over local policies could continue on electronic bulletin boards, and e-mail could be exchanged between participants of committees. It was believed that homelessness, a severe social problem that became epidemic during the Reagan era, could be ameliorated when e-mail was offered to those without a stable place to live. An e-mail address at least gave some stable contact information to those who often moved place to place in precarious economic conditions.

THE LEGACY OF PUBLIC ACCESS TELEVISION

Decades ago, community activists who took up the challenge to fight for the so-called PEG channels—the triumvirate of public, educational, and government channels—saw the value of communications democracy that would become central to future digital media developments. Though not the final answer to the maladies of modern commercial television, public access did show the potential for television. Rather than being a conduit for bland entertainment, commercials, and scatological infotainment, TV could illuminate local problems, uncover local talent, and allow for creative self-expression. In an increasingly impersonal, alienating world, the promise of public access media was that it could become an electronic "back fence," allowing the nation a chance to rediscover a sense of community.

Perhaps the most important contribution of public access television, though, and its greatest contribution to the new media environment, was its demystification of the media-making process. Public access television democratized media production by allowing anyone to come forward and get training on television production. Once a citizen was led through the process of learning how to use a camera switcher, a lavalier mic mixer, three-point lighting, and other skills of live television production, mass media mystification was greatly weakened. The participation in television production by citizen-producers was often enthralling and empowering. It demystified media production to the point at which many participants would humorously describe feeling like Dorothy in Oz, pulling the cord to reveal the great Wizard behind a seamless image-making machine. Such an empowering experience was often electrifying to new public media producers and had a huge impact on a great number of individuals, many of whom are active today in independent digital media of all types. The philosophy of public access, with its tenets of decentralized communications and participatory democracy, lies at the heart of many of today's digital projects. The impact of public access, of free radio, of microcinema, and of early community computer networks has gone largely unexamined, and with it the many contributions these movements have made: demonstrating the notion of narrowcasting, emphasizing the importance of connecting communities, building the link between active involvement and democracy, proclaiming that information should be free, and demanding the public's right to know. The tools used for electronic community building—whether through video, mini-FM radio, or computer hardware and software or through appealing to the audience's technical abilities—are really not at the heart of local community media. These tools are an important yet transient aspect of a decades-old project to reintroduce, rebuild, and reinforce communities of neighbors and localities that have been atomized, dispersed, or devalued over the decades by single television viewing, the isolation of the automobile, the subdivision of suburban development, and the general erosion of public space in American society. The bottom line is that these technologies have proven that they can help to build community in a corporal as well as an electronic way, whether it is people coming together to produce a video or to put together a radio program, or to invite people to a community meeting via a social computer network. The basic requirement of such technologies, whether it is 100-year-old radio or this year's social network app, is to reconnect the human spirit in a more honest and genuine way.

It should be emphasized that although the projects described in this chapter recover and highlight the importance of the local and community level, it by no means follows that these innovative projects suffered from a parochial worldview. To the contrary, the concerns of globalism were always pressing, whether it was acid rain or global warming, the Vietnam War or the Gulf War, global poverty or human rights. The approach taken, though, was one that flowed from the local to the global, a bottom-up approach rather than a top-down approach, giving weight to the popular slogan, "Think locally; act globally." As we shall see in the next chapter, many of these local efforts contributed to the building of communications networks that do have a truly significant global impact. These global efforts originate from smaller-scale, local projects. These artists and activists, these hackers and tinkerers, iconoclasts and freethinkers all: these local, community-based movements helped pave the way for the future of communications democracy in the United States.

3   Networking the Global Community

From the 1960s through the 1990s, activists and artists created a new culture of community and locally based DIY electronic media, which nourished a cadre of technically savvy enthusiasts and advocates. An accessible, decentralized infrastructure for production, editing, exhibition, and distribution grew tremendously, offering community media producers access to low-cost video editing and special effects, audio production, graphics, subtitling, duplicating, and other means of electronic media postproduction. The introduction of "pro-sumer" formats, such as S-VHS and Hi-8, raised the bar on public access video, while new digital platforms such as the Amiga Video Toaster gave enormous video power and creative potential to the low-budget producer. Thanks to a burgeoning demand for public access, cable television outlets for homegrown video spread to many communities nationwide, and a developing circuit of microcinemas, community media centers, and low-power FM radio stations grew an informal network for audiences hungry for something unique, real, raw, and personally relevant. Continuing advances in computer-based nonlinear editing virtually eliminated the impediments blocking sophisticated citizen media production. Video projectors dropped in price tremendously and allowed new film/video festivals and microcinemas to sprout in many cities, both large and small, in response to a growing audience for venues of independent video and film. Larger arts institutions began to pay attention to the new demand for independent audiovisual work, as local media initiatives began to coalesce around a national platform for independent production.

WE'RE NATIONWIDE! FROM THE LOCAL TO THE GLOBAL

As detailed in the previous chapter, Paper Tiger TV emerged in the early 1980s from the beginnings of a new technological infrastructure: the crisscrossing, coaxial lines of cable television. Though initially based in Manhattan, PTTV's goals and perspectives were always global. A good indication of the larger goals of PTTV is found in their manifesto, which is scrolled as screen text in every episode:

> PAPER TIGER TELEVISION IS A PUBLIC ACCESS TV SHOW. IT LOOKS AT THE COMMUNICATIONS INDUSTRY VIA THE MEDIA IN ALL OF THEIR FORMS.
>
> THE POWER OF MASS CULTURE RESTS ON THE TRUST OF THE PUBLIC. THIS LEGITIMACY IS A PAPER TIGER.
>
> INVESTIGATION INTO THE CORPORATE STRUCTURES OF THE MEDIA AND CRITICAL ANALYSIS OF THEIR CONTENT IS ONE WAY TO DEMYSTIFY THE INFORMATION INDUSTRY.
>
> DEVELOPING A CRITICAL CONSCIOUSNESS ABOUT THE COMMUNICATIONS INDUSTRY IS A NECESSARY FIRST STEP TOWARDS DEMOCRATIC CONTROL OF INFORMATION RESOURCES.[1]

While based locally in the Lower East Side of Manhattan, PPTV nurtured hopes of spreading their media-making model and electronic messages far and wide. Early on, the collective took up the task of dubbing and hand-delivering or mailing copies of the program to other supporters in other cable systems for playback, first in the other boroughs of New York City and then across the United States. The collective developed a regional and then a national system of distribution for the programs, screening regularly in Austin, Texas; San Diego, California; Burlington, Vermont; Providence, Rhode Island; Saint Louis, Missouri; Springfield, Illinois; and Detroit, Michigan.[2] A PTTV section in San Francisco sprung up to help with production and distribution on the West Coast. Paper Tiger Television was soon found on cable in San Francisco, Oakland, Marin County, Mountain View, Newark, and other Northern California environs. Dubs of the programs soon were being run around several dozen public access stations in different locales, becoming, by the popular acclaim of video activists, a form of "sneakernet." However, as the shoes began to wear thin, PTTV looked for more efficient means of distribution, finding it in the satellite distribution organization they dubbed Deep Dish TV. As with much of television technology, satellite transmission was entirely unthinkable for low-budget producers, until the mid-1980s, when there were enough satellite transponders at cheap-enough rental fees to allow mere mortals access to the "footprint" of a satellite. Other important technological changes were happening as well. By the mid-1980s, the mass marketing of the home camcorder allowed millions of citizens to have access to portable video production, essentially eliminating the need for studio equipment or expensive, cumbersome U-matic camera/deck combinations. Many contemporary video shooters today are not aware that the first generations of video cameras were not merged together with the actual video tape recording mechanisms as modern camcorders are but were actually separate camera units that needed to be connected to separate recorders. Access facilities, video co-ops, and low-budget postproduction facilities offered portable camcorders and access to video editing decks with time-base correctors (TBCs) and a few bells and whistles that permitted some simple, yet creative, editing and titling. Activists and artists worldwide captured local stories and struggles, producing home-made tapes that typically screened to a few friends and then wound up sitting on a shelf somewhere, particularly if that community did not have a micro-cinema venue. Public access producers from PTTV in New York and San Francisco, from Alternative Views in Austin and from the Squeaky Wheel in Buffalo advocated reaching audiences beyond the reach of one's own social or cultural circle, and thus creating television, not just video, and encourag-ing the public to play back their productions on local cable access stations. Groups of camcorder enthusiasts and local public access programmers began to grow in cities and towns across the United States, reenergizing stations that had become dormant and helping the public demand new ones where they did not already exist. In many towns, public access stations transitioned from being primarily a text screen of community announcements to a channel of vibrant video productions brought in from a wide variety of residents.

At the core of the public access philosophy is a belief in the importance of people making their own media and in the importance of people rejecting a predetermined role as passive consumers of prefabricated images. Many also believed strongly that a network must be locally rooted, yet globally conscious. Deep Dish TV took on the task of making an interactive, two-way video network on a national scale to the extent that the expense and techno-logical apparatus allowed. To facilitate this approach, local producers were encouraged to send in tapes to be curated together into thematically based programs that would be sent back out on the airwaves via satellite. These local groups could then download and record the feed from the dish and pro-gram the material into their own community's public access timeslots. There-fore, community groups that made a tape about their local housing struggle could sit back and watch with their participants and supporters as their story appeared alongside similar stories from all over the country on their local cable station. Thus was born Deep Dish TV, the first national public access television network. This form of TV, in which the audience produces as well as watches, ran directly counter to the predominant high-tech marketing hype of the time, where "advanced," "interactive" TV nevertheless positioned the audience as strictly consumers of visual "product." By contrast, the slogan on Deep Dish t-shirts and bumper stickers read, "Don't just watch TV, make it!"

DDTV collaborated with the Boston Film and Video Foundation to uplink its first series in 1985–1986. The series was comprised of ten one-hour pro-grams, including subjects on labor, women, agriculture, education, housing, racism, and Central America. It was offered for free to public access organiza-tions and was downlinked by over 186 stations.[3] One of the most important results of this project was a booklet that came along with the tapes, an illus-trated zine that included contact information for the hundreds of participat-ing video activists around the United States. The contact addresses were set in a mailing list template and arranged by zip code so that the list could be photocopied directly onto mailing labels and distributed via the postal service. In this pre-Internet landscape, paper, phone numbers, fax numbers, and satellite feeds contributed to a nationwide video network, forming a paper database of video activists nationwide. If an artist produced a program in Tucson, Arizona, but her friends and family lived in Albuquerque, New Mexico, she could contact New Mexico participants and ask them to cablecast the show there. Likewise, if people who lived in New York needed footage or an interview from San Francisco, they could usually find someone to do them the favor, and perhaps be asked to reciprocate sometime in the future. Video artists in one part of the country could now directly contact others in different areas for help airing programs, obtaining footage, or conducting interviews. Favors were exchanged and redeemed as individuals collaborated on projects. Many of the videos were produced by loosely knit collectives, so a spirit of cooperation was built in from the beginning. This network took root especially as people began to meet in person, often during annual national meetings of the National Federation of Local Cable Programmers (now called the Alliance for Community Media), formed in 1976 as a way for public access advocates and programmers to compare notes and strategize collectively.

DDTV produced numerous seasons of programming, with editors volunteering to put the material together in a coherent and curated fashion. After the first season of programming, Deep Dish coordinators proclaimed that it had established "a network of contacts and open lines of communication between independent producers, community groups, and access centers, between access centers and cable systems operators, and between communities all across the country." They saw this as an "ongoing network" that could fight the problems associated with public access, including isolation, publicity, and low-esteem from viewers in the face of criticism from mainstream media. As they put it, "The response to Deep Dish TV is strong evidence that an independent, decentralized television network can work."[4]

Subsequent programming seasons on Deep Dish included programs on Latino/as, humor and social change, Asia, cultural politics, AIDS, women's issues, environmentalism, antimilitarism, and many other subjects.[5] After the second season, Deep Dish had confirmed responses from 250 cable access centers that had downlinked and played DDTV programming, potentially reaching over twelve million households in forty-three states, including Alaska.[6] Judging from the mail received by Deep Dish TV, the audience also included rural viewers, using backyard dishes because they lacked access to cable systems, who were happy to see some noncommercial programming in the ether. DDTV also opened up its programming schedule to other organizations, uplinking tapes produced by workers' groups such as the United Farm Workers Union and the Amalgamated Clothing and Textile Workers Union because it was recognized that working people and their struggles rarely received fair coverage in the mainstream media. The International Women's Day Video Festival and other video festivals also chose to uplink their work through the Deep Dish Network. In 1990, in a time when the Sandinista government of Nicaragua was being vilified in the mainstream US press, the Deep Dish network took the idea of people-to-people communications a step further. In conjunction with Central America peace organizations, Deep Dish transmitted a live speech from Nicaraguan president Daniel Ortega in Managua to large US audiences, in an effort to break the blockade of free association that had been erected by the US government and the media.

Deep Dish Television initiated the first public access television network by harnessing the distributional power of satellite uplinking and downlinking, and they developed a national infrastructure around the contacts and collaborations cultivated by New York City–based Paper Tiger Television. The vision of the Deep Dish network was to continue to encourage local video producers to share stories, ideas, and solutions with other communities, recognizing that communities often faced many of the same problems. This bottom-up approach was a key aspect of what the group determined to be truly two-way media and a national movement built from grassroots. It was increasingly obvious that many of the issues investigated by local community media were national problems, such as the rise of homelessness and lack of housing, justice on the job, homophobia and the rise of the religious right, the wars in Central America, the attacks on the arts, and other pressing issues of the 1980s. An advantage of building upon local media producers, as opposed to adopting a more traditional documentary approach, was that the video material would be unique and valuable because it would be produced by people "on the inside," people who clearly knew the issues and could gain access to key participants. Video reports produced by professionals from network television, who sweep into an area for a few hours and come away with a story, may provide entertainment for their audiences but frequently leave communities frustrated or bitter about the false or uneven representation of events. Such superficial media reports almost never contain the context or historical long view that someone at the heart of an issue would have been able to convey. The success of the Deep Dish series, a growing media literacy movement, and the creation of many youth-based and educational video projects that saw video production as an important educational tool caused media production to soar in many cities and towns nationwide. The Deep Dish organizers believed these local media projects should have an ongoing, national audience. In the printed minutes of a Deep Dish meeting held in the spring of 1987, it was stated that "[d]eveloping a link between local and national interest groups and serving as a link to the broader community is another priority of Deep Dish TV. We're also aware that we are laying the foundation of a grass roots national television network and we will build into the structure an opportunity for those whose voices are ignored (or bent into unfair representation) in the mainstream media."[7] Tapping into the power of satellites in order to develop a national outlet for alternative television was a bold and audacious move for a low-budget movement that celebrated a low-tech aesthetic. By equating the "Dish" with something as wholesome and welcoming as a deep-dish cherry pie, the name "Deep Dish" was an attempt at making the satellite technology friendlier. The origins of the satellite industry were anything but friendly, however. Created by an act of Congress, the commercial satellite network—the Communications Satellite Corporation (Comsat)—included the roster of the largest telecommunications corporations in the United States, including RCA, GE, AT&T, and Western Union. Begun in 1962 in the wake of Sputnik, Comstat was originally conceived of for military purposes, in much the same way the Internet and the Interstate Highway System had been. The "open skies policy" reoriented the network to unregulated commercial use in 1972.[8] The Comsat satellites were instrumental in developing national communications for telephone, television, and data servers. When Deep Dish went forward with the tapes from their first series in 1986, it was possibly the first time alternative media had sought to access the satellite broadcasting system in the same way that network television did. The Deep Dish transmissions inspired other local media groups to develop a national "footprint." In 1989 the Chicago PBS affiliate WTTW began hosting the television show *The 90s*, produced by long-time independent video maker Tom Weinberg and the Center for Innovative TV. *The 90s* highlighted independent, eclectic video productions on a great number of subjects, some fifty-one editions in all, with a typical run time of fifty-six minutes each. Their irreverent coverage of the 1992 Republican convention in Houston by free speech prankster Stoney Burke, however, resulted in the program being cut by their PBS sponsor, who ultimately feared the wrath of the Republican-dominated Congress. In the episode, Burke boldly approached major Republican figures at the Republican convention, camcorder rolling, to ask blunt questions that broke from normal TV reporters' "softball" inquiries. For example, Burke asked Savings-and-Loan scandal-figure Neil Bush if he was going to pay back the money he had stolen, and he asked Iran-Contra scandal-figure Oliver North whether he was sorry about the people he had killed. The Stoney Burke episode, despite the censorship of PBS, played to wildly enthusiastic audiences all over the United States, thanks to microcinemas and access television. *The 90s'* coverage of the Houston, Texas, convention was a triumphal return for Weinberg, as he was part of the seminal artists group TVTV that had videotaped from inside the 1972 Miami Beach Republican convention with one of the early Sony Portapak decks. It should be noted that Weinberg was also the host of a Paper Tiger Television critique of the *Wall Street Journal*. The Stoney Burke camcorder episode from the convention floor in 1992 clearly indicated that media technology had evolved tremendously since 1972.[9] Feder reports the executive director of the Media Burn Archive, Sara Chapman, explaining that "the 1992 presidential election was a turning point in American political history, including the first uses of online media in political campaigns."[10]

Many ideas for a nationwide alternative television network were incubated throughout this time period, with some succeeding and others succumbing to budget realities. Free Speech TV, based in Boulder, Colorado, was founded in 1995, but its roots extend back to *The 90s* public television show and *The 90s Channel* on cable television. From 1995 to 2000, Free Speech TV provided weekly videotape programming to a network of some fifty community and privately leased cable channels. In 2000, Free Speech TV launched its national progressive television network when it was awarded a full-time satellite channel on direct-broadcast satellite provider DISH Network as a result of an FCC policy to set aside 4 percent of satellite channels for public interest channels.[11] In the United Kingdom, the group Undercurrents launched in 1994 from the Camcorder Action Network and developed a similar network of activist videotape producers that continues to this day.

Throughout the 1990s, local video artists strove to connect regionally and nationally through producers and programmers' groups such as the Bay Area Video Coalition (BAVC) and the Film Arts Foundation (FAF) in San Francisco and the Association of Independent Video and Filmmakers (AIVF) and Downtown Community Television (DCTV) in New York City. The Independent Television Service (ITVS) was formed by independent film and video makers in the early 1990s by a national coalition of media activists who aggressively lobbied Congress to set aside some funding for "independently produced programming that takes creative risks, sparks public dialogue, and gives voice to underserved communities."[12] The meetings of the National Federation of Local Cable Programmers (NFLCP) and the National Association of Media Access Centers (NAMAC) became important collective gatherings of video activists and media artists of all types. The Union for Democratic Communications (UDC) also brought together groups of media activists and academics.

The success of national platforms for independent media led to conversations and connections with independent media producers from other countries. It became easier to see the global implications of new media technologies in the international arena. This global vision was enriched when the Deep Dish Network and Paper Tiger launched the Gulf Crisis TV Project (GCTV), an international grassroots video project that sprang up in response to the US war on Iraq in 1990–1991. The organizers of this project were able to effectively create an alternative global television system; they were receiving, editing, and transmitting video images involving almost every state in the United States and many other nations a few short years before the popularization of the Internet and Web services that many take for granted today. The GCTV Project, and many other grassroots electronic media projects, helped lay the foundation for the global, Internet-based alternative media networks that we see expanding rapidly today.

DESERT TELEVISION STORM

Toward the end of 1990, the specter of war began to loom on the world stage as George H. W. Bush started to threaten Iraq with military retaliation after it had moved into the US-allied oil territory of Kuwait. In response to this saber rattling, the ashes of a still-smoldering antiwar movement stirred in many American communities. In city after city, town after town, US activists began to mobilize teach-ins, demonstrations, and acts of civil disobedience to raise unasked questions about US history and responsibility in the Gulf region, questions basically ignored by the mainstream media. For their part, mainstream media flooded the press and airwaves with a parade of military brass, conservative pundits, and oil-friendly business analysts. In a detailed analysis of the lists of those interviewed by CNN during the war, researcher Anthony DiMaggio discovered that "[t]here was no room in the most-mentioned list for domestic or foreign antiwar protesters, representatives of transnational humanitarian groups, dissident scholars, or even left-liberal political leaders such as John Murtha and the late Edward Kennedy who favored withdrawal."[13] Deep Dish began discussions with antiwar activists and other concerned citizens about trying to use the camcorder to capture and present the missing side of the debate. Camcorder activists nationwide had been shooting and documenting popular opposition to the war drive, scenes absent from the evening news and morning papers. The perceived subservience of the US media to the war plans of the US administration was frightening to many who often still believed in the ultimate objectivity of the "Fourth Estate." It became apparent to those who opposed the war and the proliferation of racist, anti-Arab fear-mongering that something should be done to counter the mass media's subservience to US policy.[14]

The Gulf Crisis TV Project (GCTV) was formed in the fall of 1990 by a group of video activists who put out a call for video documentation of local antiwar events, as well as for interviews with dissident experts and intellectuals ignored by mainstream media. Also welcomed were artistic and cultural works that critiqued and illuminated what was happening in the Gulf. The first four tapes of the series, edited under duress by many volunteers, were *War, Oil, and Power*, *Operation Dissidence*, *Getting Out of the Sand Trap*, and *Bring the Troops Home!* According to Dee Dee Halleck, one of the principle organizers of the project, "The series contained the work of over a hundred producers, from dozens of locations," which "ranged from rallies, to comedians, to guerrilla theater, to intimate interviews, to didactic charts and history texts. Artists included Seth Tobocman, Mary Feaster, Paul Zaloom, Papoletto Melendez, Norman Cowie, Joel Katz, Tony Avalos, and Karen Ranucci, who contributed graphics, performance, and video art. Policy and regional experts Edward Said, Noam Chomsky, Dessima Williams, Daniel Ellsberg, and Grace Paley also contributed, as did GIs who opposed the war."[15] The series captured the anger and outrage protesters felt against the war, as well as the humor, music, and drama that surrounded it.

In the fall of 1990, the first four half-hour GCTV programs were uplinked on DDTV to hundreds of local cable stations. A PBS sympathetic to the goals of Deep Dish TV, WYBE in Philadelphia, sponsored an uplink on the PBS satellite, thus making the Gulf Crisis TV Project available to millions of public television viewers, including those in New York City and

Los Angeles. The programs were also publicly shown to crowds of people hungry to see another side of the story. The tapes played in microcinemas and public venues such as community centers, movie theaters, university teach-ins, and churches. Watching the audiovisual representation of large antiwar protests collectively in public audiences helped tremendously in building confidence for further mobilization and in dispelling the "spiral of silence" and subsequent apathy and depression that frequently accompanies jingoistic media coverage.[16]

As preparation for war turned to actual war and "Desert Shield" begat "Desert Storm," the tightening of the media grew more intense, and the print dailies and large broadcasting networks meekly succumbed to military censorship of images from the Gulf. Dissenting views were essentially eliminated, and reporting of mass protest was silenced, except for rare occasions. In San Francisco, the site of a large demonstration of 200,000 people, local media outlets suppressed the extent of the protest, arbitrarily reporting the number of protesters as 15,000. One National Public Radio reporter, while preparing her live report from a demonstration, told her editor that there were over 100,000 people at one of the protests. She was told by the national news director to report neither the numbers nor the size of the protest. One television station juxtaposed an image of a handful of prowar motorcycle club members with footage of 100,000 antiwar protesters in a feeble attempt at equating both sides. A crew from the Japanese television news program *The Scoop*, a program similar to CBS's *60 Minutes*, came to San Francisco and produced an entire segment on the willful disinformation propagated by US media on the extent of public protests of the war. There was so much antiwar activity in the city of San Francisco that local activists there created their own weekly program called *Finally Got the News*. Chock full of reporting on the mass arrests, bridge takeovers, and large-scale civil disobedience occurring in the San Francisco Bay Area, it helped expose what the activists described as the media's silence and complicity.[17] KQED, the local PBS affiliate that steadfastly refused to run programs that opposed the government's viewpoint on Iraq, became the target of alternative media activists as well. Representatives of Deep Dish Television met with the head of KQED to ask why the station would not run the Gulf Crisis Series, as many other public television stations were doing. The KQED representatives said they could not air the tapes for "technical" reasons, as their engineering department determined them to be "not broadcast quality." Later that day, however, the engineers at the station let the PTTV group know that there were no technical problems; they reported that the problem lay with station management who judged the tapes too controversial.[18] As critics often point out, the limitation of public television in the United States is that it is at the mercy of Congress, which funds much of its infrastructure, and of corporate underwriting, which pays many of its bills. This often makes PBS broadcasters reluctant to rock the ideological boat. Antiwar documentarians determined to be "on" KQED at any cost showed up with a video projector and a sound system and held a public screening on a blank wall of the building that housed KQED, with the police looking on.

To further enhance distribution, the GCTV tapes were duplicated thousands of times and sold cheaply at antiwar events and through the mail. Tape owners were encouraged, in turn, to duplicate their tapes and pass them on; thus, tapes circulated by the thousands into the hands of friends, family, and coworkers nationwide, becoming, in effect, an American electronic *samizdat*, an underground distribution system of alternative information. Millions of people ultimately saw these videos in direct opposition to US policy and the US media's whiteout. All these actions added to the wholesale rejection of corporate media and contributed greatly to the desire to build an alternative media infrastructure. For their part, the mainstream media was self-congratulatory with the job they had done to cheerlead the war effort, but there is much evidence that their uncritical approach contributed greatly to weaken the trust the American people put into mainstream media.

During the war, the GCTV network grew to international proportions as the project linked with other video collectives and nongovernmental organizations (NGOs) around the world that were concerned about the war. Many of these contacts came from informal international connections that had developed from community access activism. It became clear that grassroots video organizations were growing spectacularly, not only in the United States, but also particularly in the so-called underdeveloped countries like Brazil, India, Asia, and the Middle East. In Brazil, for example, Roberto Mader wrote that "this grassroots video movement created an alternative to traditional ways of covering current affairs and brought to some screens faces hardly seen before. TV Viva in Recife is an outstanding example of alternative production in Brazil, having for many years produced a wide variety of videos screened in different town squares in the centre of the outskirts of this northeastern area. In simple, sharp language they rediscover the 'grass roots.'"[19] In South Africa, a network of activist video makers was built during the struggle against apartheid: "Workers would watch the videos at home, in factories, all over the place. Besides the union networks, videos also circulated in youth, student, church, civic, and political organizations."[20] As word of the many examples of community television projects trickled in, it was increasingly clear that the phenomenon was a truly global one. Connections with international activist media groups increased in urgency as the somber events unfolded during the Gulf War. A call went out to the international grassroots' video contacts to send footage showing documented events in their respective countries. What was the response from other peace movements around the world? Was there international outrage from other countries? What was the perspective from other peoples not subject to US media self-censorship and blind patriotism? Tapes came in to the GCTV office from all over the world, and in return tapes went out all over the world, in an international exchange of evidence of opposition to US policy in the Gulf. The GCTV Project received protest footage from Taiwan, the Philippines, Spain, Korea, and France, to name a few. Some of the Deep Dish producers had access to the large-scale C-band satellite feeds, the feeds used primarily for point-to-point uploads and downloads. These are typically used by large broadcasters to send raw material from the field to the central postproduction offices for editing. Viewing and recording the raw material from these satellite dishes revealed what the US media was willing to show its audiences versus what other countries were willing to show. Footage of blown-apart children, of bombed schools and hospitals, of grieving parents and families, and of US soldiers suffering were all routinely excised, in order to sanitize the images American audiences would receive and to build a more heroic narrative of the War in the Gulf. Some of this downlinked material was used in Gulf Crisis TV programs to demonstrate the extent of US media collusion with the US military censors. The Gulf Crisis TV series was shown all over the world on channels including the United Kingdom's Channel Four, Canada's Vision TV, and channels and public venues in France, Japan, and Germany. Some of the tapes were translated into Japanese and shown to groups of community activists and students around Japan.

The first series of four Gulf Crisis programs was followed by six more programs entitled *News World Order, Manufacturing the Enemy, Lines in the Sand, Global Dissent, Just Say No!,* and *War on the Home Front.* These tapes were broadcast on DDTV and distributed by the burgeoning network of antiwar activists and organizations. The series continued to screen, even after the war wound down. In 1993, the Gulf Crisis TV Project was included in the prestigious Whitney Biennial[21] and was later screened at the Berlin Film Festival and many other festivals and venues.

The success of the Gulf Crisis TV Project, fraught as it was with conflicts and tensions, economic difficulty, and technical limitations, illuminated the exciting possibilities unleashed by media activists who developed independent media networks that had the potential to break the blockade of ideas erected by corporate-owned media. The ability of fax machines, satellite feeds, and bulletin board services to cross borders invigorated and excited thousands of activists walled in by the corporate stranglehold of CBS, NBC, ABC, and CNN. It was a powerful feeling when people saw themselves and their beliefs represented in mass media, whether on a television set or on the big screen in front of a large public audience.

The fact that these media activities were initiated and sustained by an independent collective of artists is a strong statement in and of itself, in a field often dominated by individualistic artists and profit-driven corporations. Its collective structure often meant that the production process was rarely smooth, with frequent debate between those arguing for a "professional, broadcast quality look" versus a "funkier," home video camera aesthetic, or for appealing to an already radical audience versus appealing to a more mainstream audience. Participants also disagreed about whether to bring in younger, though perhaps less experienced, members and about how to reach out to communities of color to increase the diversity of the collective. These discussions did not always leave everyone happy and unruffled, particularly as they ensued amidst a frantic work effort, spurred by the perceived US rush to genocide in the Middle East.

Despite these problems, the collective awareness raised by this media project contributed in its own small way to the realization among young activists that corporate media was unable to deliver the truth and that a movement must have its own media infrastructure. To many Gulf War antiwar activists, the link between democratic debate over foreign policy issues and mass media became inseparable. A true democracy is, they declared, based upon an informed citizenry, and an informed citizenry was perceived as incompatible with the petro-chemical–driven foreign policy in the Gulf region. The Gulf Crisis TV Project helped develop a new way of thinking about media networks and about how such networks can contribute to democratic participation. It should be remembered, however, that this international network was built before the World Wide Web, with a small reliance on primitive e-mail tools.

TOWARD A NEW TYPE OF NETWORK

The success of the 1999 anti–World Trade Organization (WTO) protest in Seattle gave birth to a new protest movement loosely defined as proenvironment and anticapitalist. The influence of the Seattle protest can be found in many subsequent direct actions against the International Monetary Fund (IMF), the G20, the World Bank, and other international banking and trade organizations, leading all the way to the Occupy movement that erupted on Wall Street in 2011. The media model adopted by these movements originated from the Independent Media Center movement (IMC) in Seattle, which used technology that looks positively archaic by today's standards. Building the independent media centers did not happen in a vacuum, however. As Dee Dee Halleck points out, the model of collaborating through media collectives, used in Seattle and beyond, follows the model used by Deep Dish TV and the Gulf Crisis TV Project.[22]

In hindsight, compared with the tools available today, it was quite remarkable that the Gulf Crisis TV Project built such an extensive video production network at such a rapid pace, on a global scale without having the Internet and the many Web tools that are taken for granted today. The Gulf Crisis TV Project's ability to form such a network makes it clear that a network is primarily about people-to-people communications, not electronics. The network was built upon the bonds established over the years by a common understanding arrived at through a common practice. The Gulf Crisis TV Project network was developed by a shared critique of the oil economy, a knowledge of the history of colonialism and imperialism, and an embrace of established concepts of human rights. Without this shared understanding, the network of global video activists would not have gelled. As importantly, a common tenet of alternative media practice is an understanding of democratic participation and a critique of hierarchy. John Downing has also found this to be the case in his many studies of radical media:

> Can we say that, by contrast, radical alternative media are the chief standard bearers of a democratic communication structure? The argument here is yes: that, although flawed, immensely varied, and not necessarily oppositional, many such media do contribute in different degrees to that mission, and more truly than the mainstream media, in ways that are often amazing, given their exceptionally meager resources.[23]

It is for this reason that the use of the word "network" to describe Deep Dish TV was not chosen lightly. The buzzword "network" is ubiquitous in today's technological times, where it is used to describe any type of data connection. Proponents of democratic networks contend that while much of society may be connected electronically today, not much thought is given to the word "network"; in fact, not all networks are created equal.

The popular notion of a "net" has often come to signify a democratic sharing, an equal distribution of nodes, all connecting to other points, without hierarchy. Yet few networks work like that. TV broadcast networks are hierarchical, with a central locus, little feedback, and no way to communicate among its outer points. This broadcast model historically has dominated the construction of networks, as radio, TV, and cable industries have all promoted its structure. Today, the Internet is under the same pressure to conform to the centralized network model. The e-commerce economy, the stated goal for many multinational corporations, is searching for a way to force this profit-enabling structure upon the Web. The preferred Internet business model is a broadcasting model, with the central hub being distributors of electronic services and entertainment, such as Facebook, AOL, Hulu, Google, MSN, and other ventures.

There is a popular assumption that networks are inherently positive entities, that somehow all networks are the electronic equivalent of talking over the neighbors' back fence or of dealing with a friendly, local merchant. Networks, however, must be scrutinized for their social impact, in addition to their technical achievement. Like other technological creations, networks are, after all, not simply discovered or invented, but rather engineered into existence and put into place by institutions of power. Networks, and in particular electronic networks, have existed for over 100 years. The standard term "network," at least in the United States, was popularized by CBS, RCA, and what were called the "red" and "blue" networks of early commercial broadcasting. The network of telegraph lines strung up around the world at the turn of the century transformed primitive colonialism into modern imperialism. The United Fruit Company, the inventor of the "banana republic" was one of the earliest builders of AM radio networks, built in order to keep their banana plantations and shipping operations humming. Today, advanced computer network technology allows the smooth functioning of global capitalism. Cash registers' signals flow from the mall to the corporate headquarters to the offshore factories to the shipping companies and warehouses, and back again. Indeed, not all networks are created equal.

Networks can be hubs, chains, stars, or other configurations. They can also have varying levels of equality and exchange. The desire of PTTV, Deep Dish, and the Gulf Crisis TV Project was to develop a truly interactive, participatory network infrastructure that stressed democratic involvement over passive consumerism. It is not enough for Americans to be mere consumers of information; democracy requires active participation as well. The Gulf Crisis TV Project helped to promote that vision, and to point out that certain barriers to building a global, grassroots media network—such as language difference, national borders, different television standards, distance, and time obstacles—can be overcome.

A GROWING MOVEMENT FOR GLOBAL DEMOCRATIC COMMUNICATIONS

It was the culmination of years of reform efforts and alternative media collaborations, as well as a developing critique of the dominant news organizations and their control by multinational corporations that led to an upsurge in the field of media studies and a further interest in the "deconstruction" of how media operate. Critical viewing habits were coupled with a growing understanding of the economic and financial monopolization of mass media that was underway. What began as a small protestation against media monopoly by critics such as Ben Bagdikian, Noam Chomsky, and Herb Schiller became a loud chorus of protest as media companies were swallowed up by large corporations in the aftermath of rampant deregulation. The 1995 merger of Disney with Capital Cities/ABC epitomized this growing concentration, leading media critic Robert McChesney to note that "business analysts expect even more merger and buyout activity, leading to as few as six to ten 'colossal conglomerates' dominating global communication before the market stabilizes. By virtually all known theories of political democracy such a concentration of media and communication is an unmitigated disaster."[24]

The growing chorus of critiques of corporate media domination led to numerous international movements and conferences, among them the Media and Democracy Congress held in San Francisco in 1996 (organized by the Institute for Alternative Journalism), the Free the Media Conference held in New York City in 1997, and the Cultural Environment Movement begun by George Gerbner, former professor and dean of the Annenberg School for Communication. Gerbner stated in 1996 that "[f]or the first time in human history, most of the stories about people, life, and values are told not by parents, schools, churches, or others in the community who have something to tell, but by a group of distant conglomerates who have something to sell."[25]

This media-critical consciousness yielded the near unanimous verdict among many activists and artists that contemporary mainstream media, dominated as they are by a handful of multinational corporations, are structurally biased and predisposed towards representing the ideology and views of their owners.[26] For decades, social change advocates had no choice but to court hostile or indifferent media outlets in a vain attempt at squeezing out a modicum of fair representation in the large papers and broadcasting networks. In the 1990s, the rejection of mainstream media and the availability of the new tools of production and distribution combined to create a powerful new media synergy. By the time of the 1999 Seattle protests, activists were armed with an abundance of powerful new tools of media communications, and were ready to build their own media infrastructure and bypass the media's "blockade of ideas" entirely.

As alternative media networks expanded nationally and internationally in the 1990s, broadcasters and cable news operations, commercial radio stations, and other mainstream culture purveyors became increasingly hostile, propagating the notion of citizen media as untrustworthy and unprofessional. The lobbying arm of the corporate broadcasters, the National Association of Broadcasters, began litigation and lobbying against low-power FM radio, as we saw in the case of Free Radio Berkeley. News outlets began a public relations assault against what they described as biased or inaccurate accounts of news events that were gaining currency on alternative Bulletin Board Services, listservs, and Web sites. Telecommunications giants grew increasingly confrontational with public access organizations that were viewed as cutting into their audience for pay-per-view and premium channels. Governments around the globe were also increasingly uneasy and unfriendly to these new democratic media initiatives and sought ways to curb or regain control over media dissemination and curtail the possible destabilizing effects of uncontrollable media. Videocassettes and audiocassettes were easy to move across borders and slip beneath the radar of censors and regulators. The fax machine would take that ability a step further, with its capacity to transmit visual information through the phone lines, effectively eliminating borders. In the early 1990s, to demonstrate this transborder quality and to deflate the ability of the state to censor images, mini-FM radio pioneer Tetsuo Kogawa held a show in a Tokyo art gallery, starting with all blank walls. He then invited people from around the world to fax in or e-mail images that would be illegal to transport across the Japanese border, which he then printed out and hung on the gallery walls. In the 1980s, at the height of the Reaganite anti-Soviet period, an international people-to-people initiative was taken by peace activists to build a video peace-bridge across the world to bring together American and Soviet citizens in the face of official governmental hostility between the US and Soviet governments. An example of this people-to-people communication took place in the 3220 Gallery in San Francisco, funded by Plush toymaker Henry Dakin. Dubbed the "space bridge," the gallery hosted several such events with the help of an enormous satellite dish on the roof. Citizens on both sides of the world in San Francisco and Moscow would gather at an agreed-upon time to turn on cameras and meet virtually in an effort to show good will toward both sides. The ability to pull off such a spectacular, real-time meeting required, at the time, an enormous amount of money. Much of the impetus for this democratic diplomacy came from Joseph Goldin, a Russian citizen and peace activist. Goldin had earlier helped set up a Soviet-American live satellite exchange for Steve Wozniak of Apple Computer during the 1982 "US" festival, a three day high-profile rock concert conceived to be the "Woodstock" of the computer generation. Such an endeavor was a powerful way to show the potential of people-to-people technologies, though the cost and technological infrastructure of these events was far out of reach for most citizens. Goldin was very interested in these communications experiments and sought to create "interactive plazas" around the world:

> Interactive Plazas are large video screens set up in prominent public places all over the world that could constantly broadcast live images of people going about their daily lives in other countries. These large, ground-level screens will be accessible to everyone from children to top-level scientists for direct communication by random meetings or by making prior arrangements to meet at the plaza. This new form of human contact, if used wisely, could give birth to a planetary consciousness that until now has been realized only by an enlightened few. A worldwide network of satellite-linked Interactive Plazas will act as a cosmic mirror with which we, as citizens of the world, could look back at our selves and grasp our humanity and essential unity as never before.[27]

Goldin died in the late 1990s in Russia, convinced that such international communications practices would become commonplace someday.

THE WEB FROM CHIAPAS TO SEATTLE

In the early 1990s, much excitement was being generated by a new form of computer communication, a text-based method that used a government-created network of cable and computer servers to instantly communicate from a keyboard. With the introduction of the new HTML protocol and a free, downloadable application called a "browser," a previously obscure method of computer communication began to gain popularity, particularly among young people. Using a text program to write some simple code, a person could upload and "publish" words—then photos, then sounds, and, eventually, video—that could be read by a free browser program such as "Mosaic." This "World Wide Web" launched a new digital culture that celebrated its new forms of communication with new media and cultural components: magazines such as *Mondo 2000* or *Boing Boing*, dance and party scenes called "raves," user groups based upon obscure computer programming applications, and an embrace of the "geek" and "steampunk" styles. For many of the people beginning with Internet experimentation, their initial engagement lacked a clear purpose. Internet users relished building websites just to experiment, to push the limits of the technology, or to show off their skills with Unix or HTML. An international event occurred in the mid-1990s, however, that seized the imaginations of many alternative media practitioners and demonstrated a remarkable social use for new media based around the World Wide Web. Surprisingly, this event took place, not in the advanced technical centers of the developed world, but in the jungles of Chiapas, Mexico. After the signing of the North American Free Trade Agreement (NAFTA) by Canada, the United States, and Mexico, peasants and farmers of the Chiapas region took an armed stance in defense of their way of life and stood up against the Mexican ruling elite, who had signed on to NAFTA despite opposition from many Mexican peasants, workers, and intellectuals. As the Mexican army stood poised to respond with force, an electronic Zapatista presence emerged across the world, thanks to electronic media devices and a network of Web site makers and alternative Internet service providers. Suddenly, the struggle of the indigenous of the Mexican south was as close as the computer in your living room. As Dee Dee Halleck wrote, "Within a few hours after the takeover of San Cristobal de las Casas by the Zapatistas on the morning of January 1, 1994, computer screens around the world came alive with news of the uprising. By January 3, Subcommander Marcos himself was online."[28] With the eyes of the world on the developing situation, the Mexican forces of repression could not inflict their damage in secrecy. The Zapatistas and their allies seized the electronic means of reproduction and articulated their message clearly and imaginatively into the world psyche. The excitement generated by computer-based media activism inspired new forms of protest—the "digital sit-in," for example—and helped craft a new word, "hacktivism." The desire to help the indigenous people of Chiapas from the urban centers of the United States led many computer activists to experiment and develop ways of virtual participation, some legal, such as mirroring Zapatista communiqués, and some illegal, such as launching denial-of-service attacks on Mexican servers. Perhaps not since the May rebellions of France in 1968 did a synthesis of communications and popular protest make such a bold statement. The images, manifestos, and poetry of Zapatista spokesperson Subcomandante Marcos engaged a global audience directly, without the cooperation of mainstream entertainment centers, news gatekeepers, or government censors. While mainstream news did little to cover the events unfolding in Mexico, millions of people around the world were watching. From the very beginning of the Zapatista uprising, it was made clear that alternative media would be a crucial part of their battle. Summing up this battle for media, in a direct video address from the jungle of Chiapas to the Free the Media conference in New York City in 1997, Marcos said to the crowd of media activists:

> We have a choice. . . . We can have a cynical attitude in the face of the media, to say that nothing can be done. . . . Or we can simply assume

incredulity. . . . But there is a third option that is neither conformity nor disbelief: that is to construct a different way—to show the world what is really happening—to have a critical world view. . . . It is our only possibility to save the truth, to maintain it and distribute it, little by little.[29]

The possibility for direct communication with the world and for an end-run around the mass media and government was heartening. The Zapatistas were able to leap two formidable barriers: the direct censorship of the Mexican government and the self-censorship of the US media industry. Many urban young people in Mexico, the United States, and beyond saw the uprising of indigenous peasants in Chiapas, Mexico, and its poet/leader Subcomandante Marcos as especially inspiring, with its fusion of art and politics, its embrace of countercultural principles, and its youthful energy. This was not just an uprising of the oppressed, but also a vivid and inspiring fight for cultural survival. In a videotaped statement to a cultural gathering in Mexico City organized by Mexican countercultural groups and the US rock band Rage Against the Machine, Marcos entrusted the digital youth subculture with the defense of the traditions of the indigenous fighting for their survival in the jungles. Holding a guitar, he said, "We made ourselves soldiers like that so that one day soldiers would no longer be necessary, as we also remain poor, so that one day there will no longer be poverty. This is what we use the weapon of resistance for." Marcos declared that the Zapatista fight was cultural, not just military. He exclaimed, "[T]he Zapatistas have other arms" including "the weapon of our culture, of our being what we are. We have the weapon of music, the weapon of dance."[30] These words were taken to heart by many young people around the world and by many digital media enthusiasts in the United States.

It was this growing base of digital artists, media activists, hacktivists, and culture-jammers that came together to help build the protest of the meeting of the World Trade Organization (WTO) in Seattle, Washington, in 1999. In December of that year, 50,000 environmentalists, social justice advocates, and labor activists descended on Seattle in a determined outpouring of opposition to a meeting of the WTO. Many alternative media people were there among them, eager to contribute their expertise in video, radio, and Internet skills. The mass demonstrations and subsequent street clashes in Seattle caught the mainstream media off guard, as journalists expressed surprise at not only the large numbers of protesters, but also at the extent of organization and global participation evident among them. The mainstream media, as the ostensible "gatekeepers" of public news and information, had typically pronounced conflicts surrounding the World Trade Organization, the World Bank, the International Monetary Fund, and other global financial institutions as too "complex" for the public to understand. The WTO meeting had thus been deemed not newsworthy and assigned only a limited number of reporters and camera crews. According to Amy Goodman, who was in Seattle with the Democracy Now! news group, "Ordinary people were not supposed to know about this. It was all supposed to fly under the radar. The WTO was barely mentioned in the US press. The corporate media—whose parent companies had everything to gain from secret trade deals—decided on our behalf that we just wouldn't understand. It was much too complicated for an eight-second sound bite. But to the dismay of the powerful, tens of thousands of people from around the world did understand."[31] Journalists were obviously impressed by the impact of alternative electronic communication practices on the Internet that helped to articulate and propagate the importance of the WTO meeting and the need to confront it. Much of the heightened criticism of such international trade organizations came from the lessons learned during the anti-NAFTA fight, in particular the objections raised by the Zapatistas of Mexico and other organizations of the global south and by US trade unions.

While the national news media was scrambling to catch up with the rapidly unfolding events, an independent media center was already in place, sending out a steady stream of video footage, digital photos, sound files, text descriptions, and up-to-the-minute reports on the tense situation in Seattle, providing an effective end-run around the unofficial whiteout of the mainstream media. According to Jeff Perlstein of the Seattle IMC, though the group worked "in an amazingly short amount of time, with amazingly little resources," it was "able to do a significant amount as far as hooking up with each other and getting the word out, through the Web, through community-based radio, through public access TV stations [it] broadcast to every night, through print publication daily, and through all these different modes and mediums of communication."[32]

The IMC, which formed just eight weeks prior to the Seattle revolt, was put together rapidly via e-mails, listservs, Web sites, and other networking tools. For five days, WTO actions were transmitted via satellite by both Deep Dish TV and Free Speech TV to their national audiences. Many of the media activists who pulled the IMC together had never met before in person; nevertheless, they were ready to act when they set up shop in Seattle, thanks to ongoing preliminary Internet conversations. Crews of video shooters covered the streets, speeches, protests, and actions in Seattle, and crews of editors took shifts in the constant, ongoing editing of material to upload. The IMC model brought forward a new generation of collective media practice no longer limited by physical proximity and centered on new communications channels for direct action. Organizationally, this movement looked increasingly similar to the topology of the Internet itself, based on decentralized and flexible nodes, temporary autonomous zones, and affinity groups rather than traditional, large, centralized organizations. That the Indy Media Center in Seattle came together so successfully through electronic exchanges among independent media makers is testimony to the promise of such networks and gave hope that perhaps the tide was turning in the favor of democratic media. As C. Atton points out, during the Seattle protests, "Hundreds of hours of audio and video footage and hundreds of thousands of eyewitness reports, analyses, and commentary became available to activists, supporters, detractors—to 'global citizens' at large. Such independent accounts provide a powerful counter to the enduring frames of social movement coverage in mainstream media."[33]

COMPUTER TOOLS AND GLOBAL SOCIAL NETWORKS

By the time the teargas had cleared from the streets of Seattle, it was apparent to many of the media activists involved that something new and exciting had emerged—a viable option for a new, global, alternative media network. The fight against globalization from above, at which the protest had aimed, had created a counterglobalization from below in the form of a communications network that transcended borders, both politically and ideologically. While the concept of "globalization" had typically been disparaged, toward the end of the 1990s, it was viewed as having a possibly positive side. It was now increasingly clear that the new media tools based on the Internet would have a profound impact on the ability to create alternative information systems on a global scale. In 1992, just after the Gulf War had ended, Paper Tiger Television produced a program called *Staking a Claim in Cyberspace*, which was broadcast nationally on Deep Dish Television. This tape looked critically at new developments in the rapidly growing domain of "cyberspace" and the construction of the "information superhighway," as the Internet was called then. While accurately foretelling the rapid corporatization of the Internet, the program also raised the emancipatory possibilities of a universal computer media network, where every port could send and receive information, unfettered by corporate gatekeepers. The events in Seattle had provided some glimpses of that possibility. As during the mid-East and North African revolts in 2011, pundits were quick to acknowledge the Internet's role in building the large-scale Seattle demonstrations. Such a perspective, however, tended to place the technology in the center of the events, ignoring that the technical practices and experiments of independent media activists emerge from social relationships and concerted collective activity. Furthermore, this tech-centered perspective ignores the past practices and historical roots that helped pave the way for new, progressive Internet communications. The interpersonal network structure that existed beforehand to accommodate the building of this type of alternative media network remains unfamiliar to mainstream reporters and journalists. Also unknown was how the technological infrastructures used in previous alternative media projects contributed to contemporary communications practices. These underlying communications strategies are very evident in the work of contemporary alternative video networks.

The international organizing potential of the computer was imagined for many years before the launching of the World Wide Web. An earlier chapter examined how an important local project that foretold these possibilities was the Community Memory Project, a local Bulletin Board Service based in Berkeley, California, and wired around several public computer kiosks. Users could log on and enter information, news, and events relevant to the East Bay community, and it was easy to see how this could be used on a much wider scale. A pioneering example of electronic text-based communication was the French system called Minitel, a videotext service made available in France in 1982. Operating through normal telephone lines, French citizens could make train reservations, send messages, and engage in live chat, years before the primary Internet became popular. The Minitel model was also used in other countries in Europe—Ireland, Germany, and the Netherlands—but did not achieve as high a level of penetration as France. The Minitel system served millions of people but was eventually eclipsed by the World Wide Web and was formally shut down in June 2012. Minitel was possibly ahead of its time, but it demonstrated that such a system could be built on a massive scale, not just locally. It also demonstrated the activist uses of such a system, for example, when it was used to help organize a student strike in France in 1986.[34]

The value of computer networking for linking activist communications was highlighted by the creation of PeaceNet, one of the earliest such computer networks in the United States. Users of PeaceNet gained access to e-mail and standard text-based services such as telnet, file transfer protocol (ftp), gopher, and other tools. Content was posted in various archived bulletin boards, and a community of progressive computer users was created. PeaceNet was later brought into the Institute for Global Communications in 1987, where it joined EcoNet, ConflictNet, LaborNet, WomensNet, GreenNet (based in the United Kingdom), and others in the Association for Progressive Communications (APC). This group of computer activists "served tens of thousands of individuals, nonprofits, and progressive causes in more than 130 countries."[35] IGC expanded tremendously in the 1980s and 1990s, as many grassroots organizations sought their assistance in developing online computer communications, particularly in the global South. Just before the World Wide Web was launched, some of the APC nodes were Alternex in Brazil, Chasque in Uruguay and Paraguay, Ecuanex in Ecuador, Glasnet in Russia, Antenna in the Netherlands, Nicarao in Central America, and Wamani in Argentina.

In the United States, many computer enthusiasts were building Bulletin Board Services, whereby a user could log in directly into that person's server via modem and access other users' information and messages. Initially access to a BBS only gave a user an entry into the internal postings of that site, but as the Internet grew, BBSs increasingly connected to the Internet as well. According to a BBS summary in 1993, "For millions of computer users, local and regional bulletin boards represent their only contact with the global network community. These boards are themselves increasingly linked into complex global networks." "As the depth and breadth of the BBS world has grown, it has long been obvious that Internet connectivity was only a matter of time. Recent developments have brought basic Internet connections to many boards. Many more will follow soon. This is the next wave."[36] The Bulletin Board Service model, the precursor of today's social-networking sites, was the springboard for FidoNet, based in San Francisco and initiated by Tom Jennings. Jennings, active in alternative media and publisher of the zine *Homocore*, built FidoNet as a way to connect these local BBSs and to allow international exchange of messages and data among local networks. FidoNet quickly became an important communications foundation for many alternative groups around the world, before the World Wide Web. From the official archive of FidoNet, it is plain to see the activist roots of its origins:

1.1 Introduction

FidoNet is an amateur electronic mail system. As such, all of its partici-pants and operators are unpaid volunteers. From its early beginning as a few friends swapping messages back and forth (1984), it now (1989) includes over 5000 systems on six continents.

FidoNet is not a common carrier or a value-added service network and is a public network only in as much as the independent, constituent nodes may individually provide public access to the network on their system.[37]

FidoNet users regularly added improvements and additions to the core sys-tem. COBRUS, for example, gave FidoNet users easier access to the over 5000 active usenet newsgroups on the Internet: "These newsgroups include the seven major hierarchies (alt, comp, misc, sci, sco, rec, talk) in addition to many newsgroups from other parts of the world like Russia, France, Australia, Germany, etc."[38]

The popularity of the Cleveland Freenet, a locally based BBS in Cleve-land, Ohio, inspired many other areas to build similar sites. In 1989, the National Public Telecomputing Network (NPTN) was created to spread the Freenet software and methodology across the United States. Freenets sprung up in many small towns: Big Sky Telegraph in Dillon, Montana; Buffalo Freenet in Buffalo, New York; Denver Freenet in Denver, Colorado; the Heartland Freenet in Peoria, Illinois; Tallahassee Freenet in Tallahassee, Florida; and the Youngstown Freenet in Youngstown, Ohio. The Freenet model spread internationally as well; Ciao! Freenet in Trail, British Colum-bia, Canada; National Capitol Freenet in Ottowa, Ontario, Canada; Victo-ria Freenet in Victoria, British Columbia, Canada; and Wellington Citynet in Wellington, New Zealand. The Freenet model was based on the philosophy of public access, with a strong local base that connected globally. Accord-ing to the goals of the NPTN, "Freenets are successful and desirable. They are reachable over the Internet, and to many that is the end of it. However, there is another point to Freenets—to provide access to Internet-style facili-ties in a local community, to empower the community. You may want to use a Freenet and not have one locally. This is where the NPTN comes in—you can start your own Freenet."[39]

Computer networks that originally began as community and local resources increasingly tapped into the growing Internet, and it soon became apparent that computer networking had an amazing potential for alternative communications on a global scale. This was the perception even before the World Wide Web, when interaction was text-based in a Unix environment. The explosion of activity with the introduction of the HTML/browser model was already anticipated.

As the possibility for new, global alternative communications progressed, several national and international meetings were held to discuss the way forward. At the Free the Media conference in New York City in 1997, Subcomandante Marcos included in his remarks via camcorder tape the following message: "The work of independent media is to tell the history of social struggle in the world, and here in North America—the US, Canada, and Mexico—independent media has, on occasion, been able to open spaces even within the mass media monopolies: to force them to acknowledge news of other social movements." "By not having to answer to the monster media monopolies, the independent media has a life's work, a political project, and a purpose: to let the truth be known. This is increasingly more important in the globalization process. Truth becomes a knot of resistance against the lie. Our only possibility is to save the truth, to maintain it, and distribute it, little by little, in the same way that the books were saved in Fahrenheit 451. . . ."[40] The establishment of the Independent Media Center in Seattle in 1999 demonstrated that these possibilities were indeed feasible.

When media activists left the scene of the 1999 Seattle protest, they returned to their communities excited by their ability to create a large and viable international media presence based on the Internet, satellite uplinks, public access television, and community radio channels. A series of discussions and meetings led to the decision to create indy media groups (IMCs) that would serve as alternative sources of local news, but would also feed into an international portal.[41] News, graphics, video, photos, and audio could develop local alternative media presences and keep the spirit of Seattle alive. As importantly, these local centers would provide the foundation for a global media presence across borders and help to organize, inform, and unite a global grassroots effort for peace, justice, and environmental protection. The structure and strategy of the IMCs was predicated upon the work of generations of alternative media projects that emphasized action, participation, and consensus. It was also based upon a strong, international level of participation from both the developed and the newly developing world, and a continuing demand for a new world information order.

It came as a surprise to many US media activists that in many ways newly developing nations of the once-called "Third World" possessed a more sophisticated network of grassroots media than exists in the United States. There is a long tradition of grassroots organizing, primarily within the nonaligned movements (NAMs) and nongovernmental organizations (NGOs) of the developing world, to leverage some economic and political justice through the mass mobilization of peasants, farmers, workers, indigenous, and oppressed minorities. According to Armand Mattelart, "The phenomenon began in the 1960s and 1970s in three areas: human rights, multinational corporations' strategies in the Third World, and environmental protection."[42] Many of these movements relied upon decentralized systems of electronic communications that in many ways were more advanced and more accessible than similar means in the United States. Ironically, the odds of getting independent media onto the airwaves in Brazil, India, Mexico, and other developing nations was much higher than in the United States, where powerful corporations kept a firm lock on a system that jealously guards its viewers and captive audiences. Latin and Central American nations, for example, have had radio and television networks devoted to their populations of indigenous peoples for some time.

Many of the earlier arguments for creating a global independent media network came from the efforts of communications scholars, activists, and producers who coalesced around the New World Information and Communications Order (NWICO) initiative that originated from the United Nations Education, Scientific, and Cultural Organization (UNESCO) in 1976. This effort grew around many of the international meetings that were held in cities including Johannesburg and Bombay (Mumbai). The primary statement of NWICO was aimed at countering the US news monopoly and its tendency to infuse world news with pro-US propaganda. The NWICO statement was reinforced by depicting "news flow" on maps that showed that events in Africa, for example, were covered by US news crews, beamed back to the United States for processing and then rebeamed back to the Africans for consumption, in a classic neocolonial pattern. The NWICO activists articulated the idea that news should originate at the source and balance should be restored to enable a more intelligent and nuanced look at news from underrepresented nations. International efforts to develop such a plan were squelched and ridiculed by US media corporations and the US government, which proclaimed that such a policy would amount to censorship and contribute to outright propaganda. The nations of the global South also protested against the monopolization of the radio spectrum by the United States and Europe and the proliferation of satellites in orbit launched by the United States that were being used for military and surveillance purposes. The official position of the United States, from then on, would be proclaimed as the "free flow of information." To the proponents of the NWICO, it was apparent that what the United States really meant by "Freedom of Information" was the hegemonic supremacy of the US point of view. The United States was so incensed by the UNESCO position on democratic communications that it quit the organization in 1984.

The action to quit UNESCO by the Reagan administration was viewed by many nations as arrogant and perhaps only solidified the importance of building a new communications infrastructure that would challenge the hegemony of the dominant industrial nations.

In any event, it was apparent that new forms of grassroots organization were emerging in the underdeveloped world, and key to their emergence was a communications infrastructure that would develop from popular networks with the aid of new technologies. It is important to recognize the growth of these activities that in many ways paralleled the growth of such movements in the United States. As pointed out by Dorothy Kidd, "The framework of participatory communication and social change traces back to the international debates about the democratization of communication of the 1970s and 1980s. Although the larger political project of the New World Information and Communication Order was defeated at UNESCO, several of its arguments began to echo in the very different quarters of national governments, multilateral institutions, commercial media industries, non-governmental organizations, and social justice movements."[43]

In stressing the growing importance of grassroots organizations in the Third World, C. Roach contended that "[w]hile skeptics may scoff at mention of the people as a genuine force for liberation, US policy makers are now recognizing that their strategies for the Third World must take into account the new reality of grassroots groups struggling for change."[44]

This opinion was not just wishful thinking on the part of progressive intellectuals and activists. *Foreign Policy*, a conservative journal relied upon by many in the Washington power elite, also agreed with this assessment:

> Today Third World self-help organizations probably number in the hundreds of thousands, their combined memberships totaling more than 100 million. At the local level people in the developing world are better organized in 1989 than they have been since European colonialism. Community activism in the Third World is bringing new actors to international affairs . . . [and] a new generation of grassroots groups have been steadily, albeit unevenly, rising up since mid-century, with particularly impressive growth in the last two decades.[45]

The rise in these Third World popular organizations is directly attributable to the failure of democratic reforms, on the one hand, and the people's propensity and desire for self-organization, on the other. Much of the groundwork for this growth in popular organizations and "base" communities in the developing world is a result of the organizing efforts of radical organizations and liberation theologians who follow a Freirean approach to social change. B. Mody points out the importance of this approach and the use of "horizontal" communications:

> For consensus development at the grassroots level, horizontal communication comes first. This is where small, low-cost media can contribute. These decentralized local and regional media production centers are also required to convey the community's consensus upwards. Community communication is the basis of "communication popular" initiated by peasant and worker organizations in Latin America. Their process is Freirean reflection and action, their direction is horizontal, their leadership is internal, and their end is an equitable economic and social whole in which the individual is an active subject.[46]

As pointed out by P. Waterman, the search for new media strategies often leads to the development of alternative media, commonly referred to as grassroots communication, popular communication, or alternative communication, as groups increasingly turn to new technologies for more effective, direct, and unmediated communications:

> . . . [D]ramatic growth in "democratic" or "alternative" communication globally [. . .] is a result of the felt needs of social categories or interest groups which tend to criticize both capitalism and statism. The environmental, peace, women's, consumer, Third World aid, human rights, and new labour movements have been increasingly building up their own means of communication. Developing identically or analogously in the West and the East as well as the South, these new movements are customarily international and frequently internationalist. They have therefore often been actively involved in the development of cheap, direct means of communication internationally.[47]

Developing New Levels of Communications from Below

These new means of communication are practices that are outside of or in opposition to dominant communication discourses. From my own observation, I see them as falling into one of five different categories:

1. Marginal communication, or communication unrelated to organized movements, such as social-networking sites that share personal information.
2. Horizontal communication, an equal exchange between organized sectors of oppositional organizations for purposes such as joint strategy and action.
3. Anticommunication, or the willful subversion of mainstream media messages, sometimes referred to in contemporary jargon as "culture-jamming," activities such as billboard altering or jamming of radio/television signals.
4. Alternative communication, or the communicative activities of oppressed groups both within the group and towards a mass audience.
5. Internal communication, or communication among the membership of organizations or between the leadership and membership of organizations.

What makes these forms of communication different from other forms is not just that the content is different, or that they reflect the viewpoints of workers and New Social Movements, but that they tend to be structured in a less hierarchical and more democratic fashion. The importance of these communications is not just to "get the message out," but also to encourage increased democratic participation and to assist in the development of new adherents. As a result of these grassroots organizations and their use of media technologies, communication development researchers began to take greater notice of democratic uses of communications technologies. Alongside a growing critique of mass media monopolization in the United States arose case histories of grassroots media in other nations. These case studies include the Chasqui Huasi Communications group, based in Santiago, Chile;[48] the use of video by grassroots groups and trade unions in Brazil;[49] aboriginal video in the outback of Australia;[50] and use of computers by guerrillas in the Philippines.[51] With increased communication between US media groups and those in the global South, many previously localized and obscure media projects were brought to light. Deep Dish Television helped initiate this investigation with an entire series of programming featuring excerpts from some of these projects, including the indigenous television production of Brazil, the use of video in Taiwan and Korea, and the underground media in the Philippines.[52] Paper Tiger Television also highlighted key examples of alternative communications movements from other countries, such as the radio station run by the tin miners of Bolivia or the video used as a communications tool in Chiapas, Mexico. The movement of alternative communication methods began to be understood as a truly international phenomenon, illustrated by case studies of media practices by democratic activists in many countries, be it via fax, audiocassette, VHS, photocopy machine, radio, or other more advanced means. With the terrorist attack on the World Trade Center on September 11, 2001, the vital need for a global people-to-people communications channel became crystal clear. Once again, war in the Gulf loomed, and as has become well known, truth is the first casualty of war. The context of the attacks, the evidence, and the frank discussion about a US response were all buried by the Bush administration's demand to justify an attack on Iraq at any cost. The administration's manipulation of the US media and their subsequent compliance became painfully clear when the excuse of the search for "weapons of mass destruction" evaporated during the invasion and occupation of Iraq. The challenge for those who wanted to bring to light a more accurate and thoughtful picture of the situation facing a post–9/11 United States was made more difficult by the increasing stranglehold on mass media, most notoriously by the rise of Rupert Murdoch's Fox News apparatus, which had become the central locus of the American right-wing point of view. Once again, actual discussion on global politics was supplanted by a sea of flag-waving and military posturing on US television and radio. Some bright spots emerged, showing that there was still a role to be played by alternative electronic media on the world stage. Many thoughtful Web sites that examined the reality of the war in Iraq and its implications for the world went live. The ability for instant Web site posting provided the impetus for the expanded practice of Web logging, or "blogging," that allowed a quicker response to current events. One of the most trafficked sites was that of Professor Juan Cole, whose blog on the Middle East drew many thousands of those who wanted a more informed look at the region. Community and low-power FM radio stations coalesced around a few national programs that tried to avoid the Fox News approach to news. *Democracy Now!* is a show that was part of the Pacifica radio stations news hour and that began in 1996 as a daily program to discuss the presidential elections underway at that time. Moderator Amy Goodman had been a reporter on NYC Pacifica's WBAI radio when she was an eyewitness to the massacre of hundreds of East Timorese by the Indonesian military in 1991. After the election on which it was created to report was over, Goodman continued producing *Democracy Now!* and built an ongoing daily national news program that tackled subjects with a more in-depth and investigative approach. *Democracy Now!* was in Seattle covering the large protests in 1999, along with many other alternative media producers mentioned in this chapter, and later collaborated with the independent media centers set up for both the Republican and Democratic national conventions in Philadelphia and Los Angeles in 2000. After 9/11, *Democracy Now!*, building on its success as a radio show, began to produce a television component as well, and delivered the program well beyond the Pacifica Network.[53] *Democracy Now: The War and Peace Report* was produced in Down Town Community Television studios in New York City. Members from Deep Dish Television assisted in getting the television show up and running, creating a similar structure used by Deep Dish TV, which sent a satellite feed to the growing network of public access television stations, as well as to the network built by Free Speech TV. The radio portion was also uploaded and distributed to the loose network of community radio and low-power FM stations around the nation. *Democracy Now!* has thrived using this loose, national network of alternative electronic media outlets built over the years by media activists and is now broadcast on over 1000 television and radio stations nationwide.[54] According to Goodman, "Why has *Democracy Now!* grown so quickly? Because of the deafening silence in the mainstream media around the issues—and the people—that matter most. People are now confronting the most important issues of the millennium: war and peace, life and death. Yet who is shaping the discourse? Generals, corporate executives, and government officials."[55]

Other nationally syndicated radio programs using a similar distribution strategy include *CounterSpin*, produced by Fairness and Accuracy in Reporting based in New York City; *Free Speech Radio News*, a half-hour daily radio show produced by over 200 community radio producers; *Making Contact*, produced by the National Radio Project, based in Oakland, California; and *Alternative Radio*, based in Boulder, Colorado. This group of radio and television producers reflects the longtime desires of alternative media producers to build upon the strengths of local communities while developing a global outlook that bypasses the corporate model of media. The mission of such programs is not only to report on news events covered by local journalists and community activists, but also to increase the exposure of the many voices of intellectuals and experts avoided by mainstream media. To contribute to this desire for unfiltered news and information from other countries, *Link TV* was created in 1999, and gained access to both DirecTV and EchoStar direct broadcast satellite networks (later to become the DISH Network), thanks to the set-aside of space demanded by the FCC. Every day *Link TV* transmits raw sections of television programs as they are broadcast in their respective nations, offering a chance to see what others are seeing in countries unfiltered by US media corporations. *Current TV* is another progressive television network, one associated with former Vice President Al Gore. *Current TV* went live in 2005 and is attempting to build a national presence on cable and online. *Al-Jazeera English* plays an increasingly important role in transmitting a perspective that few Americans ever see, that of Arab and North African people. Although US media corporations like to denigrate *Al-Jazeera*, the network has been recognized as having a higher journalistic standard than most US news organizations. The network has also played an extremely important role in the Arab Spring movements, which is detailed in a later chapter. *Al-Jazeera* was launched in 1996, originally as a channel for the primarily Arabic-speaking countries, but it gained a wider audience after the events of 9/11. In 2006, *Al-Jazeera English* was launched as both a television service and a Web site, gaining a wide audience for its uncensored and unfiltered view of events in the Middle East and throughout the world. The success of *Al-Jazeera* and its emergence as the leading journalistic source of news from the Middle East has been hailed as a successful case of reversing the news flow from North to South, a fundamental demand put forward by activists who, many years before, had advocated for a New World Information and Communication Order. Because of its willingness to avoid self-censorship of events and opinions, it is widely perceived as an example of alternative media and has been frequently criticized or censored by the United States, Israel, and multiple nations in the Middle East. Because of its stigma, it is not widely accessible on mainstream cable channels, but is carried by other alternative networks such as Free Speech TV, Link TV, and public access channels.[56] (Note that in January 2013, Al Jazeera purchased Current TV.)

There are many reasons for the upsurge in the creation of noncorporate, independent media, ranging from oppressive military dictatorships to the self-censorship of monopoly media corporations, but the goal is the same: breaking the blockade of the free exchange of ideas put in place by institutions of power and the status quo. The foundations of new national and global alternative media projects were often built at the local and community level, and many of these global initiatives still depend upon that base. New networks of television, radio, Web, Internet, and satellite have brought together many divergent social movements, yet most still insist that these media practices remain two-way, accessible, and democratic. As detailed in the next chapter, some of the most innovative media practices have been developed by a largely unexamined social sector that is perhaps the most impacted target of the negative effects of globalization—the international working class.

4 Labor Communications in the New Global Economy

Previous chapters have made the case that the centralized, hegemonic legacy of mass communications built by the culture industries and the commercial broadcasters is being threatened by new, participatory models, originating at the local level and spreading out to the global. Many examples of these "communications from below" practices can be characterized as deviating from the broadcast model by building a system of "horizontal" communications, a nonhierarchical model that is peer-to-peer and not originating from a center. What may be surprising to observers of democratic communications is that many of these alternative means of communications were initiated by a sector of the population not normally associated with cutting-edge technologies: innovators from unions and worker's organizations. Since the beginnings of the transition to global business communications driven by computerization, industrial and manufacturing workers suffered the most from the negative effects of economic globalization. Forced to confront the electronic spread of global capitalism and the development of the global factory system, labor activists had no choice but to explore the development of alternative systems of local, regional, industrywide, and global labor communications. This early innovation by labor is an important, yet often overlooked, contribution to the evolution of new forms of local and global social networking and what constitutes an important segment of communications from below.

With the preponderance of mainstream media emphasis on the proliferation of personal communications—cell phones, social networking, and instant messaging—it is easy to overlook the largest user of telecommunications bandwidth: large corporate enterprises. Communications technology has been at the core of trade and commerce for centuries. It was the desire for improved trade (together with war, the violent accomplice of trade) that provided the impetus for improved communications such as canals, roads, postal systems, railroads, standardized weights and measures, standardized time zones, and other mechanisms that diminished distance and time and facilitated exchange. For centuries, commerce was thought of as almost indistinguishable from communication. The landmark Enlightenment 1753 French *Encyclopédie* described commerce as being in "a general sense a reciprocal communication" and more particularly "the communication that men have with each other in the productions of their lands and their industry."[1]

Current global economic trends and accompanying communications systems are evident in political economic theory dating back to the early stages of capitalist development. Classical and neoclassical economists, whose ideas still motivate business strategists today, emphasize two important profit-enhancing concepts—the division of labor and the doctrine of comparative cost advantage. In *The Wealth of Nations*, Adam Smith argues that "[t]he greatest improvement in the productive powers of labour, and the greatest part of the skill, dexterity, and judgment with which it is anywhere directed, or applied, seems to have been the effects of the division of labour."[2] Describing the manufacture of pins, Smith explains how the division of production processes among numerous workers (drawing the wire, straightening it, cutting it, sharpening it, grinding it, etc.) saves time and increases productivity. The simplification and mechanization of work and the growth in new technologies in communications and control was an enormous catalyst in spurring the movement of industries to other regions, nations, and continents, allowing the capitalist to take advantage of better terms of procuring land, labor, and/or capital.

With the division of labor taking place over a wide geographic range, communications technologies become instrumental in maintaining contact and control over distance. The French proponent of national railway networks, Michel Chevalier, saw the managerial advantages of communications systems plainly. He reported in 1832 that inventions including the railroad, the steamship, and the telegraph would enable his nation to easily "govern most of the continents that border the Mediterranean, with the same unity and the same instantaneousness as exists today within France."[3]

Lewis Mumford calls our attention to the relationship between communications technology and the geographic division of labor when he notes that "efficient administration depends upon record-keeping, charting, routing, and communication, and not necessarily upon a local overseership."[4] Henry Ford may have set a precedent for this when his assembly line led to the realization that "the making of each part was a separate business in itself, and to be made wherever it could be made the most efficiently, and that the final assembly line could be anywhere."[5] Indeed, as we see today, the final assembly line could truly be anywhere.

The discovery and development of early electrical and electromechanical communications systems tremendously hastened the geographic division of labor. In his essay on the telegraph, James Carey points out how the ability to transfer messages electrically allowed the development of the first truly multinational corporations and the ability to coordinate business around the globe.[6] With the introduction of wireless telegraphy, this power became even greater. It is no accident that the United Fruit Company, with its far-flung banana plantations in Central America, became one of the first users of wireless radio. Accompanying this stage of classical imperialism were technologies that allowed orders and messages to flow from the corporations' central offices to the outlying international outposts. Limited to overseas mail service at first, communications technologies such as the telegraph, transoceanic cable lines, wireless telegraphy, and radio grew to have extreme importance in giving orders, coordinating shipping schedules, and transferring financial data, as well as allowing colonial masters to call for military power if need be. At the earlier stages of technological development, communications were still very much linked to systems of transportation until the development of electrical forms of delivery. Carey argues that it was no accident that the words 'empire' and 'imperialism' entered the language in the 1870s, soon after the laying of the transatlantic cable because this innovation "turned colonialism into imperialism: a system in which the center of an empire could dictate rather than merely respond to the margin."[7]

The intertwining of communication systems and international business can be noted throughout contemporary history. In the 1960s, at the dawn of our contemporary information age, the rapid increase of capital into the global arena placed great demand on the ability to transfer managerial, business, and financial data rapidly and in great volume. This demand spurred enormous growth in the computer industry and created a critical dependence on international telecommunications. According to Chris Toulouse, by the 1960s "the national telephone network and the mainframe computer had made it possible for corporations to keep track of branch plants and stores supplying markets all over the country. In the 1970s, further developments in telecommunications, fiber-optic networks for data transmission, the fax machine, the desktop computer, made it possible to orchestrate production systems stretching around the globe."[8] The ability to maintain control and contact with so many disparate elements of a very sophisticated system of production is crucial to its implementation. According to Lynn Mytelka, "Segmentation and delocalization of production was a cost-reduction strategy made possible by technological innovations in unrelated industries and economic sectors" and the microprocessor made "handling information . . . economically available . . . in hitherto traditional industries."[9]

Post-Fordist manufacturing relies intensely on flexible manufacturing processes, characterized by just-in-time production and inventory techniques, decentralized managerial control, market forecasting, short production runs, flexible workforces, and product specialization. Early literature on just-in-time manufacturing techniques illustrates the dependence of post-Fordist production on new communications technologies:

> Using barcoding to capture, electronically, consumer demand at time of purchase, the data interchange technology allows the retailer to do more than just keep accurate inventory and sales records. Information about the sale is immediately transferred back through the chain to the apparel manufacturer and the textile manufacturer. With an emerging

industry standard for electronic data interchange (EDI), a true information partnership is technologically feasible; an item can be tracked at the SKU level at every point in the chain from raw material to customer.[10]

Once jobs are routinized, simplified, and mechanized, it becomes a simple matter to relocate them according to comparative advantage. The leaps in communications technology make this a painless and simple procedure.

The sophistication and proliferation of satellite networks and broadband delivery systems have melted away geographical obstacles to obtaining the best possible terms of labor the world has to offer. This has been highly evident among the manufacturing industries for many years now. It is a widespread observation that the United States "does not make anything anymore," as one sees so many products with the "Made in China" or "Made in Indonesia" label on it. Pursuing the principles of comparative advantage and the international division of labor, the service and "knowledge" jobs of the industrialized nations have also been shifted offshore. The transfer of keystrokes, numbers, voice, video, and text into digital form has made information services extremely malleable and flexible. It is by now well understood how data entry workers in Jamaica could enter millions of words daily into US corporate databases, how rote animation processes could be subcontracted to South Korean workers for the cartoons of Hanna-Barbera,[11] or how workers in India can write code for Silicon Valley–based software corporations or answer consumer customer support calls. These manufacturing and service workers, contrary to their counterparts in the industrialized Western countries, are not in the position to demand ergonomic computer screens, regular breaks, decent wages, relief from carpal tunnel syndrome, or other considerations that these jobs should provide. Today, this global labor strategy not only relies on US production moving offshore, but also on the importation of that same global workforce into its own borders. Key US domestic industries could not survive without the exploitation of cheap immigrant labor in urban, suburban, and rural areas of the United States. Even a basic industry like food production overwhelmingly depends on immigrant labor, from the fields and farms, to the packinghouses and slaughterhouses, to urban restaurants and fast food outlets.

Faced with these technological, organizational, and managerial challenges, workers both in the United States and internationally have been increasingly forced to compete in a race to the bottom to keep their jobs or to maintain a decent standard of living for themselves and their families. While old-guard American labor unions have often been blinded by national chauvinism toward workers of other nations and have smugly accepted American exceptionalism, new generations of US labor activists have emerged and have been instrumental in developing new means of communications with workers across borders. Much attention has been focused on the social networking of students, youth, and entrepreneurs, yet labor was one of the earliest practitioners of decentralized communications, developing horizontal communications as a means to cooperate in unison against an enormous corporate power seeking a complacent and cheap international workforce.

THE BEGINNINGS OF ELECTRONIC LABOR COMMUNICATIONS

To a large extent, it was the movement of industrial production to Mexico and to less developed countries (LDCs) offshore that spurred US labor to seek communication channels with workers in other nations. Multinational job flight from the North and the growing awareness of the intense exploitation of workers in the global South led significant sections of the US labor movement to realize the common interests of workers worldwide. These observations led the AFL-CIO in the 1990s to reconsider their isolation from the mainstream of international labor and connect with the global movement of workers. In the early 1990s, North American unions such as the United Electrical Workers (UE), the Teamsters (IBT), the Communications Workers of America (CWA), the Canadian Auto Workers (CAW), and the United Auto Workers (UAW) began to join forces with counterparts in Mexico such as the Frente Auténtico del Trabajo (FAT), the Sindicato de Telefonistas, and the Ford Workers Democratic Movement. As Berta Lujan of the Frente Auténtico del Trabajo stated, "A local model of unions is no longer viable when capital crosses borders and imposes its conditions at will. Labour unions will only continue being viable to the extent that they can construct a transnational force as well."[12]

Beginning with the fight against the passage of the North American Free Trade Agreement (NAFTA) in the early 1990s, labor activists discussed new strategies and tactics to coordinate activities, share resources, and establish common bonds in order to bargain more effectively with the multinational corporations. One of the early accomplishments of this labor communications activity was the creation of several computer networks dedicated to labor issues. These networks were text-based, online electronic spaces created before the advent of the World Wide Web and required a basic familiarity with a Unix-based operating system. These early computer Bulletin Board Services and networks allowed labor activists to share information, exchange ideas, coordinate actions, and make new alliances and friendships. These networks allowed autoworkers, dockworkers, Teamsters, and others to see themselves as part of an international network of all workers, not just isolated individuals within their particular industrial sectors or individual unions. Three of these early online tools were IGC/LaborNet in the United States, SoliNet in Canada, and La Neta in Mexico.

LaborNet was one of the electronic Bulletin Board Services affiliated with the Institute for Global Communications/Association for Progressive Communications (IGC/APC) network that also ran PeaceNet, the network that facilitated exchange and ideas among antiwar activists. Founded in 1991,

LaborNet was organized around industrial lines, as opposed to individual union affiliation. Doing so allowed workers from different unions to communicate with each other about problems in their plant or, perhaps, within their unions. For example, rather than having a conference on the United Steelworkers or the United Auto Workers, there were conferences on simply "auto" or "steel," as oftentimes workers in the same plant could belong to one of many different unions. The membership of LaborNet was approximately 1,400 users in the late 1990s and included union members from the Service Employees International Union, the Communication Workers of America, the United Auto Workers, and the United Farm Workers Union, as well as dissident labor groups: New Directions in the UAW, Teamsters for a Democratic Union in the International Brotherhood of Teamsters, and organizations of labor attorneys. Rank-and-file labor activists who were at odds with the official representatives of their unions often used it as a means to contact workers directly, bypassing the union leadership. A primary goal for the activists who ran LaborNet was to create cooperation and solidarity between workers from similar industries through creating direct communication channels between workers. LaborNet conferences were typically at the national and international level, allowing workers from around the nation or around the world to exchange views, contract information, or labor actions. Conferences on labor solidarity communicated numerous appeals to assist in strike support or boycott actions, either locally or from another part of the globe. A database section shared BLS reports, financial data, and other useful information to labor activists. LaborNet continues today as an independent network, having moved away from IGC a few years ago.

Created in 1986, the Canadian labor network SoliNet was one of the earliest attempts at running a labor communications system. Originally started as a computer system for public employees of Canada, it grew to include many facets of labor activism. As Marc Belanger, SoliNet moderator, stated:

> A labor union is a communications system. It exists to collect the views of its members, organize those views into persuasive arguments, disseminate them among its membership and finally communicate them to the employer. The effectiveness of a union's mission is largely determined by the success of its communications.[13]

SoliNet sponsored online conferences on the Bulletin Boards devoted to trade union topics such as health and safety, women's issues, the environment, shop steward notes, and even favorite cooking recipes. A central conference called "The Lounge" provided a place where members could talk about anything on their minds. Conferences took place on the local, national, and international levels. A national conference could be used to facilitate discussion among union members dispersed across a larger geographic area; for example, in wide-area bargaining discussions that require daily exchange of data, views, and information. The SoliNet conference on free trade developed an international profile as it helped the Canadian labor movement articulate a critique of NAFTA and other facets of globalization. The SoliNet system was also used for transmission of leaflets and organizing pamphlets across the nation to locals and activists who lacked the skills and resources to develop them locally. Shop stewards used the system for solving disputes and sharing grievance procedures. Educational courses offered members the opportunity to learn from other members throughout the system, benefiting from skills and expertise from members far away. Access to a centralized database of financial information proved useful for quick response to counter employer claims and to support union bargaining demands. Despite the success of this early electronic tool for unionists, one of the principal moderators of the system echoed a refrain heard often from unionists: "Unionists are organizers. We work with real people in real workplaces. It is this organizing which determines who we are and what we believe—not the communication tools we happen to use to pass on our beliefs. We cannot allow ourselves to be so enamored with the wonders of new communication technologies that we forget that the real source of our solidarity, now and forever, is working people talking to working people."[14]

La Neta, based in Mexico, began in 1991 as an activist Internet network provider that united activists and nongovernmental organizations working on labor and other social justice issues within Mexico. Interest in La Neta grew with the anti-NAFTA efforts, linking organizations electronically throughout Mexico. La Neta affiliated with the Association for Progressive Computing in 1993 and today hosts over a thousand organizations in Mexico.

During the fight against NAFTA, Mexican, US, and Canadian labor organizations relied heavily on Bulletin Board Services and e-mail to coordinate and exchange information on strategies to defeat the plan, which was being fast-tracked through the US Congress. E-mail allowed online labor activists to communicate regularly with others in a cheap, efficient, and rapid manner. It also facilitated personal contact and exchange with individuals at all levels of organizational hierarchy, regardless of national boundaries, affiliation, or geographic distance. Organizations like the Red Mexicana De Acción Frente al Libre Comercio (RMALC), the North American Worker-to-Worker Network, and the Canada Action Network were able to take advantage of online communications to help build a movement of labor groups that opposed NAFTA on the grounds that it was harmful to all working people. As Howard Frederick pointed out:

> This anti-NAFTA coalition is increasingly united in an electronic web of information sharing and communication. From grassroots groups in border towns to labor union headquarters in national capitals, the anti-NAFTA coalition of NGOs is sharing information, establishing mutual trust, and developing action strategies to carry out common goals.[15]

Postings kept users informed of many labor skirmishes as they unfolded, allowing union activists to keep pressure on governments and corporations via phone calls, faxes, and demonstrations. For example, after a Mexican union organizer was beaten to death inside the Ford plant in Cuautitlán, Mexico, in 1990, US and Canadian Ford workers used e-mail to help organize protests against Ford in other countries.[16]

The anti-NAFTA electronic networking fostered new cross-border initiatives that sought to address the intensive exploitation of Mexican labor in the rapidly growing maquila and Free Trade Zones spearheaded by multinational corporations. Cross-border organizing projects grew rapidly, uniting US, Canadian, and Mexican unions. An example of this is the United Electrical Workers' Strategic Organizing Alliance with the Frente Auténtico del Trabajo of Mexico. The FAT began working with the UE to unionize shops that were formerly represented by the UE but had closed and relocated to Mexico. The UE also gave assistance to the FAT in their clandestine organizing drives in maquila and Free Trade Zones and assisted in a FAT drive to organize Honeywell in Chihuahua and General Electric in Juarez.[17] In return, the FAT sent an organizer to Milwaukee to help in an ultimately successful UE-organizing campaign in a metal shop primarily comprised of Mexican workers.[18] Other groups working in cross-border organizing included Mujer a Mujer, based in San Antonio, Mexico City, and Canada, and La Mujer Obrera, based in El Paso, which was a group that formed from the garment workers who launched the successful boycott against "Farah" pants in the 1970s. These groups organized meetings and conferences to promote solidarity among female garment workers in all three countries.[19] The Transnational Information Exchange (TIE) organized conferences and delegations of autoworkers from the United States, Mexico, and Canada to initiate discussion and develop an international bargaining strategy. The Communications Workers of America established a working relationship with its counterparts in both Mexico and Canada. The Mexican telecommunications union filed charges under provisions of NAFTA against the SPRINT Corporation, accusing them of unfair labor practices when they fired several hundred people, mostly Latina, who had tried to unionize in San Francisco, California. The American Friends Service Committee established the Comité Fronterizo de Obreras (CFO) to help women in maquiladoras fight to improve their working conditions, particularly in the Zenith maquiladora in Reynosa, Mexico. The Coalition for Justice in the Maquiladoras (CJM) began organizing workers and community groups to battle against the pollutant and toxic producing maquiladoras in the Brownsville-Matamoros and Tijuana areas.[20]

Farm labor organizations have always been important cross-border labor organizers, as the US agricultural workforce has always been highly dependent upon migrant workers. In 1989 the Farm Labor Organizing Committee (FLOC) and its Mexican counterpart the Sindicato de Trabajadores Agrícolas (SNTOAC) won an unprecedented wage increase with the multinational

Campbell's Company.[21] In 1988, displaced Schlage Lock workers from North Carolina met with their Mexican Schlage Lock counterparts in a delegation organized by the Black Workers for Justice. The International Metalworkers' Federation convened a world conference of metalworkers in Peoria, Illinois, where UAW secretary-treasurer Bill Casstevens declared, "While the company is hard at work trying to divide people, we're going to unite workers from different countries to discuss common problems, plan common strategies, and work toward common solutions."[22]

Key to these new international developments was the new electronic infrastructure that helped these groups communicate across borders and promote mutual friendship, trust, solidarity, and joint action. While electronic networks have allowed cross-border labor cooperation to operate at higher levels, such international solidarity has always been an important aspect of the labor movement. Past examples include the United Mine Workers of America's assistance to their South African mineworker counterparts when they were on strike in South Africa under the old apartheid regime, and the International Longshore and Warehouseman's Union's refusal to unload cargo from either apartheid South Africa or from Latin and Central American military regimes in El Salvador and Chile. The internationalization of the workforce and the shrinking of geographical space brought about by advanced communications has rendered these foreign struggles closer than ever, bringing workers worldwide to the realization that their common efforts will be vital and essential to the maintenance of dignity, justice, and survival in the new economic order.

As a result of the new alliances built during the NAFTA fight, labor organizations have often been inspired by new social movements (NSMs) and nongovernmental organizations, strategies that have proven to be adept at mobilizing their constituencies and seizing the public's imagination. The ability for labor to survive, many began to believe, did not rest on its ability to become a large monolithic force, as in the post–World War II period, but to engage in "Lilliputian Linking" (meaning many small groups fighting together) to find common ground with other causes and build grassroots support.[23] The interests of labor activists increasingly coincided with the concerns of other organizations in terms of the environment, social justice, international affairs, women's issues, or health issues. In the early 1990s, the perspectives of activists from labor and new social movements were increasingly cross-posted on listservs and Web sites serving many different movements. Thus, news about chemical toxins found in certain products, child labor in Nike plants, exploitation of women in maquiladoras, and other information relevant to workers and the wider public began to find its way to a wide readership with many varied interests. These cross-posted, linked, and networked sites began to "go viral," making it increasingly difficult for labor information to be entirely suppressed by the gatekeepers of mass media. The interests of workers and environmentalists, social justice advocates, and other social reformers became increasingly intertwined online. As we saw in Chapter Three, evidence of this cross-pollination was strongly illustrated by the large labor and environmental presence at the Seattle demonstrations against the World Trade Organization in 1999.

WORKER-TO-WORKER COMMUNICATIONS

Computer networks, satellite transponders, e-mail, Web pages, mobile devices, and fax machines have enabled labor organizations to expand their communications capabilities internally, inter-organizationally, and toward the wider realm of the public. The ability of electronic technologies to travel instantaneously, transcend physical space, duplicate infinitely, and share information globally has been a tremendous boon for the ability of workers to communicate with other workers, whether they are in the next cubicle or across the globe. Instantaneous communications among individuals as well as large groups can help to bypass official channels of corporate or state censorship, disseminating information to interested parties around the world. Computer networks help ameliorate the bottleneck presented by older, established forms of media such as broadcast television and radio, in that any site on the network can send as well as receive. One disadvantage of electronic communication is of course, the lack of computers, technology, and infrastructure, such as adequate phone lines, in many parts of the world. This, however, is not as significant a problem as is assumed, as labor communications are primarily horizontal communications, between organizations and movements, and while individual members might not have computer access, grassroots organizations often do. The distinction should be made that labor communications is primarily horizontal communication between individuals affiliated with organizations and institutions, not only between private citizens or from a media group to the public. This is an important difference, particularly when dealing with communications technologies, which are often too expensive or too technologically complex for many people to utilize on an individual level, but may be accessible for those affiliated with an organization. Furthermore, the migration of media platforms to cellular and other handheld consumer devices has greatly increased the availability of such communications. Thus, the developers of new labor communications tend to be influenced by the tenets of appropriate technology, taking into consideration logistical, technical, or economic limitations with the use of certain technologies.

New forms of horizontal communications offer the possibility of greater democratic participation in labor union members' message and information sharing. Communications can flow between members as easily as between offices and organizations, in a nonhierarchical fashion, allowing entire memberships, not just leaders, to communicate with one another. Social-networking applications make this goal much more feasible, allowing for increased personal participation and thus a stronger sense of membership and purpose. In some cases, these have helped memberships become more deeply involved in union affairs.

THE REVOLT OF THE RANK AND FILE

It is important to realize that the US labor movement is not a monolith; it is often fractured into numerous factions and tendencies. One of the most significant occurrences in the labor movement within the last few decades has been the rise of union reform movements, built by rank-and-file members who seek to revitalize and democratize unions saddled with bureaucracies grown complacent or corrupt over the years. In fact, many of the recent changes in the AFL-CIO and other federations are a direct result of battles between traditionalists and reformers. The challenge union reformers face is heightened by the unrestrained attacks on union organizations led by corporations in recent years and by the massive export of union jobs overseas. New communications technologies have created certain advantages for strengthening a union but can also have the side effect of illuminating a lack of democracy, poor representation, or a lack of transparency within the labor organization. Labor activists shoulder the double burden of maintaining decent working conditions while also struggling against their own entrenched leadership, which is often threatened by change. It is often within the membership of these rank-and-file movements that many of the most committed and active union members were formed. From the 1970s onward, union reform organizations—such as Teamsters for a Democratic Union, Miners for Democracy, Ed Sadlowski and Steelworkers Fight Back in the Steelworkers Union, and New Directions (in the United Auto Workers Union)—have had various degrees of victory and success, ranging from defeating bad contracts to electing an international president. In any case, these reform efforts helped create a new generation of labor activists who brought a more vital vision of a modern, global labor movement. With a fresh urgency brought by the pressures of globalization and access to new communications tools, these labor activists contributed to the formation of new types of unions that fuse concepts of community organizing, new social movement activism, and traditional industrial unionism. In the 1990s, groups such as Justice for Janitors, La Mujer Obrera, the Farm Labor Organizing Committee, the Black Workers for Justice, the United Farm Workers, the Asian Immigrant Workers Association, and the Toronto Homeworkers Association developed new strategies for responding to the difficulties faced by labor.

The ability of decentralized communications to undermine traditional authority is shaking the foundations of traditional union bureaucracies, as its two-way/interactive capacity can serve to bypass the authority of union leadership. This can be extremely effective in strengthening the solidarity of the rank and file of a union, as well as bridging the gap between workers of different unions and of different countries. Democratic means of communicating among union membership can often be perceived as a threat by an incumbent union leadership out of touch with the rank and file. Some union leaders prefer that new communications be used for transferring orders from the international officers to the local leadership rather than be used by rank-and-file workers to stimulate debate or establish contacts with workers in other countries.

A more open, democratic communication infrastructure allows greater interchange among union member reformers in many different unions, as well as in many different countries. E-mail has helped to organize different insurgent caucuses in many different unions; listservs keep interested workers current on newly breaking information; databases offer newly researched findings; concerns of the rank and file are published on Web sites. Electronic networks help reform-minded union members to collaborate in writing newsletters and keeping an often geographically dispersed membership in touch. Web sites help to reach new converts to union reform and can serve as public fronts for reform organizations.

This is not to suggest that the only union reform activity is at the rank-and-file level. There are often situations where the international leadership may be more in tune with the rank and file than the local leadership. For example, Teamster reformers who have worked at the level of the international office have found electronic networks useful to reach the membership directly, bypassing the local leadership who may still be under the control of older, corrupt Teamster elements.

Sometimes the independent media activity of workers is not oppositional but more social in nature. An independent network of union members interested in collecting labor movement pins and paraphernalia exists among workers of many unions. Some workers have built their own Web pages to share their own views on their working lives and to build a sense of camaraderie. Cookbooks have proven to be quite popular on the Web sites of union members. The innovative use of communications by rank-and-file workers is an important indication that unions can gain tremendously by increasing the involvement of the members. Indeed, many union activists believe that the only way unions will survive is by democratizing and unleashing the power of the rank-and-file workers. Many activists see the present leadership structure as too bureaucratic, too constrained by old paradigms of business unionism, and too rigid to adapt to quickly changing circumstances. Labor activists believe these changes must be more than simply structural adjustments in the bureaucracy but should lead to a radically different labor movement, one that is organized and led by the working millions, not high-paid, "professional" labor leadership. To many, the modern labor movement needs to review the lessons learned during the 1930s. According to one organizer interviewed for this research,

> Problems of scale and mass approach by unions is one that is only going to be solved by the massive participation of workers and union members

[*sic*]. And if you look back at our history, as a movement back to the 1930s and 1920s, and at the times when the labor movement really did grow by leaps and bounds, it was because ordinary working people carried the load. They did the work of organizing unions. The CIO didn't get organized because they had thousands of organizers out there in the field, it was because workers themselves did it. That's the problem that the labor movement has to answer, how to do that under the conditions of today.

COMMUNICATIONS FROM THE SHOP FLOOR

In the mid-1990s, I conducted a range of interviews with over 100 labor activists from six industrial unions: the United Automobile Workers (UAW), the International Brotherhood of Teamsters, the United Electrical Workers Union (UE), the Communications Workers of America (CWA), the International Longshore and Warehouse Union (ILWU), and the International Association of Machinists (IAM). The objective of the study was to gauge labor's response to the potential of the Internet, the World Wide Web, and other new communications technologies in promoting a revitalized labor movement. At that time, the Internet was still in its infancy, and dot-edu and dot-org domains still outnumbered dot-coms. There was tremendous buzz about the growth of the new media and the "great data superhighway." I found many labor activists very excited about the potential of such communications and already using them in creative ways. In discussions about successful uses of communications in particular union battles, many examples came to the fore. Excerpts from these responses are included throughout the remainder of this chapter. The nature of the study required all respondents to remain unidentified.

The longshore workers of the ILWU cited the international effort to aid the striking dockers of Liverpool, United Kingdom, as a good example of using communications to help workers abroad. In 1995 the ports of the United Kingdom were privatized, and the dockers at Liverpool were all fired. Longshore workers internationally vowed to assist in their struggle by refusing to unload cargo from Liverpool. In the fall of 1997 word came from Labour.net, a labor BBS much like LaborNet in the United States, that a "scab" ship, the Neptune Jade, was leaving port. Communications were set up between workers in the West Coast–based ILWU, Liverpool, and international dockworkers' unions to keep track of the voyage, and workers soon learned the ship was due to be unloaded in Southern California. ILWU activists shared this information with their fellow workers and the longshore workers there refused to unload the vessel. The ship traveled up the West Coast and docked in Oakland, where the workers again refused to unload the ship. The ship then had no choice but to go to Vancouver, British Columbia, where it was also boycotted by Canadian longshore workers. Refused service on the West Coast of the United States and Canada, the ship then sailed to Japan, where the Japanese workers refused to unload it as well. An Oakland ILWU member active in the Liverpool protest spoke of the importance of electronic labor communications:

> When we had an International Day of Action in support of Liverpool and we were coordinating actions on the same day around the world . . . we were able to instantaneously be in touch . . . that day and the next day, we knew what other people were doing and did not do. What successes were had. I think that was really important to feel that. People put their butts on the line by just saying: we're not going to work today, we're going to boycott this ship . . . There are legal complications to that, different problems, jeopardy the union puts itself in to take those kinds of actions. It helps to know that everybody else is doing the same thing. . . . Well, not everybody, a bunch of people are doing it. I think it helps in that way. The instantaneous communication so that we could quickly organize and know what people want to be doing. It's definitely useful.

Shortly after the actions in support of the Liverpool dockworkers, ILWU members also demonstrated their solidarity with striking Australian dockworkers, by refusing to load boycotted Australian ships in Southern California ports. An ILWU activist stated:

> It's really important—that's one of the ways that we really keep in touch with the international movement, through e-mail. We're regularly in touch with . . . because of the dockworkers' movement. . . . [I]t's a very international movement. We're in touch with dockworkers' unions around the world not just Liverpool. Brazil, Japan, Australia—everywhere. So most of our information comes from e-mail. . . .

Another early indication of the impact of the Internet on cross-union solidarity in the United States at that time was the support garnered by different unions on strike in the "War Zone" in Decatur, Illinois, where a series of bitter strikes broke out in the early 1990s. This labor battle in the industrial heartland of America grew to include locked-out workers and strikers from Staley Manufacturing, Caterpillar Tractor, and Bridgestone/Firestone Tires. Workers in these plants were able to establish significant support mechanisms directly from other workers without having to go through the "gatekeeping" of union leaders. Workers raised money, organized delegations, and held protests as a result of direct worker-to-worker communications. E-mail, Web pages, and other communications tools contributed to building a strike support system among other industrial workers in other parts of the country. Video production helped as well, as rank-and-file workers used grassroots video productions to solicit support from their local unions. Autoworkers at the former General Motors/Toyota NUMMI plant in Fremont, California, for example, held plant gate collections to support the strikers at Caterpillar

Tractor and Bridgestone Tire. Ford workers in Ohio also participated in plant gate collections for these strikers. Sometimes these informational activities helped to educate union leadership, who may not have been aware of more effective organizing techniques. For example, autoworkers out on a picket line with striking tire workers discovered that their own auto assembly plant was mounting "scab" tires from the struck plant. Enraged that the international union would permit this, workers deluged the union headquarters with faxes, e-mails, and phone calls, eventually causing the activity to stop.

Using the Internet to reach the public directly was a prime strategy of the Teamsters' union during their successful strike against United Parcel Service (UPS) in 1997. At a time when unions were not regarded very positively by the public, Teamsters knew that the company would try to garner sympathy from the public and that any strike ultimately would be based upon the support of a wide public which relies on UPS. Teamsters cited their use of Web pages, faxed press releases, hand flyers, and other media to successfully build popular support from the public, which was crucial to their victory. Internally, their Web pages, fax machines, and phone banks made it easier to dispel doubts among their members and to counter the company's lies and threats more efficiently. International communications with other unions were also cited as a key tactic for winning their strike. One of the results of such communications was that the unions that handle UPS shipments in such countries as Japan and Holland vowed to support the strikers, a move that may have severely crippled UPS.

International communications helped a member of the machinist's union, as head of the union's human rights committee, to stay on top of developing labor struggles in other countries that might have needed a hand from US unions. Communications technologies also helped unions from other countries assist each other in research and strategies. A communications person in the IAM explained:

> We receive requests from other unions in other countries saying: "We're having problems with this company. We understand there are subsidiaries in the United States. Do any of your members work there?" Very quickly, we can search through our membership records, which are kept downstairs on a mainframe computer, and spit it out; and say Yes, No. Yes, we do. Here's the contractual language. Here's been our negotiating experience with these companies.

In international communications, the difficulty of language differences occasionally became an issue. Many union members said they expected to see some improvement in translation technologies to enable more efficient conversations between different nationalities. Other respondents stressed they would like unions in all countries to share their databases with each other, particularly so that unions in Third World countries could benefit from the databases of the richer unions in the developed world. This was reiterated by another respondent, who spoke of the need for more sophisticated databases within the unions themselves to enable unions to build cases against abusive supervisors by comparing grievance information.

The example of databases was a common one among labor activists. The ability to locate and download up-to-date information was mentioned as having a dramatic impact on how labor kept track of corporate activities, economic indicators, bargaining patterns, health and safety information, and other pertinent data. For example, a union of bus drivers in Kansas City, Missouri, electronically accessed international financial data that showed the bus company was not forthright in disclosing its financial assets, giving the union the push it needed to win a union election. In another case, a union dissident was able to access campaign information that showed how a union official unethically donated union funds to a politician.[24] In yet another example, workers in Malaysia downloaded information about proper safety procedures to follow after a toxic chemical spill, thanks to a database maintained by the European Chemical Workers Union in Brussels, Belgium. This information allowed them to refuse to clean up the spill in an unsafe manner, despite management's demands.

The possibilities offered by rapid access to electronic information continue to give labor a better hand to play in negotiating with multinational corporations, which have had access to these resources for many years. This ability to bypass official media "gatekeepers" corresponds with the capacity to transcend national boundaries as well. News and information flows along international networks just as easily as between workers of the same workplace. The result is that unions and workers of many countries are able to discuss issues and exchange views with greater ease, with little interference from national political leadership. This communication occurs between the established leaders of different unions, as well as between rank-and-file members of different international unions. The CWA has been part of the UNI Global Union active in over 100 countries and tracks the activities of global telecommunications giants, from Europe and Latin America to Asia and Africa. The IAM is part of the International Metalworkers Federation, an international body of workers representing the worldwide metals industry. Listservs and e-mail from all parts of the globe are traversing the planet and supplying news on workers' struggles everywhere. Reports of many major labor battles in the late 1990s—such as the Liverpool strike, the Han Young maquila strike, the Australian dock strikes, the Korean general strikes, and the telecommunications strikes in Puerto Rico—enabled many labor activists to follow them, though often these battles have been absent in the mass media. News about these struggles helps to create a new global consciousness about the need for a global working-class movement and for a new system of labor.

Several respondents in this study expressed surprise that many labor unions in underdeveloped nations were more technologically savvy than the US unions. A machinist involved in worker solidarity actions with Indonesian workers said that even with their meager finances and conditions of extreme repression, Indonesian unionists use computers, the Internet, cell phones, and video tape to communicate with their colleagues and with others around the world. According to this informant, US unions often resist implementing technology not because of the money involved, but either because of technical ignorance or suspicions that it could undermine the current leadership's authority. Claims about the high price tag of new technologies, one of the main arguments against them, must constantly be reexamined, as computer and technology prices continue to fall at a rapid pace. Unions may be willing to spend thousands of dollars on expensive printed brochures while balking at spending less on computer systems or an online presence.

Many union activists stated that the union bargaining process could gain significantly from electronic communications. During strikes, Web pages can be a very efficient means of keeping memberships informed, and e-mail can be effective in soliciting members' opinions on contract terms. During Master Freight Agreement bargaining with the Teamsters' union, Web pages were used to solicit Teamster members' ideas and opinions on acceptable terms and conditions. For many unions, online communication can be effective in quickly estimating cost projections on new contracts and countering corporate financial figures. The bargaining procedure for major contracts can be demystified for members by uplinking regular video reports via satellite to membership meetings around the country, which the CWA has done. The many unions bargaining on behalf of General Electric workers use e-mail extensively to present a united front to that multinational corporation. One machinist I spoke with expressed admiration for the Pilots' Union and how they used computer communications to coordinate their nationwide strike. Computer communications were important to this struggle, as pilots are located all over the country and are difficult to assemble into one meeting in one locale. Electronic communication allows pilots to exchange viewpoints on contracts while they are geographically dispersed. Frequently, corporations will engage in "whipsawing," or getting locals of the same union to compete against one another in a drive to reduce wages or eliminate benefits. Close communication between locals can prevent that from happening. Some unions in Canada are posting their entire contracts on the Web so other workers can compare their own contracts and hopefully negotiate better ones.

A primary concern of the labor movement for many years has been to organize the unorganized, and many unions began experimenting with new communication technologies for this purpose. While many union organizers contend there is no substitute for one-on-one organizing, some technologies were identified that can help facilitate these interpersonal connections. For many people fearful of approaching a union, a Web site presents itself as a nonthreatening way to gain information while remaining anonymous. Many unions claim increased contact from new people because of their Web sites. A prime target for union organizing is young people, and it is precisely among younger workers where computer access and computer literacy is found to be highest. Much of the new job growth is found among workers who use computers, making them accessible to online communications from organizers. Both IAM and CWA are interested in organizing airlines workers around the country, where a high proportion of workers are on computer terminals daily. CWA organizers, who successfully organized thousands of US Air workers, said that their Web pages made a significant difference in distributing information and stimulating interest in the union. United Electrical organizers active at the University of Iowa pointed out that a significant area of interest is in organizing university graduate students, another group of workers who generally tend to be "plugged in." In many worksites, it may be difficult to actually reach employees and hand them a leaflet, as an organizer would traditionally do at a plant gate. In response, organizers are finding ways of reaching workers at their computers, by electronically leafleting directly to their computer terminals. Even for workers who do not have good Internet connections at home, the Web can be valuable. For cab drivers who are organizing a union in Philadelphia, electronic communications are vital for staying in touch with fellow workers. According to organizer Tekle Gebremedhin, an immigrant from Eritrea, "We have 3,000 drivers. It's not easy to communicate with one another." Say Philadelphia media activists Wolfson and Mercer, "Internet access in places where drivers congregate, like the train station or the airport, would mean that hundreds of drivers could e-mail each other, get a copy of the UTWA [Unified Taxi Workers Alliance] newsletter or resolve regulatory issues that require an Internet connection." According to Wolfson and Mercer, video production has also proved valuable for organizing, as workers can tell their stories in their own languages to others in an attempt to build solidarity at work.

Although the Internet gets most of the attention, video production has also been a major factor in developing a labor media infrastructure. Grassroots video has become an important tool of unions all over the world as an inexpensive and effective means of allowing voices of workers to circulate locally, nationally, and internationally. Video is an option not only in the technically advanced United States, but also in less developed countries, such as Brazil, Malaysia, the Philippines, and India.[25] The development of new forms of television and data satellite delivery, whether analog or digital, allows a much wider range of democratic communications. With the explosive growth of YouTube and other video sharing sites, labor video can be distributed globally, inexpensively, and efficiently.

During the NAFTA battle, video became a way to illustrate more clearly what was at stake for workers. In the US/Mexican border regions, many grassroots groups relied on videotapes to expose the atrocious working and living conditions of maquiladora workers. A group of workers from Green Giant in Watsonville, California, who were laid off when their plant moved to Mexico, contributed to a video that showed children being forced to work on the assembly lines and showed raw sewage flowing into the Green Giant growing fields.[26] A group of workers from Tennessee followed their closed plant down to Mexico and videotaped an exchange with their Mexican counterparts demonstrating their solidarity and dignity as workers united against a common foe.[27]

Labor activists were some of the first initiators in creating public access programs in US cities, including San Diego's Labor Link TV, San Francisco's Labor on the Job, St. Louis's Laborvision, and Chicago's Labor Beat. UPPNET, a national labor video group, created a national network of labor video producers who uploaded union programs via satellite to public access stations nationwide. The most frequently expressed benefit of video was its ability to communicate human emotion and its stronger claim to verisimilitude, compared to e-mail and computer-based forms. According to one autoworker, "If you have the time, you can sit down and edit these things to make a pretty powerful statement, with great credibility." The immediacy of video was touted as being particularly advantageous in union struggles. A video can provide the impetus for house meetings among new members and can show them the power they have when they have a union behind them. When Ford strikers in Mexico were attacked by the military in the 1990s, autoworkers went to the plant to serve as witnesses and to pressure the government and the Ford Company to cease and desist. A videotape called *$4.00 a Day, No Way* was produced and shown in auto locals around the United States and helped generate support for the Mexican workers. Labor activists have tried to create nationwide television programs on mainstream channels or cable, a strategy with which conservative religious broadcasters have been successful for many years. *We Do The Work*, for example, was a labor show that ran on PBS for a few years on some PBS channels before running out of funding. The money needed to produce the slick, high-end types of television programming to compete with corporate media was too high a barrier for such programming and is a primary problem. Many proponents of labor video thus argue for a more local, decentralized approach for a more effective form of communications, a more personal, narrowcasting approach. As labor communicator Fred Glass said in an interview, "That's small video, which brings people into closer contact with people, as opposed to big TV, which tends towards the opposite, encouraging social atomization."[28] Radio has also been used as a venue for labor news. Many of the nationally syndicated alternative radio programs like *Democracy Now!* or *Making Contact* cover workers news, as opposed to mainstream radio, which routinely ignores it. Workers Independent News, a radio collective based in Madison, Wisconsin, produces a nationally syndicated radio program that covers labor exclusively.

Labor media activists generally agree that electronic technologies make workers and their unions much less dependent on mass media in building ties to the public as a whole. The global network of labor activists online has brought the struggles of other workers directly into the consciousness of many US union activists, and has made the paucity of worker's news in the mass media very apparent. As one union respondent put it:

> News about what's happening to workers travels from country to country faster now than it used to before, and it's not as dependent on the

mass media for news about it. If we had to depend on the mass media for news about what's happening to workers in Mexico, we wouldn't know shit. And the fact is that the unions in the labor movement here know a lot about what's happening in Mexico and in part that's due to a network of activists out there who are sort of spreading the word about it and doing it in part through e-mail and through Web pages and in part through using the progressive media and the alternative media and in part through just good organizing.

In the wake of NAFTA and as the condition of workers' standards of living worldwide began to suffer, workers' organizations were confronted with the task of revitalizing a public sphere and a participatory civil society so dear to traditional interpretations of democracy as outlined by de Tocqueville, Locke, and Marx. In an era of monolithic media conglomeration, labor organizations sought to bypass the gatekeeping role of mass media and effectively communicate with the rest of civil society in order to grow, gain converts, and stimulate social change. In the eyes of many labor activists, American mass media have been gleefully heralding the end of the industrial era and the flowering of the Information Age but rarely mention the impact of those who must bear the brunt of economic dislocation. Labor activists believe the perspectives of labor unions and workers in general have been shut out of mainstream media for many decades. While the perspectives of business are highlighted in every daily newspaper and radio or television news program, labor news is rare, with the exception of strike coverage, corruption allegations, or incidents regarding violence. This is a dramatic contrast to the post–World War II dailies, where a labor reporter was an important part of the news beat of most major metropolitan newspapers. Barbara Ehrenreich, who wrote the best-selling book *Nickeled and Dimed* about the lives of the working poor in America, bemoans the fact that magazines and newspapers solely want to please their advertisers, rather than inform their audiences. "Their advertisers want to think they are reaching wealthy people, people who will buy the products. They don't want really depressing articles about misery and hardship near their ads."[29] Labor activists believe that the contributions of labor organizations in the United States have historically been undervalued and ignored. They believe many Americans are ignorant of the fact that the rights Americans take for granted—child labor laws, unemployment insurance, the eight-hour work day, the minimum wage, health and safety regulations—are direct results of the strikes, sit-downs, slow-downs, and actions of organized workers.

Union reformers point to the ways in which unions might have maintained their membership and strength, despite the adversities of the corporate offensive and the globalization of the economy. For many years, labor unions ignored the changing nature of the workforce, which was becoming increasingly female and nonwhite. However, the primarily white, middle-aged union leaders did not open up their membership and leadership to the growing Latino/a, Asian,

African-American, immigrant, and female workforce. On the domestic level, union leadership pursued a policy of "business unionism"[30] and tied its fortunes to Democratic politicians and a labor peace that relied upon a strong economy. When US financial hegemony began to erode, the so-called business/labor coalition was tossed aside. The crushing of the Professional Air Traffic Controllers Organization (PATCO) strike in 1980 was proof of that. On the international level, US unions were often shrill opponents of democratic and militant workers' movements the world over. The AFL-CIO, through organizations like the American Institute for Free Labor Development (AIFLD), regularly supported repressive, antilabor regimes in Latin America and elsewhere.[31] The main labor organization in the world, the International Labor Organization (ILO), was shunned by the AFL-CIO, thus cutting US workers off from the community of world labor unions. US unions generally bought into the American exceptionalism point of view, whereby US workers were somehow above other wage-toilers around the world. This stance has made workers from other countries less trustful and sympathetic with US labor and alienated many international allies.

The cumulative effect of labor's conservatism was to cut the unions off from their past as a voice for the powerless and oppressed as they began to look indistinguishable from their big business counterparts. To add to its woes, the US union movement has been battered by a protracted media campaign that portrays unions as old-fashioned, ineffective, and no longer necessary.[32] This image has been very effective in helping to isolate unions from the sectors that should be their most important allies—the millions of young people, women, minorities, and immigrants who suffer the most from low wages and oppressive working conditions. A poll undertaken by the AFL-CIO in the early 1990s confirmed this hypothesis. A study of focus groups revealed that a large margin of Americans felt that unions were beneficial for workers but that only 25 percent thought that unions were concerned about all working people. The report advised, "Until unions are once again seen as advancing a broad agenda on behalf of all working Americans, they will face very serious upper limits on the possible support they can receive from the general public."[33] Labor movement activists who sought to reform US labor unions confronted two major problems—the problem posed by the globalization of capital and the weak support base found in the public at large.

IMMIGRANT WORKERS, PRECARIOUS LABOR, AND NEW COMMUNICATIONS TECHNOLOGIES

The "Battle of Seattle" was a watershed mark for labor activists, who witnessed a reemergent mass movement of workers in solidarity with other progressive sectors of civil society—environmentalists, students, and poor people—sectors not normally in sync with organized labor in the United

States. This unified show of force was clearly a result of the growth of many new channels of communication that allowed stories of workplace oppression, environmental disaster, economic injustice, and social power to flow between people all over the world, unhindered or unfiltered by mass media institutions. The new fighting spirit of labor was evident in many locals and internationals and a new feeling of optimism, which believed that the decline of labor was over, that organizing drives would increase, that labor laws would be enforced, and that new communications power would be instrumental in these efforts, prevailed. Many unions put aside historic patterns of craft difference and ideological difference and merged memberships into fewer unions and larger locals. The 1995 election of John Sweeney as head of the AFL-CIO signaled a more aggressive approach to labor organizing over a more conservative wing of the federation. The AFL-CIO president at the time was accused of not fighting harder against NAFTA and for taking a passive approach towards organizing new workers. John Sweeney had been head of the SEIU, one of the most successful labor organizations in many years, and had been credited with bringing a large amount of women and minorities into the labor movement. Sweeney came into the presidency as part of the "New Voice" slate of more progressive unions. These hopes would be short-lived with the 2000 electoral vote debacle in Florida, which saw the Supreme Court appoint George W. Bush as president and usher in a new wave of antilabor Republican initiatives. A short time later, the September 11, 2001, terrorist attacks drove the country to war and then into a deep recession, not an opportune time for labor to make any gains. US labor made significant changes in the first decade of the twenty-first century in an attempt to come to grips with dire conditions they faced. Years later, a large sector of the AFL-CIO that was influenced by many of the reform movements of the previous decade formed a caucus called New Unity Partnership, which sought to devise new strategies for organizing and building alliances with the public in the new millennium. Led by Andy Stern of the SEIU, the caucus formally split from the AFL-CIO and formed a new labor federation called Change to Win in 2005, which included large and influential unions including the Teamsters, the SEIU, the United Food and Commercial Workers, and the United Farm Workers of America.

Probably the most significant development in US labor, though, was the emergence of a new and powerful bloc of workers—immigrant workers who are among the lowest-paid and most-exploited sector of the US working class. Historically ignored or excluded from US unions, immigrant workers were increasingly seen as important allies to win over to trade unionism. Throughout the 1990s, immigrant workers were often the most active and organized component of the American working class, leading job and community actions among sheetrock workers, day laborers, farmworkers, hotel and restaurant workers, garment workers, and many other sectors. Labor scholar Ruth Milkman calls the early 1990s labor organizing activities "an embryo of the broader revitalization effort that the new AFL-CIO leadership and its allies are currently attempting to jumpstart."[34] This labor upsurge by immigrants was seen as key to reversing the decline of US labor. According to David Bacon, "Immigrant workers fought to reverse that decline. Their militant strikes often forced unions to discard old, ineffective tactics, even to reexamine how they functioned internally. People coming from Mexico, Latin America, the Philippines, and Asia often brought militant traditions and a rich repertoire of ideas for fighting employers."[35] A report issued by the Migration Policy Institute in 2003 noted that an estimated 1.8 million foreign-born workers were in unions, up from 1.4 million in 1996.[36] Much of this immigrant union adhesion was a result of the self-organization from the workers themselves, who organized themselves first and then approached unions for support. Four thousand drywall workers in Southern California went on strike in 1992 as an independent organization but later joined the Carpenters Union. "Black car" limo drivers in New York City organized as an independent organization but later joined the CWA, growing to 1,000 dues-paying members by 2005.[37] The AFL-CIO, first regionally and then nationally, took notice and changed its previous anti-immigrant outlook. With the support of many union members who cut their teeth being active with new trade union strategies, the AFL-CIO Executive Council voted formally in 2000 for "a new system that ensured a level playing field for all employers and urged amnesty for the nation's 6 million undocumented workers."[38] Many of those arguing for the rights of immigrant workers and the importance of accepting all workers regardless of immigration status pointed out that the labor movement from its very beginnings was largely founded on immigrant workers: Poles, Germans, Italians, Jews, Irish, and so on.[39] On May 1, 2006, a massive national march and strike demonstrated the power of immigrant workers when millions of immigrants left their jobs and demonstrated their collective power on the streets in cities and towns throughout the United States. Called "A Day Without Immigrants," the powerful demonstration of the ability for immigrant workers to withhold their labor sent a strong message that immigrants would no longer be powerless and afraid. This enormous and successful organizing effort was led by grassroots leaders who used innovative organizing methods and multiple communications channels with the support of many organizations and unions. At one of the largest demonstrations in Los Angeles, the SEIU and AFSCME put up money and organizers to assist in logistics and the Teamsters' union provided two eighteen-wheelers to lead off the march.[40] Although many successful labor and organizing campaigns have been led by immigrants in recent decades, these efforts were all too often seen as marginal to the mainstream efforts of US labor. Today, the contributions made to the US workers' movement by immigrant workers is recognized as a key to the growth of the labor movement as a whole.

The rise of the immigrant worker rights movement, like those of other new social movements, has significantly influenced labor and has inspired many new experimental organizing efforts. In the situation of immigrant workers, the transient, temporary, or illegal circumstances of such work means that communications strategies are key to holding these workers together. The lessons of these communications strategies are very valuable in the current conditions of employment, not just for immigrant workers, but also for many in the United States where workers are also often dispersed, work alone or in small groups, and have no regular work hours. Unfortunately these conditions are all too common in large employers such as Walmart, McDonalds, Starbucks, and other jobs. Like immigrant workers, many workers are considered to be in "precarious" situations, where work is considered temporary and workers will be expected to take jobs in any industry currently hiring, losing the ability to identify with one particular skill or vocation. Under these conditions, social networks, e-mail, mobile telephone, and other electronic communications are key to developing a network of solidarity among workers who do not share a common or stable workplace. Labor activist Michael Zweig suggests that "social-networking sites and other Internet platforms offer organizing tools. National news sources, among them *Democracy Now!* and *Worker's Independent News*, can be expanded and used as models for the many more radio, television, and Web-based resources working people will need to overcome the limitations of the mainstream media."[41] Organizers are fully aware, however, that at times the best strategy is the oldest form of communications—talking one-on-one and face-to-face. Walking up to people's homes where they live and knocking on their doors remains an important union strategy, as workers may work all over town but often live in the same neighborhood. This style of community-based labor organizing is in many ways a legacy of a union that has organized in this fashion for many years—the United Farm Workers. Organizer Cesar Chavez borrowed the community-organizer approach from Saul Alinsky's "back-of-the-yards" strategy, where house meetings and community meetings were far more viable than workplace meetings. The United Farm Workers also took this community-based strategy to a level deeper when it helped set up Spanish-language community radio stations in the communities where many farm workers lived, knowing that many workers listened to the radio during the early morning drive to the fields. In any event, marginal and immigrant workers are increasingly able to develop means of worker-to-worker communications where it was almost impossible in past decades.

Perhaps one of the harbingers of these new forms of labor organization is the Restaurant Opportunity Center (ROC) of New York City, a group that was formed by the Windows on the World restaurant workers employed in the World Trade Center. First organized as a crisis and resource center to help workers who had lost their loved ones and their jobs on September 11, the ROC transformed into a nascent labor organization that has become a model for other industries with a multiracial, transient, temporary, and immigrant workforce. ROC is currently in eight other locations, joined together in a group called ROC-United and is active on Facebook, Twitter, and many other forms of electronic media.

This new organizing model, based upon the model of "worker centers," grew rapidly in the 2000s, a strategy that organizes less on the basis of a single workforce and more upon a community of workers. In a work environment where people will have many different jobs in many different sectors of the economy, it makes more sense to organize workers as members wherever they are, rather than only as workers in a distinct factory, shop, or workplace. Ironically, this model of worker organization harkens back to a much earlier time in US history, when the Industrial Workers of the World signed up workers as worker-members, regardless of where they worked. In 2010, the Restaurant Opportunities Center, Domestic Workers United, the New York Taxi Workers Alliance, and many other innovative worker organizations joined forces to create the Excluded Workers Congress to expand their innovative organizing program on a national basis.[42] The AFL-CIO has implemented plans to organize in a similar pattern, with their Work to Live program where members are "at large" rather than in one particular workplace. In order to facilitate organization on such an amorphous and grand scale, effective electronic communications will be a necessity. As US labor activists come to grips with the new conditions of labor, new communications strategies are developed to assist. Efforts to organize Walmart, for example, rely heavily upon electronic means such as e-mail, Web sites, and instant messaging. Two groups in particular, OURWalmart and Warehouse Workers United, both backed by the United Food and Commercial Workers, have been developing campaigns to communicate with the thousands of Walmart workers coast-to-coast.[43] According to Marianne Manlilov, "Rather than organizing Walmart stores a handful at a time, the strategy is to support Walmart workers to become leaders and to have those leaders build a broad membership network across the US. The key idea behind OURWalmart's success has been to combine deep field organizing in a number of areas with an online network of volunteers who can build in areas where field organizing can't reach."[44]

Labor activists find themselves in constant struggle over gaining access to the means of communication, trying to frame their issues, protesting when their issues are ignored or distorted, staging events to get coverage, and creating their own forms of media. As William Gamson noted:[45]

> Because media discourse is so central in framing issues for the attentive public, it becomes, to quote Gurevitch and Levy (19): "a site on which various social groups, institutions, and ideologies struggle over the definition and construction of social reality."

Unions and labor organizations' have traditionally attempted to frame or reframe issues important to their goals by holding press conferences, releasing reports and studies or opinion polls, holding demonstrations or other public events, writing letters to the editor or op-eds, taking out ads in major publications, and/or producing public service announcements. Such media strategies recognize that corporate media are much more likely to use sources of information unfriendly to labor and to frame an issue along the lines of corporate ideology. Furthermore, the ability of the corporate media to saturate and overwhelm the public sphere with news, entertainment, and advertising can be a powerful weapon against labor's media interventions. Therefore, it remains imperative for labor to develop new forms of communication and at the same time to continue to seek and to pressure to reform the current mass media. A recent example of the way traditional unions have been harnessing new communications technologies can be seen in the fall 2012 Chicago Teachers Union strike. A Facebook and Twitter analysis of the strike shows that, as in the name of the report, social media acts as a megaphone and a sword in CTU strike. In just one week, the Chicago Teachers Union Facebook page picked up 16,000 new fans since the strike began and registered that 81,369 people were "talking about" the issues presented on their page. According to the "new media specialist" who runs the communications effort of the union, Kenzo Shibata, "We have focused a lot of attention on social media through this strike. We knew that we could not rely completely on traditional media to tell the story, so we empowered our members to become citizen journalists on the ground."[46] Shibata says he considers himself an "online organizer."

The strength of the union movement and worker solidarity is dependent upon strong communication channels, and new technologies are critical in building and maintaining such channels. According to one machinist interviewed for this study:

> Without communications, you cannot have a democratic labor movement. Without communications, you can't have a fight that is sustained by the members because people need to understand where they are, where they're going, what the game plan is. It has to be theirs, or you're not going to win. And communications is integral to all that.

Any successful adoption of this technology, however, remains dependent not on technical considerations, but on the strength of the organization's democratic structures. Technology employed by unions could be used to perpetuate an undemocratic union structure or to promote the participation of the rank and file. According to one organizer:

> The people themselves have to have some role in formulating what the message is. That it's not just some professional somebody or other in an office somewhere deciding, well, I think that this is what workers need to understand and know and then go out and buy airtime, studio production time, producing a message for workers in which the role of workers is to be the passive recipient and then go out and do as they're told. I think that's a really stupid use of technology and one that is bound to fail. The participation of workers is the key question.

You can't substitute for that. And the use of technology has to be oriented towards that. How does it encourage participation? And how do workers themselves learn how to use it? The use of technology which makes people into passive recipients of things or of messages is not very useful to us.

According to many respondents, effective use of new communications technology by the labor movement is highly dependent upon the ability of labor to transform itself into a new form of organization: a democratic, grassroots social movement of workers that seeks to improve the lives of all working people and of all nations. In keeping with the principles of many alternative media creators, it has to be built from the ground up, not from the top down. The reasons for this seem to be not only the limited financial and labor-power resources of unions but, perhaps equally importantly, union activists' preference for more humanistic forms of communication, such as the telephone or personal contact. The historic traditions of the labor movement weigh heavily on many union activists, who point out that the labor movement was built the "old-fashioned" way, with workers talking to workers. Most believe that this is still the way to rebuild the labor movement today.

The perceived ignorance, misrepresentation, and, oftentimes, hostility of the mass media toward organizations of working people in recent decades has led to labor's questioning of pluralist conceptions of mass media. These questions of power, hegemony, and their relationship to media have determined the direction and structure of their media strategies. Many who participated in this study stated that labor's fate is the fate of all movements for social change in the world. Few social formations have the power, the ability, or the inherent interest in fighting for social change as do labor organizations. This has been true in the underdeveloped countries as well as the developed countries. It is also obvious to many labor activists that in almost every major historical and current struggle for social reform across the world, workers' organizations have played a pivotal role in the transformation of social relations, not only in the past, but today as well. In Poland, it was the workers' organization Solidarnosc that had the power to bring their authoritarian government to the bargaining table. In South Africa the Confederation of South African Trade Unions (the COSATU), played an enormous role in defeating apartheid. In Brazil, the Metal Workers' Union is the core around which the once-opposition group, now the ruling group, the Workers' Party, is constituted. In South Korea, the ship builders' and autoworkers' unions form the primary force of resistance to totalitarianism. In the events of the 2011 "Arab Spring," it was the key role played by workers organizations that played a pivotal role in overthrowing the regimes in Tunisia, Egypt, and other nations. In the recent Occupy Wall Street protests in the United States, it was the mass protest launched by the workers of Wisconsin that set the spark to take over Wall Street.

It is this challenge that confronts those who seek to enhance the communication activities of workers, to revitalize a democratic and grassroots labor movement, and to begin to build a global movement for a better life for the working people of the world. For over a decade now, many labor organizations have approached their communications tasks with a dual purpose, attempting to influence the mainstream media while at the same time building their own system of alternative communications. It has become obvious to labor media strategists that most contemporary communications theory is inadequately developed to explain and account for these new forms of labor communications, as traditional communications theories typically explain the relation between media producers and the general public within the broadcast model. Today, with so much emphasis on the "me" of personal communications, with viral marketing, YouTube videos, and Facebook confessions, labor communications activists emphasize the potential of the collective "us" in communications. As new forms of participatory media emerge, workers continue to develop networking that is truly worthy of the name "social." Labor activists have been on the leading edge of innovative networking, and their work deserves greater recognition and a closer investigation.

5   The Fight Over Content

Much of the social history of contemporary democratic media examines new means of media production and newly created avenues for media distribution. While production and distribution are fundamental to democratic communication, the battle increasingly centers on the content of the messages themselves. The digital means of production, reproduction, and delivery has fundamentally changed the rules of the game in this regard. When Frankfurt-school scholar Walter Benjamin delivered his ideas on the mechanical means of reproduction and its impact on image making and cultural production in 1936,[1] he had no idea the extent to which this phenomenon would develop. For much of the twentieth century, the means of mass media production was technically and financially off limits to most people, as were the means of its distribution. It was considered a truism that the freedom of the press was for those who could afford a press. As barriers to media production dissolved with the evolution of new consumer-level media and recording technologies, it was control over the airwaves and cable systems that presented the barrier to a more public communications system. Now that open networks and mobile communications are eliminating roadblocks to media access, new barriers that block how we use content are quickly being erected. Historically, corporations and governments have relied upon scarcity and controlled access to media production and distribution to either generate profit or to control populations. Past tendencies to marginalize and stigmatize popular media with the brush of amateurism, as was the case with Super 8 film or with ham radio, has not seemed to diminish the popularity and impact of today's citizens' media, so the battleground has shifted to litigious, legislative, and police action. Thus lawsuits over music and film file sharing, intensified lobbying pressure to pass the Protect IP Act (PIPA), Stop Online Piracy Act (SOPA), Anticounterfeiting Trade Agreement (ACTA), and other repressive Internet legislation and police confiscation and takedowns of hard drives and computer networks are regular occurrences today. Whether it is a lawsuit to ostensibly protect the economic interest of the recording industry or to protect the moral sanctity of the populace or protect the national security of the state, the goal is the same: restrict the public's ability to freely communicate.

With the means of democratic communication falling increasingly into public hands, the battle has shifted to struggle over control of the cultural commons from which we all graze. In the contemporary information economy, intellectual property rights are the new entitlements of fortunes. The growth of the Internet, particularly with the development of the World Wide Web, has significantly threatened the traditional gatekeepers of media. This new reality provoked extraordinary legal and political efforts to clamp down on the communications practices of Internet users, with the Digital Millennium Copyright Act of 1998 (DMCA) and the Copyright Term Extension Act of 1998 (CTEA) as opening salvos. The main provisions of the DMCA enforce and criminalize those who tamper with digital rights management (DRM) technologies that impede the ability of media to be duplicated. To give an example of how quickly technology has evolved since its adoption, the act specifically mentions penalties for tampering with the "Macrovision" code used on VHS videotape. Another primary part of the act provides for "takedowns" of Web sites that link or point to material that may be infringing on copyright law.[2] According to the Electronic Frontier Foundation, "[T]he DMCA has become a serious threat that jeopardizes fair use, impedes competition and innovation, chills free expression and scientific research and interferes with computer intrusion laws."[3] The Copyright Term Extension Act of 1998, commonly called the Sonny Bono Act in honor of the original sponsor of the bill, was specifically written to protect Disney's ownership of Mickey Mouse, which otherwise would have passed into the public domain. The bill extends copyright into the distant future, and in the opinion of many, harms the public interest and damages the original intent of copyright law. Stanford law professor Lawrence Lessig, writing his opinion in the *New York Times*, put it this way:

> Can Congress really extend copyrights beyond the terms originally granted? The answer should be, "No." The Constitution gives Congress the power to hand out monopolies over speech for "limited times." The first copyright act, in 1790, gave authors fourteen years. Under the current law, the term is the life of the author—plus seventy years. This expansion written into law in 1998 is largely the product of eager lobbyists. Disney and other companies have convinced Congress to ignore the framers' intent and push the term of copyright as long as possible.[4]

Since these acts, a continuing barrage of new legal and legislative maneuvers to control content has emerged, activity that promises to expand exponentially as a media-savvy public continually searches for ways around these restrictions.

One of the central philosophical foundations of the Internet has been the policy of "net neutrality," the idea that all content must be treated equally, without preference, bias, or restriction. Net neutrality stems from long-standing battles between the public interest and the early telephone monopoly whereby it was agreed that while the phone company may charge for service, it may not do so based on content. For "plain old telephone service" (POTS), as it is known, the telephone line provider has no business determining what will transmit over the telephone line. A slow talker gets charged the same as a fast talker, for example. The telecommunications companies prefer a model instituted by the cable industry whereby different content can be charged at different levels. The cable industry model allows the company the right to control what material will be coming though that cable, to charge at different levels, or to block the content at will.

Those who would destroy net neutrality work hand-in-hand with those who prefer the centralization of content in order to effectively control content and increase the ability to profit. Comcast, for example, is often accused of violating net neutrality by restricting the network speed of some of their customers. Accusations have surfaced over charges that Comcast discriminates against Netflix users and privileges customers who use their proprietary Xfinity service.[5] Comcast has also fought in court for the right to deliver slower speeds to customers using BitTorrent and YouTube.[6] Verizon has also lobbied heavily against net neutrality, to the extent of arguing that net neutrality violates their first amendment rights.[7] Both of these companies have a poor record when it comes to protecting the rights of the public and their customers. In the recent past, Comcast has purposefully blocked traffic for users of the file sharing, peer-to-peer protocol BitTorrent; Verizon Wireless was found to have blocked a prochoice organization from sending text messages to members; and AT&T censored comments by Pearl Jam singer Eddie Vedder that were critical of President George W. Bush.[8] The telecommunications companies are claiming the right to develop a parallel Internet structure to offer greater bandwidth for content delivery for those who pay more. Such a move would threaten the democratic and egalitarian nature of the Internet and relegate smaller, independent Internet projects to a marginalized existence of stuttering playback speeds and long download times. Critics of such a plan argue that if the Internet were constructed to accommodate only the large, established, multinational corporations, none of the innovative companies that have risen to the fore in recent years would have had a chance to succeed, citing YouTube, Google, Facebook, and others. A centralized content system free of net neutrality and built around traditional broadcasting models would allow for easier enforcement of new restrictions on copyright and trademark especially if backed by the Internet restriction legislation that has been proposed by the entertainment and cultural industries.

The Stop Online Piracy Act/E-PARASITE Act (SOPA) and the Protect IP Act (PIPA) stem from an earlier proposal entitled the Combating Online Infringements and Counterfeits Act (COICA) that would have created a blacklist of Web sites. The various bills provide for blocking blacklisted sites by interfering with the Internet's domain name system (DNS), which translates names like *www.papertiger.org* or *www.nytimes.com* into the IP addresses that computers use to communicate. If SOPA had been made law, copyright holders who discovered their work on a site could have forced payment processors to cut off payments and advertisers to cut ties with a simple warning notice. All of this would have allowed someone claiming infringement to shut down a site, without due process, by making its domain impossible to find and by cutting off its financial resources. These bills target Web sites whose users supposedly violate copyright, yet they use vague definitions that would have included many neutral Web sites that simply pass along or aggregate material posted by their users. Though these prohibitive legislative bills were shut down by a massive display of public anger through e-mails and Web postings, similar legislation still survives and is being pushed heavily by entertainment and telecommunications industry lobbyists, often under new names with different descriptions. In response to the introduction of legislative acts calling for Internet censorship, eighty-three founders and engineers who helped build the Internet wrote a letter to Congress that included this passage:

> The current bills—SOPA explicitly and PIPA implicitly—also threaten engineers who build Internet systems or offer services that are not readily and automatically compliant with censorship actions by the US government. When we designed the Internet the first time, our priorities were reliability, robustness, and minimizing central points of failure or control. We are alarmed that Congress is so close to mandating censorship-compliance as a design requirement for new Internet innovations. This can only damage the security of the network and give authoritarian governments more power over what their citizens can read and publish.[9]

"DISNEY IS A LANGUAGE"

The issue of intellectual property rights has been predominantly framed around one of economic necessity and protection of financial value. Though the entertainment conglomerates have paid lip service to the artistic integrity of cultural creation, that claim appears increasingly empty, as it is often the case that creative artists do not own their own work. A well-known case in point is the hundreds of Beatles songs that are not owned by the artists, but by Sony/ATV and the estate of Michael Jackson. The argument around economic and financial value, however, fundamentally obfuscates the real issue concerning the use of these cultural products. The images, sounds, icons, ideas, and creations emanating from our vast cultural apparatus—whether corporate, organizational, or individual—are the symbols and language that we use today.[10] They are part of the foundation of our culture and our communications systems and are essential to any form of conversation we need to carry on as a society. Standardization of words, phrases, icons, symbols, and other representations allows the human race to communicate about the contemporary world around us. In a free culture, we would no more allow a corporate entity to lock up references to the Beatles, *The Grapes of*

Wrath, James Brown, or *The Wizard of Oz* than we would allow a business entity to lock up the letter *C* or the word *free*. This very subject was the focus of a lawsuit between media-collage band "Negativland" and the Irish rock band U2, involving copyright over the letter *U* and the numeral 2. This legal wrangle is the subject of avant-garde filmmaker (and microcinema producer) Craig Baldwin's film "Sonic Outlaws."[11] In our media saturated culture, songs, ad jingles, blockbuster movies, celebrities, billboard campaigns, and other cultural products are the building blocks and reference points of how we carry forth daily discussion of the state of our society. In 1984, presidential candidate Walter Mondale acknowledged this when he famously asked, "Where's the beef?" in a political comment based upon a popular Wendy's commercial. When a public is bombarded with slogans, images, and sounds that are designed to permeate the collective consciousness, it is inevitable that these will become part of the language and culture. "Got Milk?," the Energizer Bunny, the Budweiser Frogs, the Jolly Green Giant, Tony the Tiger, and a host of other creations are riffed on, added to, spoofed, and generally incorporated into daily use. For a quick gauge to measure the impact of fictional creations on American culture, take a look at the millions of little copyright and trademark violators roaming the streets on All Hallows Eve. There you will see a throng of Harry Potters, Teenage Mutant Ninja Turtles, Darth Vaders, and other icons of popular culture. The attempt to lock up or control common linguistic tropes by claiming copyright or trademark is nothing new; it has been attempted generation after generation by those wishing to claim ownership and control of ideas. British Parliamentarians, at the turn of the eighteenth century, entertained the following thought while discussing such a prospect:

> What property can a man have in ideas? While he keeps them to himself they are his own, when he published them they are his no longer. If I take water from the ocean it is mine; if I pour if back it is mine no longer.[12]

In our current media-saturated environment, for example, fictional characters are utilized as stand-ins for political figures and archetypes. A political cartoon, circulating at the time of the 2012 presidential election, portrayed Mitt Romney with the upper class, one-percent of America—depicted as Homer Simpson's boss, the top-hatted gentleman from the Monopoly game, Scrooge McDuck, and cartoon character Richie Rich: symbolically potent images but potential copyright infringement cases. Popular songs become part of everyday conversation due to their social and political significance, ad campaigns become iconic images, and television shows are referenced as moral barometers, social indicators, and demographic trends. We can speak of "McJobs" and "Walmartization" and know what we're talking about. In a period when millions are on the Internet, have video cameras and recorders, have some basic audiovisual editing tools, and are media-savvy, our rich media artifacts are increasingly incorporated into music and video mashups, visual gags, Photoshop spoofs, and other violations of copyright laws in a collective effort to converse about our current social condition in this large and complex nation. Media that is swapped, traded, recut, and mashed up all end up as part of the great din of active communications in our public sphere. Copyright restrictions and intellectual property regulations should take into account that today's media is part of our language. The rights of the public should play a significant part of any conversation regarding intellectual property rights today. The language of "fair use" recognizes this responsibility, but media corporations have been very effective in weakening the interpretation of "fair use" as it is currently invoked. First among these attacks on "fair use" is the practice of sending cease-and-desist letters, alleging copyright and trademark infringement, and threatening dire punishments, to everyone from artists and social critics to commercial competitors. These threatening actions have grown dramatically with a growing culture of shared media accelerated by the Internet.

THE CORPORATE PLUNDER OF PUBLIC IDEAS

There are few more cherished ideas in the West than the individual as the source of invention, discovery, and creativity. Our folklore and historical narratives are full of inventors and artists who are credited with being the pivotal force in technology and culture. This "great man" theory has become generally accepted as the lynchpin to understanding much of our history. Thus Thomas Edison invented the light bulb, Alexander Graham Bell invented the telephone, and Jonas Salk discovered the polio vaccine. Unfortunately, this perspective—part of the social construction of knowledge—ignores the decades of other innovations that led up to these particular interpretations and implementations of technology. Regarding world history, this framework constructs World War II as a struggle between the wills and egos of Churchill, Roosevelt, and Stalin allied against Hitler, Mussolini, and Tojo. Thus fascism becomes reduced to a single bad man, rather than resulting from the complicity of the millions of people who formed that mass political movement, along with the social, political, and economic realities that helped create it. Subsequently, the masses that fought fascism are relegated to being little more than the pawns of great men, be it Patton, MacArthur, De Gaulle, or other military commanders. This propensity to individualize significant developments—referred to by some as the "Columbus effect," in honor of the man who single-handedly "discovered" America—is a modernist method of stripping social and collective context from individual contributions.[13] Kathy Burke LeFevre summarizes Fernand Braudel and Michel Foucault by saying, "Such perspectives suggest that traditional views of an event or act have been misleading when they have presumed that the individual unit—a speech or a written text, an individual hero, a particular battle or discovery—is clearly separable from a larger, continuing force, or stream of events in which it participates."[14] This prejudice is very much a part of trademark and copyright assumptions today. Jim Thomas writes that the very act of publishing tends to "fossilize" an idea by printing a name of ownership on it. He says that "the print technology through which this communally developed knowledge is typically delivered—distanced, fossilized, abstracted from the network of interconnected minds that formed it—continually enforces the opposite message."[15] As our culture moves away from print technology and more toward an interactive, networked one, it creates the possibility for a more accurate reflection of the interconnectedness of knowledge production. Unfortunately, this may not be so beneficial for those whose profit depends upon individual ownership of ideas.

In the twenty-first century information- and service-based economy, this emphasis on the individual has substantial repercussions for the financial fortunes of those credited for new and old cultural commodities. The US economic system—with its intricate and ponderous system of patents, trademarks, and copyrights—rests to a large degree on such emphasis. Corporations, considered as "persons" for many decades now, and formally recognized as such by an act of the US Supreme Court in the 2010 Citizen's United case, benefit tremendously by this ahistorical and simplistic perspective. Though the United States likes to consider itself a "nation of tinkerers," in the Ben Franklin motif, the overwhelming majority of the patents, copyrights, and trademarks are held by organizational entities, not citizen-inventors.

Patent protection has long been incorporated into law, as early as the Constitution of the United States of America was written. It was put in place as a critical means by which to promote technological progress by protecting the economic interests of the developers of new mechanical and physical devices and systems. Copyright, on the other hand, was instituted to protect the creative work of authors, for work that ostensibly had no "functional" value. Trademark was ostensibly set up to protect consumers of products and to aid in correctly identifying commodities. The fight over patents that typified much of the industrial era, such as RCA's legal maneuvering to be credited with the invention of radio circuitry or Edison's battle for control over motion picture equipment, has become primarily a battle over copyright and trademark rights as we move deeper into the so-called Information Age, which places less weight upon "things" and more weight on "ideas." This conflict, which began in earnest with the birth of the mass media, becomes increasingly heated when we enter the digital domain, when work can be digitized, transformed, and distributed without limits.

Though there has been increasing public discussion about intellectual property and copyright, the current debate does not upset the individualistic worldview. The discussion so far has been narrowly framed by those with the most economic interest at stake. Critics of copyright law typically argue for a more limited interpretation of copyright, such as a speedier entry into public domain, while the bulk of legal challenges center around which individual or entity can rightfully claim to be the creative source of a creative property. Missing from the discussion is the possibility that many cultural and creative properties belong not to those currently claiming ownership, but to our collective culture. Many cultural products currently being fought over in the courtrooms and boardrooms spring from the streets, subcultures, indigenous societies, and collective practices of social groups and not from the cubicles of corporations and entrepreneurial capital, nor from the isolated garrets of artistic geniuses. This collective and public culture is culled, prepared, commodified, packaged, and resold to a global market for consumer consumption. Hip-hop street culture, a phenomenon that originated in North American barrios and ghettos, has generated hundreds of hot commodities that can now be found in suburban malls across America. Likewise, punk music and its paraphernalia, despite its origins as a strident critique of consumerism, is often found incorporated into consumer products and advertising campaigns that seek to incorporate its irony and "coolness." Many other cultural appropriations are visibly and sometimes humorously apparent to the average consumer. The worn-out Levis of bohemian subcultures can often be found as high-priced, pre-"fatigued" fashion items in the windows of boutiques. To promote "street cred," students are hired to chalk product graffiti around urban areas. Billboard ads are purposely marked to look like graffiti. The work of avant-garde and experimental artists, often initially dismissed or ridiculed, routinely shows up in mainstream advertising campaigns. Contemporary "edgy" art, whether it's the low-grade video images reminiscent of early video artists or the collages and cutups of today's Dadaist-inspired collagists, is bound to be refined and brought into the repertoire of mainstream image making by commercial industries that are increasingly devoid of new ideas, elevating the vocation of "trendspotting" to high status in many creative firms. It is a given that the image makers of corporate advertising and branding routinely plunder our cultural commons to appropriate the latest trends. But corporate cultural plunder goes way beyond contemporary street culture. Classical works of art are routinely featured in high fashion ads from cologne to handbags and from evening gowns to shoes.[16] Making such an association with high art is essential, as the business of selling extravagant accoutrements for large sums of money is sometimes considered boorish, so evoking the timeless mystique of a Rodin or a Botticelli is a clear path to consumers' acceptance. Allusions to indigenous cultures and Third World cultures, also popular for capture and incorporation into consumer products and for brand naming, are often useful in associating a product with strength and ruggedness or with a sense of adventure. In the frenzy of our contemporary branding culture, untold millions of dollars flow from corporations into the legal system in order to claim ownership of cultural products to which they have no legitimate right.

In summary, it has long been understood that corporations tremendously profit from publicly funded innovation and infrastructure. Corporations often decry taxation but profit handsomely from it when it funds everything from the interstate highway construction that moves their goods, to the

Interstate Commerce Commission that regulates such transportation, to the banking system that ensures solvency, to the police and army that protect it all. But the benefits of collective cultural production are far more obscure.

The problem with many copyright and trademark laws is they are often enforced for the sole economic enhancement of business portfolios and not for the protection of the creative individual or for the common good. Until these discrepancies are resolved, this century will witness countless skirmishes between those who wish to use our common languages, images, and sounds for social communication and those who wish to lock them up for private gain.

In the mad stampede for branding, intellectual property restrictions are pushed to an extreme by an increasingly parasitical business environment intent on cornering any marketable ideas that emerge from the popular consciousness. Many examples border on absurdity and become fodder for popular humor, such as the monopoly of the prefix *Mc* by the giant burger chain or the claiming of the phrase "fair and balanced" by right-wing media giant News Corporation/Fox. These extreme and public examples deflect from the more egregious and damaging examples of corporations that borrow from the public domain while working to block similar access to the public. Perhaps even more hypocritical is the use of copyright law to deliberately destroy the intent and meaning of the original creation, though its original intent was to protect the integrity of the creator. Such examples abound in advertising where images, music, and lyrics are torn from context to promote ideas antithetical to the artists' original intent. In either case, the current intellectual copyright foundations are all about monopolizing culture for financial profit and little about either creative origination or artistic integrity. In the public realm of entertainment and politics, artistic integrity and the rights of the artist do not seem to matter much to the politicians and political leaders who so avidly support legislation to strengthen the rights of intellectual property holders. The Pretenders' song "My City Was Gone," written by lead singer Chrissie Hynde, was for many years used as the opening music to right-wing radio entertainer Rush Limbaugh's show, even though Hynde, left-wing and anti-Rush, frequently demanded that he desist, to no avail.[17] Bruce Springsteen's song "Born in the USA" was used for many a Republican political backdrop, particularly during the Ronald Reagan campaign, despite Springsteen's complaint that he was an outspoken critic of Reagan's brand of politics. Bruce Springsteen's public rebuke of the GOP has not stopped politicians from hitching a ride on the popularity of popular music, regardless of the conflicting messages. Some additional cease-and-desist complaints spurred by recent election campaigns, almost always Republican, include John McCain's use of John Mellencamp's "Pink Houses," Van Halen's "Right Now," the Foo Fighters' "My Hero," and Jackson Browne's "Running on Empty"; Mike Huckabee's use of Boston's "More Than a Feeling"; Sarah Palin's use of Heart's "Barracuda" and Gretchen Peters's "Independence Day"; Mitt Romney's use of Survivor's "Eye of the Tiger";[18] Michelle Bachman's use of Tom Petty's "American

Girl"; and many others.[19] A memorable distortion of artistic integrity was witnessed during a nationally televised tribute to John Lennon just after his death, when the lyrics to his popular anthem "Imagine," which originally said to "imagine no religion," were changed to "imagine one religion," most likely due to the network's fear of the strength of the then-powerful "Moral Majority." At New York City's gigantic 2012 New Year's celebration in Times Square, popular musician Cee Lo Green committed the same offense, changing John Lennon's lyrics from "nothing to kill or die for/and no religion too" to "nothing to kill or die for/and all religion's true."[20]

The immense Hollywood film companies, represented by the Motion Picture Association of America, the principal lobbying and trade arm of Hollywood, are one of the most militant forces leading the charge against intellectual "theft." As many scholars of Hollywood are aware, the founders of the film industry based in Southern California are historic violators of patent law. It is notable that the reason for the centrality of Hollywood to film production, as opposed to New Jersey or New York where the US film industry was born, is directly related to the evasion of patent restrictions on motion picture equipment. The advantage of the barren landscape of the tiny outpost of Hollywood, California, besides the good weather, was the distance it placed between the film producers and the Edison patent lawyers who demanded tighter controls and payment for film production. According to Paul Spehr:

> The move to open spaces was also spurred by the intense rivalry between the established companies of the Motion Picture Patents organization and the upstart "independents" who chose not to comply with the trust's "arbitrary business restrictions." To escape the trust's detectives it was necessary to be free to move to unexpected locations and near to open countryside.[21]

Besides the irony of its current concern over copyright enforcement, Hollywood is also noted as a prime beneficiary of the appropriation of collective culture. Perhaps Disney is singled out too often to represent the dark side of the Hollywood system. Yet it comes up frequently in such debates because of its militant legal activity in defense of what it claims as its own property rights. The irony is too great to pass up: even its very first production, *Steamboat Willy*, was a direct takeoff on a popular film of the day. This Disney cartoon imitates the Buster Keaton film *Steamboat Bill, Jr*. Such a derivative violation would certainly raise eyebrows among copyright lawyers today. Almost the entire repertoire of classic Disney productions outright plunders work from the public domain. The vast bulk of their core animation films is almost entirely work from authors in the public domain or from popular folk tales and fairy tales too old to be accorded to any one author. How is it that such common tales such as *Snow White and the Seven Dwarfs*, *Cinderella*, *Sleeping Beauty*, or *Beauty and the Beast*, all based on oral cultural traditions hundreds of years old, can be closely guarded by Disney as their properties?

How can work such as *Pinocchio, Jungle Book, Lady and the Tramp*, and other works whose authors received not one dime for their work, now be widely considered as Disney creations? In *How to Read Donald Duck*, one of the most important pieces of cultural criticism ever written, Ariel Dorfman and Armand Mattelart explode the Disney myth: "Like the natives and the nephews in the comics, Disney workers must surrender to the millionaire Uncle Scrooge McDisney their treasures—the surplus value of their physical and mental resources." Commenting on Disney's plunder of the creative commons, they state, "Literature, too, has been obliged to pour its treasures into the great Disney money bin. Disney was, as Gilbert Seldes put it many years ago, the 'rapacious strip-miner' in the 'goldmine of legend and myth.'"[22]

Even beyond such bald-faced appropriation of public work, there is a second tier of appropriation: the thinly veiled copies of archetypes from literature, characters that are clearly pulled from other creative sources, characters as "Scrooge" McDuck or the alter-egos of "Jekyll and Hyde" or the many references to "Merlin" the magician, and other recognizable characters. Again, today's copyright lawyers would have their hands full from so much replication of derivative archetypical creations. The law though, works in industries' favor, protecting corporations from outside claims, but punishing individuals who transgress upon the property supposedly belonging to corporations. In the past, editions of the book *How to Read Donald Duck* have been seized in the United States and banned in Chile, the country where it was first printed. Perhaps the most famous Disney infringement case was brought against the commune of underground cartoonists led by Dan O'Neill, who founded Air Pirates, in order to critique Disney for its "corporate seizure of the American narrative." Their creative work, *Air Pirates Funnies*, was banned after a protracted legal fight.[23]

Narrative texts and visual imagery are not the only materials fought over in copyright courts; music is also a highly contested medium. The rich traditions of American music are fertile ground for corporate plunder, as music is a tremendous source of emotional attachment and relevance. Perhaps musician Tom Waits said it best in a letter he wrote to the *Nation*: "Songs carry emotional information and some transport us back to a poignant time, place, or event in our lives. It's no wonder a corporation would want to hitch a ride on the spell these songs cast and encourage you to buy soft drinks, underwear, or automobiles while you're in the trance."[24]

Business interests have long recognized the timeless value of music, perhaps even more so than many struggling musicians. It is for this reason that so many television jingles are snippets of beloved, popular music, often to the disappointment of viewers who resent that such memory-laden and emotional content is used to sell automobiles or beer. Many artists lose control of their music in the same copyright system that was supposed to protect the artistic integrity of their work. Beatles songs initially led the charge, when most of the rights to their music were sold to the highest bidder. Many popular musicians' songs followed, from Led Zeppelin to Marvin Gaye.

Some holdouts remain, however, such as the supergroup the Doors, who refused to sell to corporate buyers. In an interview about Jim Morrison with John Densmore, a founder of the Doors, Densmore spoke about the primary objection to commercialization: "Integrity. Jim really went crazy over 'Come on, Buick, light my fire' [when Buick wanted to use the Doors' hit "Light My Fire" in a car commercial, but Morrison adamantly refused to allow it]. Well, Jim was flipping out. What does it mean? It means he cares about the entire [Doors] catalogue and what it represents. And you know, when you're young and trying to pay the rent [it's tempting to take those kind of offers], but Jim thought, 'We don't need to pay the rent [by selling our songs for use in commercials].' He cared about the legacy of the band."[25]

But with the financial stakes so high, few can hold out.

Another insidious example of a violation of artistic integrity due to the nature of the copyright system is the use of John Fogerty's Creedence Clearwater Revival song, "Fortunate Son," whose antiwar lyrics are twisted to sell patriotism and blue jeans. Fogerty, a veteran, was inspired to write the song upon reflecting on the photos of Republican youth from the Nixon family, whom he imagined would never have to fight in the wars their parents had launched. The lyrics sarcastically associate flag-waving patriotism with the hypocrisy of upper-class politicians who send other people's sons and daughters to war. The Wrangler Jeans group, who bought the rights to use the song, lifted only the first lines, "Some folks are born made to wave the flag, ooh, they're red, white, and blue," playing them over an American flag sticker stuck on the buttocks of a jeans wearer. Thus a strongly stated antiwar song became an anthem for blind patriotism and consumerism. Fogerty protested, but the copyright system protected the owner and not the creator.

These examples of loss of artistic integrity do not even begin to document the countless examples of music coming from original composers who were never compensated for their original work. Examples would include the Beach Boys' hit song, "Sloop John B," which originated from a field recording taken from Caribbean sailors in the 1930s, or "The Lion Sleeps Tonight," an African song that reached number one on the American charts, whose writer died a pauper, having sold the rights of the song for less than two dollars.[26]

That music is a collective product of generations of songwriters, poets, balladeers, composers, and cultural producers is an accepted fact by many musicians but is rejected by those whose ownership of songs means profit. Perhaps one of the most important contemporary American songwriters, Bob Dylan, acknowledges the debt musicians owe the socially produced legacy of American music. In an interview with *Rolling Stone* in 2012, he admits that he borrows much inspiration from old Protestant hymns, poetry, and other cultural traditions. In the interview, he says, "You borrow a tune here, then change it a little bit. You borrow some words there. Then add to them. You don't claim to be original."[27]

Such appropriation of common works is commonplace today, and corporations shamelessly "trademark" persons, places, and things pulled from centuries-old, common cultural legacies. Rich literary sources—Shakespeare, the Brothers Grimm, the Arthurian legends, and oral histories and folk tales, popularized in the American West, the Medieval period, or ancient civilizations—have provided a rich treasure trove for corporate appropriation; corporations borrow freely from our shared culture for financial gain. One study of the contemporary relevance of the King Arthur tradition notes:

> Twentieth-century America, in particular, proved a rich breeding ground for the Arthurian mythos, not only in film and high or mid-culture fiction (novels, short stories, fantasy fiction, science fiction), but in such areas of popular and mass culture as television, gaming, advertising, material goods, comic books, musical theater, pop music, and an assortment of esoteric genres.[28]

A quick stroll through any shopping mall will reveal many of the names and products gleaned from such sources, from Round Table Pizza to Merlin Telephones to Excalibur Electronics. With this in mind, it is not hard to imagine the impetus and the sense of righteousness of contemporary consumers, artists, and media makers who feel free to feed off the fat of the land when it comes to popular media. The popularity of MP3 downloads, torrent feeds and the burning of DVDs and CDs makes perfect sense in this regard. Users of this media typically see themselves as legitimate users of popular culture, not as thieves. Until this is understood by such trade groups as the Recording Industry Association of America and the Motion Picture Association of America, there will doubtless be little letup in this kind of activity, even though many members of the public understand that cultural works are increasingly locked up and restricted by corporations and media conglomerates, creating a condition called the "permission culture" by Stanford legal scholar Lawrence Lessig, who stated, "The consequence is that we are less and less a free culture, more and more a permission culture."[29] In the permission culture, the public conversation is reduced to a situation where permission must be granted to speak, replacing a more democratic culture of speech. When expression is repressed as in this manner, citizens will continue to exchange ideas, although they will be forced to go "underground" and continue in less conspicuous places, placing millions of people in the category of outlaws. As the imbalance grows between public access to media production, on the one hand, and a territorial, possessive, and ubiquitous corporate media on the other, an emergent and popular subculture arises that adopts the stance of cultural jujitsu and a David-versus-Goliath strategy of using the force of the larger opponent against itself. In this way, participants can discuss, address, and comment upon the nature of our society and our culture by using the images, sounds, and meanings it produces, despite the fact that it is increasingly illegal to do so.

Outlawing culture has produced a culture of outlaws in this regard. What began as a small phenomenon led by artists, political provocateurs, and hip-hop and punk enthusiasts has now become a major presence on the Internet, particularly gaining adherents in the fan culture that makes its home online. Fans who edit their own versions of *Star Trek* episodes and share them with thousands of other *Star Trek* fans have convinced many people of the fun and creativity of the re-edit, disregarding the grey area of the law it places them in. Cutting together a scene of a new *Batman* release that replaces Batman's voice with that of cookie monster from Sesame Street is great fun, but makes no friends in copyright courts. The popularity of cutups, mashups, re-editing, fan fiction, and the phenomenon popularly referred to as "culture-jamming," has become mainstream, as have more technical practices that I refer to as "technopranks."

TECHNOPRANKS AND MEDIA HIJINKS

There have been few attempts to unify activities such as hacking, pranking, and culture-jamming. I believe they spring from a similar desire to inject public input into a closed communications system that drives other practitioners of alternative media. In the United States, we have eroded the public sphere in favor of a system of one-way communications, in essence eliminating public discussion in favor of the mass reception of messages from the centers of power. In an age in which public space is disappearing and the public main street is replaced with the private property of the mall, prankster forays into the mediascape seem increasingly inevitable and indeed have won over a wide range of avid advocates. The spirit of communications-from-below that incorporates humor, graffiti writing, technical showmanship, grassroots activism, as well as DIY, punk rock, or hip-hop aesthetics has emerged in a great many of these media interventions. Rather than serving as mere background noise to cultural, social, and political life, these seemingly disparate practices have contributed to a growing movement to bypass the blockade of ideas now restricting democratic access to culture and communications. While culture-jamming is, I believe, commonly understood as a general term, I would like to delve more deeply into the area I call "technopranks," a media practice that requires perhaps a more skilled and concerted group of practitioners.

In an attempt to make sense of technopranks, I have categorized some primary areas of activities and offer some examples to illustrate them. The two main divisions reflect two primary camps of media activism—those choosing to focus on disrupting and critiquing corporate media and those working to build alternative channels of information. I refer to these two areas respectively as "Breaking the Façade" and "New Electronic Spheres." These activities are generally, but not always, produced anonymously, or they are crowd-sourced and are directed to the widest sectors of society. Many of these activities skirt the murky borders of illegality. Whereas culture-jamming tends to fall within a more localized media context, such as billboard alterations or graffiti campaigns that are place-based, techno-pranks lean toward a more global campaign, where the goal is to reach millions around the globe, riding on the power of media and social networks. As we will see here, the activities of workers have also had a special role to play in this type of subterranean communication.

It is hard to ignore that the American public is subject to a constant barrage of commercial messages, public relations ploys, political spins, and other modern propaganda techniques. "Breaking the façade" refers to the types of hijinks that chip away at the smooth veneer of these manipulative practices. Whether consciously or unconsciously, the traditions of Dadaism, Surrealism, and Situationism contribute to the ways electronic pranksters expose the fallacy of mainstream media objectivity, corporate responsibility, and the benevolence of the state, often while violating the public's "common decency." Where culture is increasingly trademarked, and life itself seems to be branded, it seems natural that many people want to speak back to the logo. When we live immersed in a media environment saturated by advertising and brands, corporate icons and symbols become just part of the environment and fair game for commentary. When corporate power has surpassed state power, as many scholars believe has happened, logos become political and ideological symbols, not just abstractions for products. The Coca-Cola logo, for example, has represented the neocolonial power of the United States abroad for many decades, as has McDonald's and Bank of America, and now Nike and Starbucks. Many members of the public are increasingly incensed at what these logos represent, evoking anger at seeing the drugstore on Main Street close because of Walmart or having their local coffee shop pushed out of business by Starbucks, or seeing their own culture appropriated from them, to be repackaged and sold at retail outlets at the mall. To appropriate a logo and turn it around on itself may be illegal in some instances, but in many ways, it represents the only way to make one's voice heard. To use yet another metaphor, the logo is the Achilles's heel of many a large and powerful corporation whose power often resides in its brand. Borrowing the logo or other representative symbol from a powerful economic or cultural force in order to make a statement is considered fair game in the ethical philosophies of many a culture-jammer. It is also part of what many of them would see as art or, certainly, entertainment. In the words of many culture-jammers, "Copyright infringement is your greatest entertainment value," although they would admit that it is an increasingly litigious one.

CUT-AND-PASTE COMMENTARY (THE JACKALOPE TRADITION)

Although Photoshop and other computer-based image tools make photographic collage simple and quick, by no means did this practice emerge from the computer age. There is a long tradition of photographic collage in the cut-and-paste commentary tradition going back to the beginnings of photography, where blade and glue were just as effective tools as Photoshop at turning the meaning of an image back onto itself. Perhaps the most well-known practitioner of this was the artist John Heartfield, whose biting satirical collages attacked the rise of fascism in Germany. For example, in one of Heartfield's images, the slogan "millions stand behind him" combines with an image of Hitler with his hand in the fascist salute while bankers behind him place millions in his open palm. In the United States, there is a long tradition of using such technique for comic effect. One of the most recognizable is the "jackalope" trope, which at one time could be found in rural gift shops across the nation. The elusive "jackalope" was a doctored image of a giant rabbit pasted in a bucolic meadow scene with a large rack of antlers. The "jackalope" follows in the same vein as "the one that got away" image, depicting a monstrous-sized rainbow trout caught by a victorious fisherman in a tiny rowboat.

These images follow a grand tradition of tall tales and satire, a blend of tongue-in-cheek and cut-and-paste, frequently mixed with a dark sense of humor. Today, doctored images flood the e-mail boxes of millions and represent a large amount of the images popping up on Facebook sites and other image-sharing and social-networking platforms.

An early Photoshopped file that demonstrated the power of image doctoring powered by the Internet was a cleverly constructed photo that showed a backpacker on top of the World Trade Center while a jetliner loomed in the background, ostensibly someone's last photograph found in the rubble of the twin towers. This photo reached such a wide distribution that mainstream press felt the need to step in and point out that it was a fake. While this example demonstrated the ability for an image to deceive, it also demonstrated the speed at which a single person could deliver an image to such an enormous global audience. Another somewhat astonishing example is the case of how *Sesame Street*'s Bert from Bert and Ernie wound up on posters held up by angry Bangladeshi demonstrators in the pages of *Time*. After the attack on the World Trade Center and the retaliatory strikes in the Middle East, demonstrators in Bangladesh wanted to voice their condemnation of the attack on Afghanistan by showing support of Osama Bin Laden, the equivalent, perhaps, of burning the American flag. As Osama Bin Laden was a private person, there are not many pictures of him, so the protestors did what most people would do in the digital age—they conducted a Google search for an image of him. Unfortunately, they found the satirical and humorous web site, *Bert is Evil*, which depicts the Muppet with evil people throughout history, including Osama bin Laden. They downloaded that image, not recognizing that the image of Bert was in the picture. That photo was printed on thousands of posters for demonstrators to carry, and their march was photographed and printed worldwide on the wires of the Associated Press and Reuters, thus sending the image of Bert and Osama full-circle around the globe in a true demonstration of the power of global media.[30] The problem this represents to corporate America is that many of these cut-and-paste images often violate copyright and often depict commercial products and their logos in a negative light. A more contemporary example of the global proliferation of a Photoshopped social commentary is the now famous "meme" of a police officer causally pepper-spraying students of the University of California at Davis, who are passively sitting on the ground. An artist Photoshopped the cutout of Lieutenant Pike into a famous work of art and began an avalanche of artwork depicting the pepper-spraying officer in historical images, popular films, and historical moments in time, including the Disney film *Snow White*, an album cover of rock band Pink Floyd, Lego constructions, and among many other copyrighted scenes and products. The speed at which these images appeared was shocking, not only to corporate holders of trademarks, but to the University and police officials who desperately wanted the subject to fade into obscurity. Today, when images become "memes," there are sites such as Tumblr, Pinterest, Reddit, and other sites where they can be quickly displayed, shared, and downloaded among global audiences.[31]

Since these digital works of social critique are often created anonymously or collectively and distributed at top speed, there is little a corporation or politician can do to stop them, at least at the source or at the individual receiver. It is for this reason that the importance of the centralized broadcast model becomes critical, as there will then be a central gate at which digital media can be stopped, filtered, investigated, or charged. The decentralized peer-to-peer model does not allow this. Thus peer-to-peer networks or sites using bit Torrent have faced the harshest police actions, from lawsuits to brutal invasion of homes and seizures of hard drives and computers, as in the cases of networks like the original Napster, LimeWire, or Pirate Bay.

Of course, the manipulation of images for social commentary is only a small part of the enormous exchange of manipulated media that goes on today. Video and film clip manipulation and commentary, music mashups, voiceover replacement, phony subtitling under television scenes, and much, much more comprise a large part of what is flowing through the Internet today. It could be truthfully stated that much of this material is just for entertainment, but it would be hard to sort that part out from the large amount of media manipulation that is commentary, social activism, or critique and criticism of commercialism, political hypocrisy, and our current political and social situation, all of which—unlike entertainment—would be protected by the provisions of fair use, without facing copyright restrictions. New laws pushed by mass media lobbyists aim for a chilling and restrictive media environment, carefully controlled by centralized gatekeepers who will drastically impinge such a free exchange of media exchange regardless of its intent.

COPYRIGHT AND OUR CULTURAL COMMONS

There are of course many legitimate reasons for copyright and trademark protections. Certainly the financial protection of creative development, as well as protection of artistic integrity, is important. But there are other reasons that common words and phrases should have some protections from commercial exploitation—to protect the integrity of culture as a whole. A popular source of cultural plunder is the indigenous cultures of North America: Native American tribes that never got around to copyrighting their icons and symbols centuries ago. One can buy Crazy Horse Malt Liquor, named after the famed Oglala Lakota Sioux Chief. One can buy Cherokee Jeans, or a Washington Redskins warmup jacket, or a Jeep Cherokee automobile, or a Dodge Dakota truck. Also for sale: Mohawk Carpets, Mohawk Oil, or Mohawk Paper products. The US military is armed with United Technologies Blackhawk Helicopters, named after an Indian chief, updating the Iroquois Helicopter line. The US military relies upon Apache helicopters, developed by McDonnell-Douglas, now built by Boeing. The military uses Tomahawk Missiles, which took up where Nike missiles left off, Nike being one of the most contested of global corporate brands. Nike, of course, is the Greek god of victory, whose image branded early Nike sneakers. The word *Amazon* is actually owned by Amazon.com as is the word *Denali*.[32] There are literally thousands of corporate brands that owe their images to indigenous cultures around the world, yet these companies boldly claim ownership to the ancient words, symbols, and icons.

There is a belief among some indigenous cultures, regarding the taking of images of people and sacred objects and places, which has historically been presented as proof of their primitivism and backwardness. Crazy Horse, for example, reportedly refused to be photographed. Perhaps it is time to review some of these ideas as a form of cultural and personal copyright. It is increasingly common for advertisers and corporate branders to heist images of individuals that represent qualities they would like to project for their products. A prime example is the use of Charlie Chaplin's image to promote IBM products. In many of these situations, the photographer has the right to distribute the photos, not the person whose picture is taken, particularly if the figure is a public person. Should society allow a lifetime of work, struggle, and achievement by an individual to be seized in a flash of a camera and then sold to a corporate bidder to sell products? The use of a photograph of United Farm Workers founder Cesar Chavez in a national ad campaign to sell Apple computers was one of many such examples. Che Guevara's image shows up on dozens of consumer products, from beer to t-shirts. Perhaps the conviction that a person's visage belongs to him- or herself makes more sense than allowing it to be taken by a stock photographer for commercial value, and who then owns the copyright to it.

As the public's ability to share, circulate, and comment upon popular cultural products is taken away, it begins to reemerge in areas of semi-legality and illegality. As this book makes clear, the desire for free communications forces the public to reenter the public sphere in new and innovative ways. The Internet and the technologies that ride upon it are rife with cracks and crevices that can be taken advantage of to skirt roadblocks and make a point. Some of these practices are condemned as "hacking," but, in fact, there are still many gray areas yet to be characterized. One of these examples is the practice of "Google bombing," a method of coaxing Google's ubiquitous search engine to deliver an audience to a site that makes a political point. Google bombs are very effective in delivering satirical answers to rhetorical questions or key words. Google bombs can direct queries on the popular Google search site to phony error pages or to other sites that usually provide a humorous response to a key word or question. News of these hacks is often relayed along the same distribution networks used by Photoshop pranks, circulated among networks of friends and colleagues who prompt each other with the right search terms to ask. One of the most notorious was the suggestion to type in "miserable failure" in the Google search window, which for a long time returned the Web site of George W. Bush. Google has made claims that it has defeated the ability to Google bomb, but evidence suggests otherwise. During the 2012 election season, Googling "Romney" brought up a Google bomb site, a Web page that only contained a large dictionary description for "Romney"—"Romney (rom-ney) v. 1. To defecate in terror." This definition was a joust at Romney for a reputed story of how he had transported his dog on the roof of his car during a twelve-hour trip to Canada, causing the dog to get diarrhea. A Google analyst noted that it is an impressive stunt to rise to the top of Google in less than a month. Knowing the importance of linking to raise popularity of a site, the analyst noted, "Wow. Not one person links to this site, and yet it makes it so high in Google."[33]

Following in the parody and satire vein, disinformation Web sites remain very popular and confounding to those parodied. Since the Web began, grabbing a Web site in the typical first-come, first-served way proved a convenient way to humiliate the party that was too slow to grab its own domain. For a long time, the site *whitehouse.com* was owned by a purveyor of pornography. To add insult to injury, these sites usually visually imitate the object of satire and serve to confuse and agitate innocent visitors. The Yes Men, a media-pranking group of people who wish to call attention to egregious corporate activity, regularly use deceptive and imitation sites to convey their messages. Some of the most well-known parody sites have included Dow Chemical, the World Trade Organization, and Bank of America. Recently, a site called *arcticready.com* spoofed Shell Oil to raise attention about the impact of global warming and oil exploration in the arctic.[34] In the early days of the Internet, the domain name system maintained by the US government was simple and straightforward, not necessarily deferential to powerful interests with a stake in copyright and trademark. The management of names was privatized and entrusted to the Internet Committee on Assigned Names and Numbers (ICANN), in large part to reassert control over online naming rights. ICANN's attempt at such a policy was drafted in close cooperation with the World Intellectual Property Organization (WIPO), and the result has now become known as the Uniform Dispute Resolution Policy (UDRP). Powerful interests involved with the ICANN have reasserted control over naming by linking domain names to the laws around copyright infringement.

When Web sites are outlawed only outlaws will have Web sites.

Though the incidences of outright hacking, cracking, and electronic crimes are soaring, the only concern of this book centers on acts of illegalities that involve the desire to communicate. Sometimes those who seek to communicate will initiate outright Web hacks that range from focused political education to electronic graffiti. Sometimes the work can only be described as vandalism. Because the perpetrator must crack security and surreptitiously replace files on servers, this type of practice gets much publicity on account of its illegality. Regardless of the swapped content, the result of such intrusion can be called the "Wizard of Oz" effect, in that it punctures the omnipotent strength of the victims. When hackers replace the public Web sites of the CIA, FBI, Pentagon, and Department of Justice, they certainly diminish the power the sites' owners would like to project to the public. Frequent Web site attacks have substantially degraded the once-powerful images of these organizations and have added to the notion of "breaking the façade."

NEW SPHERES OF DISCUSSION

The strategy that often accompanies the "breaking the façade" activities is the creation of new electronic spaces for the free exchange of information and discussion. The eternal guiding principle held dear by many of the pioneers of the Internet has been "information seeks to be free," a philosophy infuriating to official gatekeepers of information in the powerful media chains and in the governments. The increased tension between control and freedom of information is heating up daily and has a dramatic impact on world events. Truth often begins to emerge in these spaces and crevices where unfiltered information can be deposited for public investigation, outside the realm of established media and governmental filters. Once a critical mass of the public begins to recognize and discuss the information, mass media often feels obliged to wade in with its spin and avoid the embarrassment of being left behind on an issue that excites or concerns the public. That citizens can publish original documents, images, evidence, and entire original sources unfiltered by mass media on such a massive scale is something new. WikiLeaks is of course one of the primary spaces of this kind, but there have been many before. Earlier Internet publishing projects of this kind include the release of damning files from cigarette companies detailing their targeting of youth, purloined documents on the instability of software for electronic voting, and the health risks of eating at McDonald's. This type of activity is probably the most frightening for powerful corporate and governmental interests because they allow hard data to be viewed by the public and bypass the "spin" put on the issues by public relations and the mass media. Some of these releases of information may be obtained illegally, some not, but publishing them instantaneously worldwide makes them impossible to retrieve.

A CULTURAL NETWORK OF WORKERS

Visualize a cartoon image of a group of line-drawn characters doubled over with laughter, and one of them is saying, "You want it when?" This image has been Xeroxed, posted, faxed, and passed along from office to office, from warehouse to warehouse, and from factory to factory for many years. Decades even. You can usually find one, not facing outward to superiors, foremen, or customers where all can see, but inward toward the workspace, where it is shared as a communal joke among workers. It is not an example of management-approved humor, but rather a small expression of a griev-ance understood by many workers, an "in" joke. It is a proven source of aggravation to higher-ups, who not only resent the implicit threat it poses, but who also recognize that it was most likely duplicated on company pho-tocopy machines on company time. Often designed by creative but bored office workers, these images proliferate on the distribution model created from a loose network that arose primarily to share jokes via Xerox and fax machines. Who created this image, no one seems to know. Recent blog dis-cussions have claimed various sources, and some report seeing it as early as the 1960s. Over the years, it has elicited chuckles from millions of workers, at least in the English-speaking workplaces of the world, as it has circulated back and forth across the nation.

Workplaces throughout the United States are incubators of creative expression—in media, in art, in jokes, and in folklore, ranging from the cre-atively intelligent to the demonstrably vulgar. Notice the cubicle spaces, the workstations, even the toolboxes of workers who have no dedicated work-space, and you will see touches of play and creativity that help define the workers as individuals who claim those tiny spaces as their own. Outsider art has a huge venue in the workspaces of Americans. Consider the collec-tor of manufacturing ends and leftovers, the desktop sculptor in the office, the collector of misshapen machine rejects, the sketcher and cartoonist, the Photoshop artist whose wry mashup commentary appears on the bulletin boards, the prankster whose messages resound through the office public address system. Their spirit is reflected in the song sung by Johnny Cash, about the autoworker who assembles an entire automobile in his spare time from smuggling out parts of cars over a lifetime on the assembly line.[35] This is all creative energy that happens at work, not only for one's creative self-expression, but also for the community of fellow human beings whom our current economic system has chosen to lump together. *Processed World Magazine*, a popular zine of the 1980s and 1990s, published anonymous "Tales of Toil" from workers in the evolving information age along with much of the workplace-made cutups, montages, cartoons, and illustrations that critiqued the conditions of work through sarcasm and humor.[36]

As noted in previous chapters, the contributions of workers are rarely recognized in relation to cultural exchanges on social networking, yet workers have played a long and vital role in building a shared communications tradition of jokes, images, anecdotes, and observations about the nature and conditions of work, typically under the radar of employers and managers. These preconditions transition easily to a more electronic form of workers' social networking, whether an informal means of sharing cultural products or a more formal networking for jobs, the function that sites like LinkedIn are trying to commercialize.

Almost everyone has a desire and a need for creative expression and play, although most people will never have an opportunity to indulge in such activity as a full-time occupation. There are exceptions of course, such as former cubicle-dweller Scott Adams, whose doodles and ruminations became the cartoon strip *Dilbert*, or Matt Groening, whose *Work Is Hell* series spawned a generation of workplace pushpin and eraser sculptures. The creative urge remains, however, and typically manifests in seemingly unproductive ways: checking Facebook at work, texting jokes, or posting humorous images on Web sites. It is no secret that the working day has spilled over into traditional free time in the last decade. The extent to which e-mail, social networking, and mobile communications has invaded free time has become a given. For many occupations, there is no escape from work. For many people, surrender is inevitable. Answering e-mails on a weekend or updating Facebook late at night blurs the boundaries between leisure and labor, as friendships blur together with work contacts. That these activities are perceived as "fun" is good news for US corporate enterprises that rely upon ever increasing levels of volunteer labor and productivity.

What is lost by the enclosure of free time into the domain of social and entertainment commodities is still not clear. The long-term economic benefits of activity are also unclear. What is clear, however, is that the conflict over work and leisure time does not represent any significant break with the recent past. The struggle over the length of the workday has been an integral aspect of the capitalist system since its beginnings. Though the type of work performed has changed dramatically, much of the "new" economy is still based upon marketing and direct advertising, dependent upon cultivating and holding audiences and selling products that are still manufactured or grown in more traditional workplaces.

The desire for one's labor and creative effort to be recognized is a long-standing one, going back to early craft workers who branded or initialized metal work, pottery, or woodwork. In an era of global labor, where pieces of labor come from disparate corners of the globe to be assembled and mass-marketed, individual recognition for work is almost nonexistent. This is particularly true in the software and entertainment industries, where the name Disney or Microsoft subsumes the creative talent of tens of thousands of workers. Workers leave evidence of individuality in many of these products, however. Some spaces in which workers leave their mark operate like "permission" walls for graffiti, where management looks the other way and ignores the transgression. Other worker marks surface later, often to the embarrassment of the megacorporation. Programmers often like to leave telltale signs of their labor and participation in the software development, leaving behind "Easter eggs" and "trapdoors" that can be accessed by those in the know, a form of electronic geo-caching. Animators have slipped in single-frame images that push the boundaries of good taste and become points of bragging rights. Notorious examples have included quasi-pornographic imagery in Disney cartoons, from films like *Roger Rabbit* and others. Electronic circuit designers have included various doodles and cultural imagery that skirt the laws around trademark infringement. When a microcircuit is designed, the artwork is shrunk and etched on a tiny wafer of silicon, making the original invisible to the naked eye. When the chip is cracked open and viewed under an electron microscope, the image becomes visible. Treasure hunters of these microscopic graffiti works search for these images and post them to collectors' Web sites. The collection is a repository of trademark infringement: Mr. T, the Marshmallow Man, Dilbert, and probably most insulting, the Linux penguin that will power many computers running Microsoft and other proprietary software.[37]

THE WAY FORWARD

Ultimately, what is the impact of such activities? While some pundits like to dismiss them all as the trivial work of isolated individuals, the total effect of technopranks is having a substantial impact on public life. Exchanges between workers about conditions of labor mixed with sarcasm or absurdity develop pathways of communication that deepen the level of conversation in the public sphere. That is not to say that all this sharing is limited to humor. Workers have been on the leading edge of developing new and direct channels of information for the public sphere. The leaking of sensitive information is typically done not by outside investigators, but by workers who are confronted with the knowledge of terrible things they feel compelled to share with the public. Probably the most infamous leak in current memory is that of the Pentagon papers. The nefarious activities of the United States in Southeast Asia were brought to light thanks to the conscience of Daniel Ellsberg, who arranged publication of documents to which he had access when he was working at the Rand Corporation. The irresponsibility of the nuclear industry was leaked thanks to the work of Kerr-McGee employee Karen Silkwood. The massive WikiLeaks release of documents related to the Iraq-Afghanistan wars was reported to have originated from an employee of the US armed forces with direct access to classified documents. Contrary to popular notions of anonymous computer hackers ferreting out information in the middle of the night, most whistle-blower data and media are released by workers with in-depth knowledge of the subjects. Workers' communications activities on social networks bring benefits ranging from sharing raw documents directly to the public, to questioning and satirizing powerful interests, to deflating the omnipotent power of corporations and government, to building horizontal links between millions of people. The electronic communications activities of workers will continue to flourish, although no doubt under the radar of mainstream media. The growing social links between students and youth, activists, workers, artists, scholars, scientists, and citizens of all nations are transforming the ability to communicate freely in an increasingly global culture.

While the infrastructure that permits this communication is expanding, what people talk about or share with one another is increasingly threatened. A posting of a clip of a favorite soap opera may seem a far cry from the posting of a classified document, yet they are united by the fact that their content is under increasing scrutiny by governmental and private organizations with the clout and police power to intervene. In some countries, it is the multinational corporations that are leading the charge on Internet restriction, while in others, it is authoritarian governmental regimes. One can find a plethora of examples that illustrate these restrictions. In the United States alone, there are many hundreds of Web sites that have been seized and shutdown by the Immigration and Customs Enforcement agency (ICE) through their Operation In Our Sites campaign, with the ceremonial seal of ICE placed on their homepage positions. According to the American Civil Liberties Union, "ICE has been shutting down Web sites allegedly involved in illicit online activities on very little legal basis, without any adversarial hearing and without providing notice until weeks or months later. Court orders permitting domain name seizures are made on the basis of ex parte affidavits, meaning that only the government presents evidence and Web site operators have no opportunity to be heard or to respond to allegations until after their Web sites have been shut down. As several legal scholars have pointed out, this violates the Fifth Amendment's due process clause and the First Amendment."[38] Some of these seized sites are part of copyright infringement disputes, but others are simply attacks on the very premise of anonymity on the Internet. Corralling Internet communications into the centralized models government and corporation prefer means eliminating the possibility for privacy that many have depended upon. It is this anonymity that has enabled people around the world to speak out without facing punishment, an ability that many governments celebrate even as they attempt to eliminate that kind of privacy. In the spring of 2012, federal authorities removed a server operated by three long-time progressive ISP groups based in New York City as part of a criminal investigation. According to a statement issued by the Association for Progressive Computing (APC), "The FBI has effectively shut down service to hundreds of users and their harsh actions can only be interpreted as threatening to anonymous use of the Internet. 'Like other anonymizing services such as the

TOR network [the Onion Router network], these remailers are widely used to protect the identity of human rights activists who place themselves and their families in grave danger by reporting information about abuses,' the ISP statement continues. Remailers are also important for corporate whistle blowers, democracy activists working under repressive regimes, and others to communicate vital information that would otherwise go unreported."[39] The APC statement was endorsed by many individuals and groups active in democratic communications, including Deep Dish Television, Richard Stallman, Free Network Foundation, National Lawyers Guild, and Programa LaNeta. In China, using keywords such as "China democracy" in a search engine can reroute or shut down a computer connection. While that may seem somewhat Orwellian, this manipulation of the search process is also operational in the United States, as Google has bent to pressure from corporate interests who want to ensure that their products rank higher than those deemed to have a negative impact on their brand. Google has announced that copyright complaints based upon provisions in the Digital Millennium Copyright Act (DMCA) will be a factor in search logarithms, even though complaints may be unproven or spurious. Business reporter Thomas Claburn wrote in *Information Week*, "Google Search should not participate in copyright enforcement any more than a hardware store should restrict the sale of hammers to prevent a potential crime. It should not circumvent the judicial process by passing judgment on Web sites just because someone complains. The legal system presumes innocence until guilt is proven; Google should make the same presumption."[40] Many constitutional rights that Americans take for granted are not valid in the new Internet environment. Assumptions about innocence before guilt are not operational when Web sites can be taken down simply by having a complaint filed. Protected forms of privacy that require a search warrant are ignored as well. Nevertheless, democratic communications are hard to resist, especially when so many people have experienced their benefits and have learned the appropriate skills to evade censorship and political filters.

This chapter discussed two primary types of activities under the headings of "breaking the façade" and "new electronic spheres of communication." There will doubtlessly be many new forms of alternative communications that exploit the loopholes in new laws or violate them completely. In the near future, these new practices will make it necessary to expand, amend, or toss out the categories of communications resistance I have proposed. In any case, it is abundantly clear that activists building the new democratic communications environment will be up against powerful economic, political, and military forces that recognize that the one who controls the means and content of communications will win the day. Recent events on the world stage suggest that democratic communications will be the ultimate victor.

6   The Shape of Things to Come

The current communications environment in which we live would certainly seem like a science fiction scenario come to life from the perspective of someone like H. G. Wells, steampunk icon and preeminent science-fiction writer from the end of the nineteenth century. As Wells prophesied in his 1898–99 serialized work *The Sleeper Awakes*, "After telephone, kinematograph, and phonograph had replaced newspaper, book, schoolmaster, and letter, to live outside the range of the electric cables was to live an isolated savage."[1] Jules Verne, another legendary science-fiction writer from the same period, wrote of "piano-electro-reckoners," "telephotes," and "phonotelephotic" communications, devices that would allow instant computation and personal audiovisual communications at great distances.[2]

In the twenty-first century, we move in a cloud of data, clutching personal televisual electronics, plugging listening devices into our ears, and accessing and sending information instantly to and from distant corners of the globe. Wells and Verne would no doubt be surprised to see that many features from their own age would still be recognizable. The means of human communications are still considered commodities to be bought and sold within a marketplace. Powerful monopoly interests still wield their financial and political clout to accumulate and control their communications markets. In many cases, these monopoly powers bear the same names: AT&T, Western Union, and General Electric, for example. Our futuristic communications technologies may seem radically new, but their roots grow in the same ground as they did at the beginning of the electromechanical era. In order to consider the current directions of media and communications, it is essential to understand the role played by telegraph, wireless telegraphy, film projection, sound amplification, telephony, AM and FM radio, television, cable, satellites, and computer networks. These seemingly separate technological milestones are in fact part of the same trajectory that links today's iPhone, Facebook, and YouTube users. These histories and the paradigm they have created still weigh enormously on the promise of new democratic avenues of public communications. New media technologies and their role in revitalizing public discourse have certainly risen to the fore in recent years and show no signs of abating. Creators of democratic media on the local level, the global level, and among a newly awakened and globalized working class show much promise in this regard. As this democratic tendency rises, so, too, does resistance against it on the part of those in powerful political, economic, and military positions who benefit from controlling the means of communications.

SURVEILLANCE AS MASS MEDIA

One of the most contentious challenges posed by new media technologies is the invasion of one's personal life and the threat that technologies represent to personal privacy. It is increasingly apparent that at any moment of day or night, our voices, images, actions, and coordinates can be observed, recorded, networked, digitized, stored, and shared. The cameras are watching when we drive through an intersection near the change of the light. The cameras stare through grey, plastic lenses when we withdraw money from the ATM. They track us when we enter the airport, train station, or bus station. They stare down from the ceiling behind the cash register when we make a purchase at the convenience store. They can note whether we take the elevator or walk down the stairs in our offices or workplaces. They watch us as we walk to our parked cars in the parking lot.

Our data trails are equally marked. Cached and duly recorded on servers and databases across the planet, it is noted when and where we made a bank deposit, bought a particular product, took a trip, rented a video, crossed a tollbooth, or checked out a book. Rather than simply record these mundane transactions, some systems go a step further—analyzing, postulating, and making assumptions about their meanings. How much a person drinks alcoholic beverages. What kind of laundry detergent a person prefers. What genre of media entertainment a person likes. Outcomes could determine what coupons to offer, what prices to charge, or what products or services to offer for sale. They may also lead to more judgmental questions. Why did he buy two different types of toothpaste if he lives alone? Why did she buy a bottle of Jack Daniels, when she says she doesn't drink? He says he's healthy, but he purchased a prescription drug at Walgreen's last week. She's been looking at job search Web sites this week. He's been Googling self-help sites. Her cell phone log shows lots of calls to New York. "If you are looking up the word *cancer* on a health site," says Dan Auerbach, a staff technologist at the Electronic Frontier Foundation, a digital rights group in San Francisco, "there's a high probability that you have cancer or are interested in that. This is the sort of data that can be collected."[3] These invasions of personal privacy have many consumers' rights groups arguing for a stronger "do not track" option built into Web browsers, an option that has the advertising industry up in arms.[4]

Not only are our activities being monitored by external mechanisms, but our own personal devices are betraying us as well. Our cell phones reveal our present whereabouts and record our coordinates up to years at a time. Radio-frequency identification (RFID) tags on our credit cards and driver's licenses can transmit our data trail as we move through a maze of RFID readers. Our computers reveal our unique identification numbers to central servers, routers, and Internet service providers. Global Positioning System (GPS) units track our driving locations. Even our home computer printers have hidden codes that can reveal a user's identity.[5] These details do not even take into account the many times a day we willingly and purposely reveal our actions, thoughts, travels, and other personal information in our tweets, Facebook postings, Instagram uploads, and blogs. This self-posted information is now routinely read by potential employers and police investigators. Our visual, aural, network, and data information leave a shadowy trail of our activities, habits, purchases, health concerns, and other evidence that create a composite picture of who we are. Not just who we want people to believe we are, but also who we are in our private lives. Many people have come to believe that having centralized records, which could become available for inspection or purchase, is a strong violation of our right to privacy and our right "to be left alone," a central tenet of the US Constitution.[6]

This rapidly expanding system of surveillance and data-veillance has been compared to a high-tech panopticon, the engineering solution popularized in the 1800s that creates a central point from which a viewer observes all activities taking place in any location without being observed him- or herself. From its origin as a tool of incarceration, the panopticon has become ubiquitous, extending from the prison and the factory to the shopping mall and the town square, an ideal mechanism engineered by those in power to keep an eye on the potentially disruptive lower classes and the have-nots. The goal of the panopticon is not only to observe, but also to transfer self-control to the subjugated. The premise is that the mere idea that the subject is being watched is as effective as actually watching him or her. Our new electronic panopticon extends the visual control system beyond the physical and architectural domain of structures, streets, and dwellings, to the electronic observance of personal habits and activities peculiar to the commercial, medical, entertainment, and personal transactions of the populace. In the relatively tranquil political environment of the United States, where the population is largely rendered politically apathetic through the ideological and cultural manufacture of consent,[7] the value of consumers' activities and economic choices is perhaps more relevant than their political ambitions. Nonetheless, whether the terrain is the battle site over market share for a particular consumer brand or for ideological and political allegiances, a similar seizure of information and data is desired. In the lean, globalized, just-in-time production system driven by point-of-sale data streams, information on the consumers' minutest twitches becomes a valuable commodity. This realization has led transnational corporations to covet the data and analysis of contemporary consumers' buying habits, dredged from electronic card swipes, online activities, product registrations, and other gimmicks. This same process is equally valuable to political campaigns that strive to understand and respond to the "buying" trends of the American electorate. This access to personal data, oftentimes harvested through "cookies" planted via Web browsers, reached a pinnacle in the 2012 presidential election, when campaign callers were "guided by scripts and call lists compiled by people—or computers—with access to details like whether voters may have visited pornographic Web sites, have homes in foreclosure, are more prone to drink Michelob Ultra than Corona, have gay friends, or enjoy expensive vacations."[8] It is this access to personal data that has placed Silicon Valley giants Google, Facebook, Yahoo, and other online sites in the Wall Street speculative spotlight. The question of how to turn personal data access into stock market gold nags the nervous stockholders of these relative newcomers to the stock exchanges. Facebook's reliance upon harvesting data is key to its attempts to assure investors of its profitability. According to the analysts, "Facebook's new forays reveal the rich trail of data that consumers can leave, often unwittingly, every time they buy groceries with a loyalty card or when they longingly eye a pair of shoes online. All of that data can trickle back to Facebook: with nearly a billion users, the company can find those consumers when they log on to Facebook and direct tailored ads to them. In an experiment that stirred some controversy, Facebook linked arms with Datalogix, a data-mining company, to glean what individual shoppers buy at offline stores. Datalogix says it gets this information from loyalty card data and other sources."[9]

As a society, we have grown accustomed to such personal inspection. In the early days of the Web, several revelations began to surface that momentarily angered many Internet users. There was an outcry when it surfaced that many Web sites secretly inserted "cookies" onto computer users' hard drives that could send back information on the user to the Web site producer. There was a similar outcry when it was reported that many Web sites were running third-party software applications in the background of browsers that took note of links Web surfers clicked on. Another revelation that quickly blew over was the realization that the Apple iPhone tracked and stored the geographic coordinates of their users over long periods of time.[10]

There has been resistance to the blanket of surveillance thrown upon the planet. Google's Street View maps have been banned in places, where even the sight of Google's roaming camera-vehicles has produced assault and vandalism by angry crowds. Hostility to the Google vehicles has grown after it was discovered that the Google vehicles were gathering data from wireless networks active in the areas they recorded.[11] Facial recognition software used by Google, used in conjunction with digital images, is also subject to restriction by nations who fear the loss of anonymity in public.[12] Devoid of any concrete, articulated reason to oppose it, the majority of the US public, however, tends to accept the invasion of privacy. The majority believes there is no reason to oppose these measures because "they have nothing to hide." To oppose such surveillance may also invite suspicion, particularly as governments typically use either pornographic trafficking or terrorist activities as reasons to excuse privacy invasion. So, many people self-consciously pose for cameras in public spaces, and aware that they are always within earshot, they watch what they say on their cell phone, careful not to get caught doing something they may find embarrassing or that could embroil them in legal problems.

Such logic is hard to argue against. In a post–9/11 world, there are terrorists to trap. There are also legitimate businesses that want to capture the public's demographic urges. Many citizens prefer not to consider the subtle effects that follow from surveillance measures that wear down, inhibit, and degrade the privacy rights of citizens. For beyond the obvious invasion of privacy lies an even darker result, a long-term erosion of spontaneous, popular expression and public activity.

It has been long surmised that the realization that one is being looked at leads to the development of a strong sense of self-censorship, enforcing a regime of personal inhibition, and leading to a subsequent withdrawal from public activities. Over time, this internalized sense of being watched will cause a populace to "perform" at all times and behave according to an assigned script of expected behavior, a prescribed mode of behavior, so that one subsequently abandons a true sense of being a free agent who possesses free will. Such a chilling effect is a perfect accompaniment to an already well-established system of mass media that encourages passivity, detachment, and futility.

Though many bemoan this degradation of privacy, the technology that supports it continues to grow by leaps and bounds, seemingly moved along by unseen hands. Like a Frankenstein with a video camera, the technology has, according to many, taken on a life of its own. Progress has its price, after all. Libertarian ideologues and technological fetishists alike wring their hands as if nothing can be done, as if there are no human hands that hang the cameras, mount the microphones, tap in the code, or execute the commands. According to this popular position, technology cannot be stopped, nor can it be regulated. Critics respond that technology does not have a life of its own, despite the Promethean myths that surround it. To use a popular cinematic metaphor, there is a wizard behind the curtain, pulling the levers and calling out the orders. It only takes someone to pull the curtain aside to then discover that the people behind the curtain are prominent players in governments, corporations, and institutions that benefit from intrusions into citizens' personal lives. Beyond the edifices of their corporations or organizations are real people who have names and addresses, social security numbers, and phone numbers. But revealing that, of course, would be a violation of their privacy.

In the classic dystopian vision, illustrated in countless popular books, television programs, films, and music—*1984*, *Brave New World*, *The Wall*, *The Prisoner*, *Brazil*, *V for Vendetta*, and *Invasion of the Body Snatchers*, for example—the citizen is stifled by an omnipresent layer of cameras, microphones, and electronic intrusions, making it difficult to do anything but go along with the preordained rhythm of the masses. After all, no one wants to stand out, or struggle against the state-imposed "spiral of silence." This level of surveillance already feels natural to many because communications have always been centralized and dominated by institutions that remain out of the control of the average person. A strong assumption is that "there is really nothing anyone can do" because the citizen typically has no business challenging the technological and communications decisions made by experts. With this bleak assessment, frightfully illustrated by popular culture, it is altogether too easy to fall into the dichotomy of perpetrator/victim that pits the passive populace against the aggressive, authoritarian central corporation or government. In fact, the situation is far more fluid and complex than that and is changing rapidly. I would argue that our contemporary information, communications, and data environment is not yet our dystopian prison but, more realistically, a contested terrain, a contestation that is in great flux, with both victories and defeats for different interests. It is, in fact, part of an information war that has been brewing for many decades.

Embedded in the history of communications lies the dormant hope of developing a media system that is truly democratic, a two-way system that propagates from sender to receiver and from receiver to sender. In contrast, our contemporary media model is constructed around the broadcasting model, enabling a centralized power to control the flow of information and ideas outward to the populace. The audience then participates in a weak "feedback" loop, returning information back to the centralized core, whether with responses to programming, consumer activities, voting habits, or personal data. The consumers of media send in purchase cards, participate in surveys, join focus groups, get retail "club" cards, and submit the details of their lives to centralized databases. A small percentage may even submit the occasional "letter to the editor." Thus the American people participate in "two-way" communication.

But all is not bleak.

Surveillance is a double-edged sword. The modern means of surveillance have often been used to repress, harass, exploit, and subjugate citizens and workers across the planet, especially those who refuse and resist their assigned roles and status in life. But in many instances, these same tools have also been used to fight back against powerful forces, in an attempt to reassert free association, open the democratic process, and promote social justice. The question over who is watching whom will be at the heart of a global struggle to determine whether our communications technologies will be used as weapons to suppress the populace or as tools to empower them. A cell phone video that records police abusing a citizen, a WikiLeaks release of cables that expose bribery, a hacker's stolen cell phone transcripts that publish corporate malfeasance: all are manifestations of a fight back against secrecy and a stand for the people's "right to know." Now that both sides of this media equation have roughly the same access to the same tools, surveillance initiated by the public will be much harder to control. Thus there will be a strong push for new legislative, judicial, and technological means to outlaw, marginalize, and restrict the means for democratic communications. The strategy that supports corporate media interests will be rife with contradiction, as it will not aim to ban the technology but to impact its intent, its use, and its control over obtaining, recording, and analyzing visual, aural, and informational data. The arguments will come down, in a decidedly anti-democratic fashion, to a question of political, economic, and police power. Yet the linking of democracy and communications power is increasingly connected in the public's mind, and that association will be hard to roll back. When people begin to articulate their own media agenda and generate their own investigations and discussions, the agenda of mainstream media can be diverted, to the chagrin of entertainment executives, official public relations officials, advertising executives, and spinmeisters, who profit from their dominant media positions. The public's construction of its own media power began decades ago as a little stream, and now has become a torrent and one of the prime factors of the decline of the centralized and monopolized system of state/corporate power over information. In recent history, a steady progression of communications technologies have contributed to equalizing the balance between the people's investigative power and corporate/state surveillance, from instant photographs and photocopy machines, to camcorders and computers, to networks and cell phones.

COUNTER-SURVEILLANCE AND POPULAR POWER

In the mid-1960s, G. William Domhoff wrote a book called *Who Rules America*, an innovative work that was as much research as it was counter-surveillance.[13] Following in the tradition of muckraking journalists like Lincoln Steffens[14] and insurgent sociologists like C. Wright Mills,[15] Domhoff revealed the US elite, not as an abstract, theoretical concept, but as people who rule the United States in their work, socializing, and entertaining. One such investigation revealed to the public the existence of the infamous Bohemian Grove gatherings, the annual, highly secretive social gathering of the highest echelons of people who controlled political and ruling-class power in the United States.[16] It was a rude intrusion into the personal lives of the US upper classes, who have always been pleased to have access to scholars who study the social demographics, patterns, and habits of less powerful people, but certainly not happy to have their own secrets, haunts, and mating habits revealed, as if they, too, behaved as a class and not as individuals. New trends during the 1960s emerged as part of the radical student movement that challenged traditional practices of not only sociology, which typically examined the lower social classes, but anthropology as well, which paternalistically looked at Third-World societies from the perspective of the industrialized West. Turning this academic lens around revived a long tradition of power structure research, which investigated the interlocking ties of those who sat on the boards of directors of major corporations, universities, think tanks, and powerful institutions. Power structure research was a strong tool for trade unions, environmentalists, antiwar activists, and others who sought to pressure offending institutions and push for social reforms by uncovering the individuals hiding behind the cloak of the corporation. Revealing the class contradictions of American society in such a stark manner demystified the workings of a system that often remained shrouded in monolithic and secretive corporate, social, and institutional entities.

Such an approach became an integral part of those seeking to challenge the monopolies of the media as well. Professor of journalism Ben Bagdikian was instrumental in developing power structure research of the US mass media in his collection of essays, *The Effete Conspiracy and Other Crimes of the Press*,[17] and in his later *The Media Monopoly*.[18] In these works, Bagdikian made the then-blasphemous observation that the mass media was influenced and controlled by an upper class through its ownership of corporations, and thus structurally conveyed their ideologies through the media they sell. Paper Tiger Television, which once featured Bagdikian in one of its video productions,[19] produced many tapes on the subject of who owns media, from magazines such as *Time*[20] and *Vogue*[21] to the television networks.[22] One of Paper Tiger's numerous publications included a chart illustrating ownership of the three major television networks in a spread titled, "Know Your Connections."[23] Herbert Schiller, an influential professor of media, contributed work that exposed the corporate and governmental manipulation and control of what he referred to as the "culture industry."[24] Bringing power structure research into the World Wide Web age, Web designer Josh On's *They Rule* is an interactive Web site that uses corporate and government data to reveal the connections between major corporations and the military-industrial complex.[25] With the rapid advancement in online research tools and databases, investigations that follow data trails that wind through financial statements, political appointments, interlocking directorates, and foreign bank accounts have become much easier. But power structure research is not the only type of investigation that has proven valuable to confronting a misbalance of power. Physical evidence and counter-surveillance have proven valuable as well and have become major symbols of the clash between the secrecy of authoritarianism and the openness of a democratic society.

The Black Panther Party (BPP), perhaps the most influential political movement of the 1960s, began as a counter-surveillance project.[26] The founders of the BPP—Huey P. Newton, Bobby Seale, and others—then students at Merritt College in Oakland, decided that the single most important action they could take to assist the Black community was to trail police officers' cars through the ghetto and to document cases of harassment and brutality. The Oakland Police Department, which admittedly spied on Oakland's Black community for years, could not bear the thought that the lens could be reversed and turned back toward them. Much of the enmity and hostility that arose between the Oakland Police and the Black Panthers originated in the confrontations that erupted when Panthers members simply followed the police as they cruised through the overwhelmingly African-American community of Oakland. Community self-defense organizations in cities across the United States adopted similar tactics, and citizens' counter-surveillance became a common strategy for emboldening communities that had been historically abused by police. Progressing from film cameras and early Portapak video units to digital camcorders, cell phones, and computer-based distribution networks, grassroots counter-surveillance activity has fundamentally altered the balance of power between rogue police departments and communities of color.

In 1992–1993 a public video festival and exhibition was mounted in Buffalo, New York, by the Hallwalls Contemporary Arts center called, *Video Witnesses: Networking in the 90s.* Some of the titles shown included *Cops and Camcorders* by Barbara Lattanzi and Jim Hartel, *Hands on the Verdict: The 1992 Uprising* by Los Angeles Video Activists (including Liz Canner and Julia Meltzer), *Witness This!* by Lynn Hughes and Milwaukee Newsreel, and *Feed*, a compilation of off-air video moments from the 1992 New Hampshire presidential primary intercepted by satellite television feeds taken by artist Brian Springer.[27] The installations and screenings brought attention to the developing power of citizen video and its ability to aid in exposing injustice to the rest of the world. This eye-opening program helped develop the idea that repression does not need to remain invisible, and the public does not have to be on the losing end of surveillance. Perhaps more importantly, *Video Witnesses* demonstrated that there was a developing global community interested in both viewing and contributing to an exchange of citizen surveillance. The Los Angeles uprising in 1992 sparked by the video capture of the beating of Rodney King is perhaps the most famous manifestation of the video as witness. There are, in fact, hundreds of videos captured on small-format videotapes that have been passed around samizdat-like during that decade preceding cell phone cameras and social networks, including one in which this author was personally involved. A physical struggle between Western Shoshone Native American elder Carrie Dann and a federal Bureau of Land Management agent in the desolate high desert of central Nevada was captured on videotape by a traveler who had just happened to be visiting the Dann ranch. The tape was quickly brought to Mission Creek Video in San Francisco by writer Rebecca Solnit after the incident. The tape was edited by myself and cablecast repeatedly on public access television channels across the United States. Snippets of the tape were broadcast on CNN, and over 100 copies of it were mailed to leaders of American Indian tribes and members of Congress, thanks to an emergency video duplication grant offered by a nonprofit foundation. Further videotaping was completed and edited into a documentary short entitled *Newe Sogobia Is Not for Sale!* and exhibited in many film festivals across the United States.[28] The footage of two elderly Native American woman and one elderly Native American man fighting off federal agents on horseback resonated deeply with viewers. The response was an upsurge of public support for the Western Shoshone people in their 100-year-old battle against the federal government for self-determination.

The ongoing struggle of the Western Shoshone clearly demonstrated the spread of new communications tools in the videotape era.[29] The Shoshone elders were no strangers to technology and were actively engaged in deploying a string of their own surveillance tools to monitor and report back on Bureau of Land Management maneuvers on their land, using radiotelephone units and roving reconnaissance volunteers. The Shoshone also scanned police band frequencies for any hint of activity in the area. Fax machines and other devices helped them to stay in touch with supporters in the metropolitan areas, far from their trailers and offices in the middle of the high desert of Nevada. When the rural, elderly, Native American Western Shoshone embraced electronic communications to defend their traditional way of life, they broke several strong stereotypes: that new technology was only for the young, that rural people have no use for it, and that technology has no place in traditional cultures. These globally publicized events in the desert proved that social networking was in place well before the public embraced the Internet.

THE FREEING OF INFORMATION

The introduction and embrace of the World Wide Web brought a powerful new set of counter-surveillance tools and distribution methods. The same type of electronic tools that benefit the global economic empires of transnational corporations can also be of value to those who choose to push back against corporate abuse and governmental repression. Controversial documents, which in the past would remain in dusty archives, have been exposed to mass audiences and have taken on great new significance in public debate. Though many people associate electronic whistle blowing and data dumping with the contemporary WikiLeaks, there is a long, well-documented history of releasing public documents through controversial means. Early in the 1990s, an anonymous person or persons dropped off boxes of purloined tobacco industry documents from the Brown and Williamson Tobacco Company to the University of California, San Francisco, Tobacco Research Center. A veritable "Pentagon papers" of the tobacco industry, the revelations delivered a powerful blow to the tobacco industry's claims of ignorance about the health risks associated with their products. The UCSF researchers digitally scanned the documents and posted them on the World Wide Web for everyone to see. By the time the disappearance of the documents was noticed and reported stolen, the researchers had already published the files electronically on the Internet. Today those files can still be viewed at the Research Center.[30] Likewise, purloined e-mails exchanged between technicians working for the Diebold Corporation and posted to the Web instantly pushed the dangers of electronic voting onto the public agenda. In the e-mails, the technicians noted how easily their systems could be broken into and how voting tallies could be manipulated. Rather than be concerned about the shortcomings of their product, Diebold fought to keep their problems private, even though the flaws could impact national elections. According to the *New York Times*, "Diebold Election Systems, which makes voting machines, is waging legal war against grassroots advocates, including dozens of college students, who are posting on the Internet copies of the company's internal communications about its electronic voting machines."[31] What made these claims even more damning was the revelation that the Diebold Corporation has strong ties to the Republican Party.[32] Diebold used copyright provisions of the Digital Millennium Copyright Act in its attempt to punish publishers of the files. Revelations of the fragility of electronic voting caused many states to move away from electronic voting and place renewed insistence on paper-based back up. Public access to data and documents is not always as dramatic, yet it can yield critical results to significant groups of people. Instant access to data allows trade union negotiators to quickly tap into the financial statements of corporate representatives during collective bargaining, and industrial workers can access the databases of chemical manufacturers for more accurate information about the health risks posed to those who work with dangerous substances. Corporations may bemoan their loss of data monopoly, but it has become clear that increased public access to information levels the playing field for many in the new data-driven environment.

What has accelerated the amount of electronic whistle blowing and the unveiling of secret documents is, of course, the exponential growth of social-networking computing sites and the now ubiquitous availability of computational network tools. From Facebook, Twitter, and YouTube to Archive.org and WikiLeaks, these sites are Holy Grails for media activists who have long chafed at the contradiction of having many new tools for media production but few means to reach a mass audience. These electronic spaces are proving integral to the continuation of the counter-surveillance models that began with the early video witness movement. The success of such screen-based portals flies in the face of the many broadcast industry experts who for a long time insisted that high definition (HD) programming and surround sound will be the future for media. Industry experts wince at the thought that the new video platform may not be expensive new HD flat panels, but the tiny, low-fidelity cell phone, which acts as both camera and monitor. Industry leaders are expressing a rising panic that the market will shift away from computer screens altogether, as millions adopt the convenience and mobility of smart phones. There is strong evidence that the shift to mobile platforms deflated the initial stock offering of Facebook, a platform that up until now has been strongly invested in users accessing their network via a computer screen.[33]

YouTube has grown to be a major headache to politicians and to law enforcement agencies since it has become a central location for exposing and sharing evidence of the abuse of authority in the United States and across the globe. By now a legion of infamous YouTube exposures have been seen by millions of viewers worldwide. An early effective public video posting was the documentation of a politician from Virginia, Senator George Allen, chiding the student of Indian descent who was videotaping him with the epithet "macaca," meaning "monkey."[34] Viewed many hundreds of thousands of times, Allen's racist language, aimed at the young person of color who wielded a video camera, played a large role in the Senator's reelection defeat. The beating of William Cardenas by the Los Angeles Police Department,[35] and the shooting of a student with a Taser gun in the University of California, Los Angeles, library[36] have sealed the reputation of the cell phone video as a central tool for counter-surveillance by a vigilant public. A landmark case that demonstrated the might of YouTube exposures was the tragic shooting death of Oscar Grant in an Oakland, California, Bay Area Rapid Transit station on New Year's Day in 2009. Video postings from cell phone operators on the scene at the station showed the horrible scene unfold as police officers pinned down and shot the young man in the head.[37] The video footage electrified the city of Oakland and created numerous large and sometimes violent protests. The roots of the Occupy Oakland militancy are often traced to the energy generated from the Oscar Grant episode. Such video recordings have become normal aspects of courtroom and judicial proceedings. In a high profile case in New York City, a nineteen-year-old man named Luis Solivan was charged with assaulting a police officer and spent two weeks in jail awaiting his hearing. His case was dropped when a grand jury watched a video Solivan's acquaintance had shot through his Bronx apartment window. While the police claimed that Solivan attacked both officers and tried to take their guns, the video showed the police brutally beating Solivan, using pepper spray, and slamming his head against a wall while handcuffed. The *New York Times* reported that "Ilann M. Maazel, a lawyer representing Mr. Solivan, said that but for the video, 'I think there's a real likelihood that the grand jury would have indicted him.' 'What it shows is shocking,' Mr. Maazel added. 'It revealed that the police did not tell the truth and they wanted to put an innocent man in jail, potentially for many years.'"[38] One would think that examples of video use would be beneficial to the upholding of justice and of innocence before guilt has been proven, but police departments and governments are conducting serious efforts toward technology that will disable mobile cameras when they deem "necessary." Apple has patented technology that would do just that. According to Apple, "[C]overt police or government operations may require complete 'blackout' conditions." Apple says that "as wireless devices such as cellular telephones, pagers, personal media devices, and smart phones become ubiquitous, more and more people are carrying these devices in various social and professional settings. . . . The result is that these wireless devices can often annoy, frustrate, and even threaten people in sensitive venues."[39] The technology would give authorities the ability to shut down the capacity for cell phones to take photos or video, thus ending the remarkable tide of citizen media intervention that has captured brutalities, injustices, and unlawfulness around the globe. At least that is what is hoped for, although undoubtedly technically savvy alternative media activists are already looking at ways to hack the technology. Still, the power of citizens' cameras continues unabated, knocking down and exposing powerful corporations and politicians. The video capture and posting of presidential candidate Mitt Romney at a private fundraising event dismissing "47 percent" of US citizens as unimportant is another damning example.[40] Animal rights activists and healthy food advocates have also have championed the use of personal video capture. The "pink slime" video taken at a meat processing plant in 2012 and linked to what eventually becomes fast-food meat products is either credited or blamed with shutting that entire industry down in what has now become a major legal case.[41]

As the power of public communications expands, police, corporate, and governmental representatives recorded in acts of illegal or compromising activities often attempt to "spin" or contextualize these crimes and misdemeanors; nevertheless, the visual and aural power of video is overwhelmingly clear. Loss of media control has not been positive for authoritarian and anti-democratic forces. The conflict between espousing the free flow of information and attempting to squelch that free flow of information has been growing for many years. Two examples have taken center stage in recent years that put this contention in high contrast. Only a few years ago, WikiLeaks was a relatively obscure Web site where whistle blowers could release documents anonymously to be distributed to as wide a public as possible. With the release of the Iraq-Afghanistan papers, WikiLeaks rocketed from obscurity to center stage in a heated debate over governmental secrecy and the public's right to know. The WikiLeaks release was also an embarrassment to mainstream journalism, which had been bested by a renegade Web site that provided extensive and valuable background to the public about the US role in the Middle East, even though much of the information released was already accessible to journalists who could have taken a more aggressive investigative approach. The WikiLeaks release put the official US public relations stance of "freedom of information" in an awkward light, as the US government's actions suggest that freedom of information only applies to other countries, not to the United States. The government's response to the WikiLeaks release was draconian: shutting off the group's financial means of survival, incarcerating Bradley Manning, who is accused of sending the files to WikiLeaks, and threatening to extradite and issue the death penalty for Julian Assange, the founder of WikiLeaks. Though WikiLeaks is primarily linked in the public mind to the Iraq-Afghanistan leaks, the site has been a treasure trove in many ways beyond that limited area of conflict. Starting what is now called "Cablegate," the site also released a voluminous collection of cables and communications between the United States and Central and Latin American nations, which may prove as damning. According to Peter Kornbluh, who analyzed the cables, "From the United States to Argentina, communities have been empowered by a better understanding of what our governments are doing—in our names, but so often without our knowledge. What we citizens of the Western Hemisphere do with that power will become the ultimate legacy of the WikiLeaks experience."[42] The irony here is that despite the outrage and threats of violence and incarceration directed towards WikiLeaks founder Julian Assange, there is no real indication that what they have done is illegal. In fact, the basic justification of their cause is contained in the passing of the Freedom of Information Act, signed into law by President Johnson in 1966.[43]

Nor is what they have done unique, as can be seen by reviewing the released documents published in the pages of publications like *CounterSpy* or *CovertAction Information Bulletin*, later called *CovertAction Quarterly* (CAQ),[44] a whistle blowing publication cofounded by ex-CIA employee Phillip Agee. The activities of CAQ so infuriated the US political establishment that Congress passed a law "aimed at the Phillip Agees of the world"[45]—the Intelligence Identities Protection Act of 1982. According to the *Washington Post*, "The private papers of Philip Agee, the disaffected CIA operative whose unauthorized publication of agency secrets thirty-five years ago was arguably far more damaging than anything WikiLeaks has produced, have been obtained by New York University, which plans to make them public next spring."[46] An earlier successfully published release of secret police intelligence documents was the "liberation" of the FBI files stolen from the FBI office in Media, Pennsylvania, in 1971. The documents were delivered to newspapers and magazines and revealed the existence of the COINTELPRO authorization of police subversion of civil liberties of American dissidents.[47] As we have seen repeatedly, when efforts to bring to light valuable public information are thwarted or outlawed, citizens who seek the truth will develop organizational and technological end-runs around information blockades constructed by institutions hiding behind a veil of secrecy. New tools of information have greatly accelerated this process. The threat represented by WikiLeaks and groups like it runs counter to the growing insistence that all Web and Internet activity be susceptible to either monitoring or shutdown by governments and corporations. The ability to maintain a Web site that keeps its users and data private and that allows anonymity to contributors is increasingly untenable for the status quo. While authorities increase attacks on "rogue" Web sites, many longtime computer enthusiasts active in the digital rights movement counter those attacks, and continue to stand by the watchwords, "information wants to be free," the foundational slogan of the early personal computer movement. On the legal end of this battle are the Electronic Frontier Foundation (EFF), the Free Software Foundation (FSF), and the American Civil Liberties Union (ACLU) DotRights group, which contest clampdowns on digital freedom with legal activity and online protests. The collective "hacktivist" group known as Anonymous, which many people believe originated within the Web community 4chan where most posts tend to be "anonymous," is an example of an outside-the-law response to government repression and secrecy in the computer age. The amorphous, loosely organized Anonymous group is reputed to have accomplished computer-cracking feats such as accessing and publishing Sarah Palin's e-mails and launching denial of service attacks on Visa in retaliation for Visa's compliance in cutting off WikiLeaks's source of funding.[48]

While governments and corporations struggle to corral public computing practices into a centralized broadcasting model—placing themselves at the central axis of the means and content of media, successful public computing projects have taken root and flourished as alternatives to centralization. Yet principal sources of information and public sites of knowledge have shifted increasingly away from private control to the stewardship of the public. The benefits of crowd-sourced knowledge are many and are increasingly relied upon to solve complex problems quickly and accurately. According to James Surowiecki, "The idea of the wisdom of the crowds also takes decentralization as a given and a good, since it implies that if you set a crowd of self-interested, independent people to work in a decentralized way on the same problem, instead of trying to direct their efforts from the top down, their collective solution is likely to be better than any other solution you could come up with."[49] An early example of the success of this collective knowledge philosophy is the open-source computer movement, which led to the operating system GNU (Gnu's Not Unix) and to the development of Linux as a collectively maintained and collaboratively updated operating system. The foundations of the Free Software Movement are based upon these conditions:[50]

- Freedom 0: The freedom to run the program for any purpose
- Freedom 1: The freedom to study how the program works and adapt it to your needs with access to the source code as a precondition
- Freedom 2: The freedom to redistribute copies so you can help your neighbor
- Freedom 3: The freedom to improve the program and to release your improvements to the public so that the whole community benefits with access to the source code as a precondition

Probably the most well-known example of a wide-scale public collaborative project, however, is the crowd-sourced knowledge base of Wikipedia. The Wikipedia project sprung from an earlier endeavor called Nupedia, which took its inspiration directly from the open-source/free software movement initiated by Richard Stallman and others. Wikipedia was started in 2001 with the goal of becoming a collaboratively produced, free knowledge base for the world. It is one of the most heavily trafficked sites on Earth, typically ranked as the sixth most trafficked.[51] In another coincidental reference to science-fiction writer H. G. Wells, Joseph Reagle notes that the Wikipedia idea can be traced back to Wells's proposal for a "World Brain" whereby the encyclopedia could solve the "jigsaw puzzle" of global problems by bringing all the "mental wealth of our world into something like a common understanding."[52]

While Wikipedia and other crowd-sourced knowledge bases focus primarily on collective knowledge and referenced sources of information, other projects have arisen to counter the deleterious effects of aggressive copyright and restrictions to cultural legacies. In the spirit of free information, projects like the Internet Archive, Project Gutenberg, and Creative Commons have solidified their role as foundations for a new culture of public ownership. The Internet Archive, which also operates the "Wayback Machine," was founded by Brewster Kahle in 1996 to "prevent the Internet—a new medium with major historical significance—and other 'born-digital' materials from disappearing into the past."[53] The Archive has already digitized millions of books and archived over 150 billion Web pages in its efforts.[54] Project Gutenberg, founded as early as 1971, claims to have originated the idea of e-books. The Project undertook to electronically duplicate the world's great literature and make it available regardless of national borders or financial burden. Michael Hart, the founder of Project Gutenberg, conceived of the digitizing project when he was given free time on a Xerox Sigma V mainframe computer at the University of Illinois. He then decided that "the greatest value created by computers would not be computing, but would be the storage, retrieval, and searching of what was stored in our libraries."[55] He then proceeded to type in the US Declaration of Independence, which he sent to everyone on the network. Project Gutenberg stores all texts in plain text, or ASCII, to make them easily searchable and accessible worldwide. Creative Commons allows artists and creators to take proper credit for their creations but also to allow them to enter them into the public sphere without the harsh restrictions of conventional copyright. All of these nonprofit entities form a large part of a new electronic sphere being built in contradistinction to the commercialized and centralized model promoted by corporations. A vital part of this open culture of sharing is based upon crowd-sourcing and peer-to-peer networking, a thoroughly decentralized means of sharing information. As Internet Archive founder Brewster Kahle says, "I come from the Internet generation, and the things we've seen work have not been these closed, walled gardens. . . . And what we're really about is having no centralized points of control."[56] Peer-to-peer sharing helps to build a culture of mutual respect and responsibility, as it depends upon leaving a computer folder open for others to access, an anathema to those who work so hard to commodify and control information. Many of the core technologies, including the Internet itself, are based upon peer networks. According to Steven Johnson, "In other words, it's impossible to overstate the importance of peer production to the modern digital world. Peer networks created and now maintain the Linux operating system on which Android smart phones are based; the Unix kernel that Mac OSX and iOS devices use, and the Apache software that powers most Web servers in the world (not to mention the millions of entries that now populate Wikipedia). What sounds on the face of it like the most utopian of collectivist fantasies— millions of people sharing their ideas with no ownership claims—turns out to have made possible the communications infrastructure of our age."[57]

Polemics about public information, the elimination of secrecy, and public access to the means of communication can seem somewhat theoretical at times, as arguments sally back and forth about ethics and policy, business models, and legislation. What has brought ideas about democracy and communications to life and placed them on the global stage has been a series of social eruptions on local and global levels that have changed the face of history. The inspirational role played by democratic communications is central to understanding the so-called "Arab Spring" and the examples it provided to movements for social change around the world.

TECHNOLOGIES OF PROTEST

On December 19, 2010, an unemployed young man selling fruits and vegetables in the town of Sidi Bouzid, Tunisia, was accosted by police, who confiscated his stall and publicly humiliated him. The young man, Mohamed Bouazizi, decrying rampant unemployment, governmental corruption, and personal humiliation and despair, set himself on fire outside the doors of a governmental building. His act of desperation triggered a demonstration of a few hundred young people who empathized with Mr. Bouazizi. As the demonstration led to clashes with police, the images were captured on cell phones, shared widely on the Internet, and were eventually broadcast on Al-Jazeera.[58] The result of that and subsequent video footage of demonstrations against long-standing corrupt regimes in the Arab world is credited with unleashing a torrent of revolutions and social unrest that swept through that part of the world and dramatically transformed its political makeup. In Algeria, Mohsen Bouterfif set himself on fire, echoing the self-immolation that had ignited a revolution in Tunisia.[59] Algeria also soon exploded in violent protests and calls for revolutionary change. The Arab Spring spread into Egypt, Libya, Yemen, Bahrain, Syria, and the entire region on a flood of video, texts, Facebook postings, and Internet exchanges. The massive occupation of Tahrir Square in Egypt during the uprising that ousted long-time Egyptian leader Hosni Mubarak was especially emblematic of the enormous changes taking place in this part of the world and especially highlighted the importance of independent, democratic media. A reporter in Tahrir Square reported, "It's amazing, the days, you know, when you show—when you pull out your camera, how many people want their voices to be heard. They've been stifled for so long, it's been such a clampdown for so many years, so many decades, that when you do pull out a camera, people are just scrambling to try and get their voices heard, to say their part."[60] From another reporter in the Square comes a description of an important part of the encampment where "there's a media tent . . . that's been set up for the past week. And they're disseminating—collecting stories of people within the Square, people who were wounded, people who were attacked, people who were injured, and just ordinary people who are within the Square, asking them why they're there and creating an archive of this and trying to distribute it all over the world so that people get a true picture of what's going on inside, even as international journalists are being cracked down on and not allowed to get in."[61] A viral video of a young Egyptian woman, Asmaa Mahfouz, captured in particular the power of social media. In the video, the young woman speaks directly to her camera about the Egyptian crisis and urges everyone watching to use every channel of alternative communications open to them to build for a massive protest in the following week. As importantly, she urges her viewers to physically bring people to the protest, urging people not to passively watch the events on Facebook and other media. She faces the camera directly and urges, "Go down to the street. Send SMSs. Post it on the Net. Make people aware. You know your own social circle, your building, your family, your friends. Tell them to come with us. Bring five people or ten people. If each one of us manages to bring five or ten to Tahrir Square and talk to people and tell them: 'This is enough. Instead of setting ourselves on fire, let us do something positive'; it will make a difference, a big difference."[62] The protest that took place on January 25, 2011, that she had been building for became one of the largest protests in Egyptian history, and many credit her viral video as a tremendous catalyst for getting people on the street. The events in Tahrir Square in many ways epitomized how the conflict between an authoritarian regime and a new political movement played out in the realm of communications.

While the protesters were busy uploading photographs, tweeting messages, and posting support of the uprising on Facebook, secret police and military operatives were also busy photographing activists for later reprisals and punishment. Forces of repression in all nations of the Arab Spring were also relying upon the online activities of dissidents to identify and incriminate activists for future punishment. In nations that are populous and without the enormous funds necessary to create a large secret police force, online surveillance becomes easier than more traditional infiltration and eavesdropping work, establishing social media as a double-edged sword for social change.

The clash between democratic communications and state-controlled communications was perhaps no more visible than in Egypt, where the Mubarak regime fought to shut down the communications tools upon which activists were relying to organize their protests. At the height of the protests, according to the *New York Times*, Mubarak "ordered that Egypt be essentially severed from the global Internet and telecommunications systems."[63] Twitter, in particular, recognized the precarious situation it faced and posted the following message to its users: "We can confirm that Twitter was blocked in Egypt around 8 a.m. PST today. It is impacting both Twitter.com and applications."[64] Even with this draconian response, video, pictures, and texts still leaked out of Egypt and showed the world what was happening there. Leaked videos "from Cairo and other major cities showed protesters openly defying the curfew and few efforts being made to enforce it."[65]

According to many Arab Spring activists, it was necessary to "think small." At a forum on the Arab Spring, the consensus was that "you don't have to link every device to the Internet; you just have to transfer your photo of the government thugs' latest atrocity to somebody else's device before your phone gets confiscated."[66] In skirmishes close to border regions of other countries, activists were able to harness networks in those nearby nations. Small, mobile communications systems were also set up, allowing media to be dispersed.

According to a blog reporting on the Egyptian crisis,

> The Internet crackdown began in earnest on January 28 when the government, amidst extremely large-scale demonstrations, moved to fully restrict the Internet and cellular forms of mobilizing demonstrators. Internet and cell phone connections had been disrupted or restricted in Cairo, Alexandria, and other places, cutting off social media Web sites that had been used to organize protests and complicating efforts by news media to report on events on the ground. Some reports said journalists had been singled out by police, who used batons to beat and charge protesters. One cell phone operator, Vodafone, said on Friday that Egypt had told all mobile operators to suspend services in selected areas of the country. The British company said it would comply with the order, Reuters reported.[67]

While Egypt clumsily tried to shut down communications, there was no doubt that many other nations anxiously awaited with their own self-interest at heart to gauge their success on shutting off public access to their own media.

While advocates of democratic media were thrilled with the centrality of media tools to the uprisings, caution was also raised about awarding them too much credit. As detailed in previous chapters in this book, media tools can be vital accompaniments to social change, but they are not its cause. There are, of course, countless examples of revolutionary uprisings that relied upon traditional social networks and analog media without the help of the Internet. When the Arab Spring first burst into the headlines, some media and governmental quarters were to quick to insist the revolutions were the direct result of the Internet tools themselves, dubbing the events the "Facebook revolution" or the "Twitter revolution," belying a common conceit that Western governments and corporations often espouse bringing "civilization" to the hinterlands, particularly to the Arab world. Concurring with this enthusiasm, Sara Reardon says, "The Western world was quick to celebrate the success of new media, and the idea of the Arab Spring as a 'Facebook revolution' spread as fast as the tweets."[68] The myth of these revolutions being delivered courtesy of US technology were quickly picked apart by those active in the events, who acknowledged the advantages the technology offered but insisted that the events were driven by material conditions and long-standing personal networks, not by computers and cell phones. Social media can certainly act as important accelerants, but communications alone do not overthrow governments. Ultimately for those uprisings to succeed, the people had to go into the streets, fight bullets and tear gas, and face great personal danger. Computer scientist Huan Liu of

Arizona State University in Tucson says, "Social media wasn't a catalyst. The events it describes were the catalyst." Filippo Menczer of Indiana University in Bloomington agrees: "We have a history of thousands of uprisings without social media," he says.[69] And according to a recent study by the US Institute of Peace, as cited by Camille Crittenden, new media "acted like a megaphone more than a rallying cry."

Although online tools served as an important bridge to mainstream media and diplomats outside the region, social media took a backseat to more traditional organizing techniques to spark participation for direct action on the ground.[70] The derisive term, "clicktivism," was deployed to critique the rather widespread misconception that great social change will come about merely by clicking on electronic petitions, clicking "like" on Facebook, or clicking on any of a great multitude of online actions. The enthusiasm lent toward activism without leaving one's computer or mobile screen is perhaps a result of the great attention paid to the celebratory promotion of the Twitter and Facebook "revolutions." The central anticlicktivist manifesto, if there is one, can be found in the magazine *Adbusters*, which has helped critique reliance upon the computer for social activism. This anticlicktivist manifesto, in part, reads, "Dazzled by the promise of reaching a million people with a single click, social change has been turned over to a technocracy of programmers and 'social media experts,' who build glitzy, expensive Web sites and viral campaigns that amass millions of e-mail addresses. Treating e-mail addresses as equivalent to members, these organizations boast of their large size and downplay their small impact. It is all about quantity."[71] The real impact and promise of technologies is of course somewhere between the revolutionary and anticlicktivist perspectives.

A deeper understanding of the role played by new technologies in the social upheavals of the Middle East will support a more realistic evaluation of the advantages digital communications offer to democratic movements. A good place to start is with the "like" feature on Facebook, which has come to signify the banality of social network "action" online. When considered more carefully, however, such a feature can play a valuable role in building a movement for social change, particularly in repressive societies with tightly controlled media outlets. In its essence, such a feature can become a valuable means by which the public can test ideas for agreement. Those who control the state, on the other hand, use mass media to attempt to control populations by eliminating discussions of more radical solutions or by downplaying ideas through derogatory language; protestors become "hooligans" and "criminals"; their sympathizers become "traitors" and "unpatriotic." Oftentimes, official opinion polls can play that role: when using manipulative language to achieve intended results in public opinion, the published results effectively will alienate those who believe the opposite opinion, in a tendency known as the "spiral of silence." As Michael Hardt and Antonio Negri point out, "There is, of course, something strangely circular in the notion that opinion polls tell us what we think. At the very least, opinion polls have a centripetal psychological effect, encouraging all to conform to the view of the majority. Many on both the left and the right charge that the media and their opinion polls are biased and serve to manipulate and even fabricate public opinion."[72] If one could post a controversial idea that then gets thousands of additional "likes," the impact could be an emboldened public who now know that they are not alone. It was simple features such as this that helped get people on the streets to take action, knowing that others would follow. In Egypt, according to Merlyna Lim, "[P]eople shared a yearning to oust Hosni Mubarak, but each person was afraid to step forward. Once they saw how many other Egyptians agreed with them, they grew bolder."[73]

Viewing the influence of media and the Arab Spring using the template of the outline of this book will prove useful to understanding the events. Moving from an undemocratic and centralized media system to building local communications structures, giving them global reach, synchronizing them with the organized workers' movement, and sharing information that is hidden from public view is at the core of the Arab Spring. Any analysis of the catalytic influence of social networking in the Arab Spring needs to recognize that the technologies themselves are not well integrated into the fabric of everyday life. In fact, the penetration of Facebook and Twitter in the Arab world is not that high, mostly limited to young people who are both educated and better off financially. According to Zoe Fox in a quantitative analysis of social-networking demographics in Arab countries, "Social media has often been touted for the role it played in the popular uprisings that have spread across the Arab world since December 2010. Despite the buzz, you may be surprised that only 0.26% of the Egyptian population, 0.1% of the Tunisian population, and 0.04% of the Syrian population are active on Twitter."[74] The young street vendor who set himself ablaze in Tunisia is emblematic because he was a young college-educated graduate who was unable to find work to support his family. As earlier chapters detailed, small media operating horizontally can be extremely effective in encouraging and then connecting potential leaders and organizers for action against large and powerful adversaries. Social media did not have to reach a mass audience to be effective. Many organizing strategies of both labor unions and nongovernmental organizations understand the importance of connecting with and communicating with a small group of influential and persuasive leaders, who act as catalysts and communicators among a larger mass of people. Facebook played a valuable role in sharing opinion, organizing demonstrations, and amassing a critical mass of support for a plan of action. Twitter played a valuable role in keeping the movements informed on a minute-by-minute basis and in letting people know "where to go and what to do." The communications activity was magnified by its global audience as well, spreading news of what was happening not only locally but also globally, motivating acts of international solidarity and political pressure from foreign governments. According to Saleem Kassim's analysis of social media during the Arab Spring, "We use Facebook to schedule the protests," an Arab Spring activist from Egypt announced, "and we use Twitter to coordinate, and YouTube to tell the world."[75] The acts set in motion by social media tools motivated more traditional media channels, in particular broadcasting network Al-Jazeera, which has built a reputation for fairness, accuracy, and knowledge of the affairs and history of the Arab world. Television and cable networks played an enormous role in spreading the upheavals because they have an entry point into the home of masses of lower- and working-class citizens who aren't on Facebook or social networks. Google executive Wael Ghonim, active in the Egyptian uprisings, acknowledged some of the class barriers that online communications present, when he noted that "[r]eaching working-class Egyptians was not going to happen through the Internet and Facebook. Youth groups that had mobilized through the Internet printed fliers of the January 25 invitation and distributed them, together with the SMS messages."[76] Mobile technology in particular was used effectively to convey footage to the outside world, where it was magnified exponentially on television screens around the world. The role of workers' channels of communications, so often ignored by the narratives constructed by mass media, must also be appreciated. Mobilizing thousands of students and young people in the streets is an impressive and potent force for social change, but when organized groups of workers put their muscle into social change, their force can be even more powerful. This they did in many of the countries of the Arab Spring, and many activists credit the participation of labor with dealing the final blow against the repressive regimes. In the Egyptian uprising, much credit is given to the participation of the Egyptian independent labor organizations that led many workers on strike during the uprising, in defiance of the established state-controlled Egyptian Trade Union Federation (ETUF). According to a report published by the Carnegie Endowment for International Peace, workers in Egypt "were quick to mobilize in the early stages of the groundswell that eventually unseated Hosni Mubarak, and they deserve more credit for his ouster than they typically receive. Soon after the uprising began, workers violated ETUF's legal monopoly on trade union organization and formed the Egyptian Federation of Independent Trade Unions (EFITU)—the first new institution to emerge from the revolt. Labor mobilization continued at an unprecedented level during 2011 and early 2012, and workers established hundreds of new, independent enterprise-level unions."[77]

In September of 2012, the AFL-CIO awarded the George Meany-Lane Kirkland Human Rights Awards to the Tunisian General Union of Labor and the General Federation of Bahrain Trade Unions. The AFL-CIO reports that at the ceremony, AFL-CIO President Richard Trumka recognized labor movements throughout the Arab region for their ongoing role in the struggle for democracy and honored the "brave working people of Bahrain and Tunisia, who transformed a wave of protests into the mass movement of democracy and economic equality that has come to be known as the Arab

Spring. Unionists are a leading voice against corruption, for women's rights, and for a robust democracy with the rights of working people at its core."[78] The ability for workers' movements to communicate and coordinate in order to quickly respond to mass protests in their countries is a testament to their abilities to build their own unique channels of communications.

Finally, in the consideration of the role of the freedom of information, it must not be forgotten that one of the opening acts of the Arab Spring was the release of the cables between the United States and the Tunisian regime by the group WikiLeaks. The WikiLeaks group, often reviled today by US politicians, weakened the Tunisian regime by revealing the weakness and corruption of the regime vis-à-vis the US government. In 2011, Amnesty International singled out WikiLeaks for its positive role in setting the events of the Arab Spring in motion. The UK-based *Guardian* newspaper noted at an awards convocation that "the rights group singles out WikiLeaks and the newspapers that pored over its previously confidential government files, among them the *Guardian*, as a catalyst in a series of uprisings against repressive regimes, notably the overthrow of Tunisia's long-serving president, Zine al-Abidine Ben Ali. One example highlighted by the Amnesty International's Salil Shetty was Tunisia, where WikiLeaks's revelations about Ben Ali's corrupt regime combined with rapidly spreading news of the self-immolation of a disillusioned young man, Mohamed Bouazizi, to spark major protests."[79] Other WikiLeaks cables sent shockwaves through other nations as well, provoking its citizens to rebel against their oppressive and secretive regimes.

We see in the series of chain reactions that we now call the Arab Spring that information really is powerful. The skirmishes that developed during the Arab Spring between forces of democratic communications and repression provide an indication of the direction the global struggle will tend toward between forces of democratic communication and those that insist on centralization and control. In the uprisings of Tunisia, Egypt, Bahrain, Algeria, and other nations, the freedom to communicate freely was never assured. By controlling the servers, cables, and routers of the networks, military and police proved that they have vital weapons in their arsenals to muffle public communications. Cellular networks were shut down, as were huge swaths of the Internet in an effort to curtail speech and quell the revolt. The support of international solidarity activists who rallied to the Arab Spring proved very beneficial, as there were tasks that could be completed outside the borders. Many hacktivists and media specialists around the world assisted the Arab Spring by launching alternative layers of communications, building mirror sites for passing on media and information, and launching computer attacks on repressive governments. Hackers from other countries were also sometimes effective at gaining access to software and filtering blockages in the networks, reversing them to allow information to flow once again. The global structure of the Internet has often proved bewildering to those who are accustomed to quelling dissent only within the borders of the nation-state. The struggle over control of the Internet is emblematic of a global information war that will certainly continue to grow, as antagonists and protagonists prove their technological acumen and determination in the conflict between free and locked-down communications.

The events of the Arab Spring are energizing and inspiring for many people around the globe who are also looking at how communications technologies and media can rebuild democratic spirit in their own countries. In the United States, the tweets, videos, and postings from Tunisia, Egypt, Algeria, Bahrain, and other nations fired the imaginations of many activists, who stayed glued to their mobile phones and computers awaiting the next moves, in much the same manner that many Americans monitored the "Green" revolution in Iran in 2009.[80]

Back in the United States, in Wisconsin, a move by Republican governor Scott Walker to ban trade union collective bargaining sent many young activists into motion, where they proceeded to launch their own "Wisconsin Uprising." Using the power of communications tools like Facebook and Twitter, an alliance of workers, students, teachers, and farmers began an occupation of the state capitol building in Madison that reached epic proportions. At the heart of the mobilization were the American Federation of State, County, and Municipal Employees (AFSCME); the teachers unions; and other groups of organized workers, who relied upon their own communications tools to mobilize their memberships and build support for their cause within Wisconsin and around the globe. The occupation of Madison was an enormous success and fired up computer activists around the nation. Many of the people who were enamored of the new tools were introduced to them through the grassroots effort to elect Barack Obama, a phenomenal mobilization that spurred a great number of new electronic mobilization efforts. MoveOn. org, in particular, used these tools to great advantage, allowing voters to get involved at any level of commitment, from making a few phone calls in a few, spare minutes of time, to hosting major calling events in their homes. Organizing electronic get-out-the-vote meetings, calling parties to mobilize voters or other MoveOn members, and harnessing MoveOn members' cell phone capacity to call voters around the country, MoveOn built a group of millions who committed themselves to using all the tools at their disposal to spread support for Obama far and wide. Much of this enthusiasm simmered after the election and fueled the frustration and disappointment over the collapsing economy and the perception of corruption on Wall Street. Success in massive mobilization in Wisconsin helped prime the pump for action over these frustrations, and when suggestions were made to "occupy" Wall Street, many jumped at the chance. The date set for occupation was propelled through the culture-jamming magazine *Adbusters* and went viral through many channels of alternative communications. Proof that communications can equal bodily participation can be seen in the massive outpouring of support for the Occupy movement that began on Wall Street and spread to hundreds of communities, large and small, throughout the United States. The Twitter hashtag #occupywallstreet was one of the first of many to propel the Occupy call across the nation, as thousands of Occupy camps were pitched across the United States. Once in place, the Occupy forces developed many new and advanced forms of communications to bypass the mainstream media, who ignored the protests as long as they could. According to a Reuters analysis of Twitter use in the Occupy Wall Street protests, "The notion of Occupy Wall Street was out there, but it was not gaining much attention—until, of course, it did, suddenly, and with force. Social media experts trace the expansion to hyper-local tweeters, people who cover the pulse of communities at a level of detail not even local papers can match."[81] Social networking and texting technologies have their flip side, however, as was witnessed in the Arab Spring events where the authorities hacked, phished, and spied upon protestors' data. Videos of protests that went viral could often come back to haunt the protestors, whose faces and identifications were being documented for police actions later. Some video posters began to blur the faces of protestors and others opted for less public means of communication. In a recent trial in New York City, Twitter was ordered to hand over months of tweets in an Occupy Wall Street protestor's trial, which they proceeded to do.[82]

In many ways, the Occupy movement mirrored the Independent Media Center's efforts a decade previously in Seattle, though this time the technologies were much faster and more efficient. Many of the Occupy camps had live streaming video coverage, where viewers around the world could see exactly what was happening regardless of whether it was reported by mainstream media or not. Once the alternative streams of information went viral, mainstream newspapers and television operations began to get involved in coverage or risk being left out of the story. Television, radio, and newspaper coverage amplified the movement even further, reaching those outside the bounds of computer access. Media was a central part of most Occupy sites, with a media booth often in place besides a food distribution table. Many Occupy sites also hosted a lending library of books for occupiers to read. In addition to the video cameras set up for live streaming, low-power FM radio stations were also a common sight. Tumblr, Facebook, YouTube, and other sites became major venues for media produced by Occupy. Newsletters and newspapers, signage, and other print media were also common media tools generated from Occupy, not only from Occupy Wall Street but also from streets, commons, and universities across the United States.[83] For many Occupy encampments, the act of physical protest was made synonymous with acts of independent, grassroots communications, and movements for economic and social justice became increasingly fused with movements for media democracy.

HACKERSPACES AND DIY DEMOCRACY

An interest in DIY media has also emerged from a larger culture of DIY technologies that has been growing in the last several years, as the notion of "hacking" becomes less construed as breaking things and more associated with "making things." In the 1980s and 1990s, activists primarily oriented towards anarchism created collective spaces called "info-shops," local storefronts and workspaces that served as centers for media creation, distribution, and self-directed learning. Info-shops helped spread a culture of shared spaces for tinkering, making art, and sharing tools and ideas among activists. During this period, a massive shift in the US economy from manufacturing and engineering to services and finance sparked a renewed interest in "making" things again. Growth in garage tinkering and small-scale manufacturing on the DIY level has grown rapidly in recent years, witnessed by the rapid growth in "hackerspaces," "makerspaces," and collective workshops and tool-sharing garages around the country. Notable spaces include Noisebridge in San Francisco; Hacker Dojo in Mountain View, California; and NYC Resistor in New York, only a few of the hundreds of hackerspaces around the United States and the world.

An indication of the growing synergy between hacker/DIY communities and that of democratic communications is the recent Hope conference *Hackers on Planet Earth: US Department of Hopeland Security*, held in New York City in 2012. A conference held every other year by groups associated with the hacker publication *2600*,[84] the conference catalog demonstrates the wide range of activity that reflects many of the concerns and practices highlighted in this book. In addition to small-scale technical instruction, workshops and talks held at the conference included "Occupy the Airwaves: Tools to Empower Community Radio Stations," "Anti-Censorship and Anti-Surveillance Tools," "The Emergence of Hacker as Artist and Artist as Hacker and Hacktivism," and "Tools and the Arab Spring." A description for the "Kill the Internet" workshop, notes, "As grassroots Internet culture grows and flourishes, pushing out into international mainstream recognition, top-down cultural models are threatened and fight back, while governments attempt to quash and chill dissent empowered and organized by the Internet."[85]

Grassroots DIY and hacking activity has attracted the attention of the US Defense Advanced Research Projects Agency (DARPA), the government institution that produced the original call for proposals that created the Internet. While DARPA evidently recognizes the importance of DIY tinkering and is proposing funding hackerspaces and linking them to educational institutions, many in the hackerspace community criticize funding from the Defense Department as antithetical to the political stance of many hackerspace members. A cofounder of Noisebridge in San Francisco had this to say about the funding: "Having these programs in schools is fantastic, but the military calling the shots in American education? I don't see that as a positive move."[86] Many hackerspace participants were active in Occupy Wall Street activities, though they typically remained out of public view. Many hackerspace enthusiasts emerge in mass spectacles of art and technology in the Black Rock Desert during the annual Burning Man festival, and at the Maker Faires held at various fairgrounds around the country, where many thousands of DIY makers convene to demonstrate projects and learn from each other. These physical, tangible, electronic, and mechanical projects often involve media technologies. Building FM radio transmitters is often a popular project for makers, along with ham and shortwave radio relay systems. Innovative visual display systems are popular, too, as are video surveillance robots, and other video-centric artistic works. DIY makers often share a strong affinity with alternative media producers and these synergies result in projects that enhance democratic communications. In Egypt during the Arab Spring, as cell phone towers and wifi routers were shut down by the government in an attempt to kill communication channels, electronic tinkerers considered how mesh networks—portable, battery-powered wifi towers—could build an open network over and above the ones in place. Mesh networks were operational at the Wall Street occupation, and in other sites, in preparation for a time when alternative Internet communications may be necessary due to governmental interference. The concern over control of the Internet has spurred a new movement of mesh network enthusiasts, following in the footsteps of the movement of pirate radio enthusiasts. As public access to network hardware becomes threatened, media activists are developing methods and strategies of surmounting the blockades of servers and routers. Many other hardware hacker electronic projects have proven popular in recent years, fusing electronic know-how with communications. Surprisingly, many of the DIY communications technologies are primarily to serve local, not global, needs. Portable loudspeaker systems are a common site in street demonstrations, mounted on hand trucks and powered by car batteries, effective when authorities cut electrical power in order to quell amplified speech. Demonstrating the philosophy of appropriate technology, one of the most vivid communications technologies present at Occupy rallies was perhaps the least technological: the "people's mic." When amplification is not an option, the active speaker speaks in short clips, which the crowd repeats in an active, call-and-response mode. To turn on the "people's mic," one must call out "mic check!" and wait while the active audience prepares for the task. Thus an old communications practice most known for its origins in the churches of Black America, and already noted as an innovative developer of communications in the face of repression, resurfaces under new conditions. Taking advantage of new forms of local media that accentuate the power of street protest, laser and optical light systems have become increasingly popular. One such device is called the "Illuminator," a powerful signage display system that can project slogans on building walls from far away, a sort of "bat signal" for demonstrators. The Illuminator team is currently working on mass-producing the Illuminator for demonstrators across the United States. A host of new software options have been developed not only to spread messages far and wide, but also to assist in immediate logistical support for street actions. Text messaging systems like Twitter are very useful for purposes such as the following: summoning demonstrators at a moment's notice; sharing the objectives of the action with people on the ground; disseminating legal information in case of arrest; mapping the position of police forces; alerting the presence of tear gas or other weapons; and reporting injuries, arrests, and deaths. Such immediate information not only helps crowds outmaneuver police and military tactics, but also helps to control the panic and misinformation that leads to injuries. While tools like Twitter have proven invaluable, history shows that versions of fast message response have been used in the past, before the availability of Internet and cellular tools. In the mid-1970s in San Francisco, for example, the International Hotel was an aging, single-room occupancy hotel full of primarily elderly Filipino men who had fought against eviction for many years, thanks to the support of a large coalition of young activists. In order to fight the threat of police eviction, a "phone tree" was used to great effectiveness as the "Twitter" of the day. One phone call to the top of the phone tree would activate that person to make five or more calls down the list, summoning supporters that an eviction was in progress. Those five or more people would in turn each call the people on the list below them. Those people would begin their calls until there were thousands of people gathered in front of the Hotel ready to block police from evicting the tenants. People's Park in Berkeley, California, offers another example of "old-school" analog communications being used for street actions. During massive riots in support of the People's Park occupation, radio station KPFA cut into its normal programming to cover the demonstrations in the streets of Berkeley. People on the street reported in from pay phones, which were ubiquitous at that time, and KPFA put the callers on the air to broadcast up-to-date news. Some people in the crowd had radio-telephones and walkie-talkies, through which they could communicate to the on-air broadcast as well. In that manner, marchers walking with portable FM radios could be informed of what was happening and where. These examples show that democratic communications spring from creativity, determination, and perhaps most importantly, collaboration—not advanced technology. A recent upheaval in the German Parliament by a radical political party, the Pirate Party, humorously demonstrated this distinction. Pirate Party members used instant social media to communicate with each other from Parliament, provoking senior Parliament officials to ban laptop computers. According to NBC News Digital, "Young and Internet-savvy factions like the Pirate Party advocate dissemination of information using the likes of Twitter and Facebook, but the Council of Elders deems it a 'parallel debate' and therefore bans such activity." In response to the ban, Pirate Party members brought in a portable typewriter instead, to the consternation of officials and laughter of the public, thereby reversing the ban.[87] It is easy to see that a DIY attitude is all the rage today, but many DIY-ers feel it is easy to confuse the true spirit of DIY media and technology with a marketing trend that promotes consumerism on an individual level. The consumerist version of DIY is epitomized by the "i-trend," whether of the Apple variety or any other manufacturing brand—a strategy to sell an illusion of personal empowerment that is based on the yearning for uniqueness in a massified global society. The media and technology innovators who are the initiators of the DIY trend insist this was not what they had in mind. A more accurate acronym, they propose, is DIO, or do-it-ourselves, a stress on collaborative activity more at the heart of what the DIY movement is all about. DIY media, radical media, and alternative media, they contend, are not marketing brands but strategies chosen by sectors of marginalized society that fight for genuine democracy, justice, equality, and social change.

THE FUTURE OF MEDIA AND DEMOCRACY

With the rate of technological change moving at blinding speed, it is easy to be overwhelmed and swept away by claims of personal empowerment linked to the consumption of consumer electronic products. Media corporations and governments appealingly entice the public with their preferred vision of a future communications lifestyle—a centralized and secured environment of enclosed electronic social space driven by advertising revenue and constrained by governmental control and surveillance. Democratic communications activists, however, promote another option: to continue the path opened up by generations of media activists, computer hackers, labor organizers, video artists, DIY makers, and others who have worked long and hard to nurture systems and networks that enable democratic, two-way communications. Rather than viewing communications practices as a profitable venture, they frame them as fundamental to a healthy and participatory democratic society. By taking a longer view above and beyond the Facebooks, Twitters, and YouTubes of today, one can see the recurring, constant dynamic that binds the capabilities of human communication to the social, economic, and political limitations of our political-economic system. These limitations must be realized and surmounted to maintain and further develop the democratic infrastructure that has been built to date. Surveying the long history of democratic communications practices allows today's social-networking users to appreciate the depth and commitment to democratic practice necessary to move us beyond a recurring trap of centralization and commercialization and to continue to build a strong participatory democracy as opposed to a passive, "thin" democracy, as described by Benjamin Barber.[88]

In the organization of this book, I have presented a structure to understand the context and history of communications democracy in our current age. To begin, it is necessary to consider the weaknesses of the centralized broadcast system of media monopolies and to understand the technological implications of broadcasting and computer networks in permitting such centralization. Large-scale monopolization of media spurred the development of many local initiatives to reestablish community and local media. Successes of local networking led to global connections and to more powerful methods of worldwide communications from below. These new ways of communicating have undermined media blockades established by corporations and governments and disrupt the typical one-way flow of information.

In particular, and despite the impression that they usually lack access to digital communications tools, workers and their organizations have taken a leading role in creating a global voice for those on the bottom rungs of society and those often left out of the media discourse. The new channels of information, both local and global, have challenged what can be said and shown and have built networks and a new culture of sharing video, music, information, and data in defiance of secrecy and censorship. These new ways of communicating are changing the world from the bottom up, but not without great conflict with those who would choose to remain in control.

The threat represented by the corporate acquisition of media and the Internet by powerful multinational corporations cannot be overemphasized. Media conglomerates are major players in the world today, and they are responsible for much of the news the world needs to know if citizens are to make informed decisions about life-and-death issues. It is well documented that traditional venues of news have changed dramatically in recent years, as the reach of newspapers, radio, and television declines. Recent studies point to the growth of online sources of news and entertainment, particularly within the demographic of younger people. According to a 2012 poll conducted by the Pew Research Center, approximately the same number of adults less than thirty years of age received their news from a social-networking site as from television.[89] These quantitative findings can be deceiving, though, as the major sources of news and entertainment often originate from the same media monopolies. Whether one reads news on Yahoo! or in the pages of the *USA Today* is irrelevant if that information is entirely the same. Though much attention is paid to blogging, particularly in the world of politics, it is noted that many large-audience bloggers are the same pundits that already have a presence in traditional media outlets; they are often the same voices and opinions one hears on AM talk-radio or reads in newsprint, promoted by the same media monopolies. While acknowledging the power of citizen blogging, researcher Mathew Hindman concedes that most bloggers are "well-educated, white, male professionals. Nearly all the bloggers in our census were either educational elites, business elites, technical elites, or traditional journalists."[90] Unfortunately, investigative journalism that looks at the monopolization of media ownership and corporate privatization is not on the news agenda for corporate media outlets. In traditional one-way fashion, the mainstream media proclaims the right to survey and comment on the business of the public but is not receptive to the public's view of the business of the media. The privatization of the Internet that involved many media corporations in the early 1990s was virtually invisible in mainstream media and occurred without public scrutiny. One of the most important media policy decisions in many years, the 1996 Telecommunications Bill, faced a virtual whiteout in the mass media, as public input was clearly not desired by media giants who stood to benefit financially from the bill. Subsequently, the story of the Telecommunications Bill was chosen as the top-censored story of 1995 by the anticensorship group Project Censored.[91] Since the beginning of broadcasting, there has been a constant struggle between corporate interests and representatives of the public over who controls the airwaves. In the search for profit, corporations lobby for full control or ownership over this valuable resource for the realization of maximum financial gain. Information the public needs to know about spectrum allocation is routinely ignored by media industries, which profit from spectrum allocation. Not long ago, the portion of the spectrum currently used by wireless telephony lay dormant and was relatively cheap to obtain. Those with control of such frequencies today now find themselves sitting on a veritable gold mine, with the explosive growth of the cellular telephone industry. In the United States, vast portions of the spectrum were allocated to commercial broadcasters to enable them to transmit high definition television (HDTV). The US public, by giving all this spectrum away, may have missed out on a great opportunity to allow more public access to the airwaves and a greater diversity of programming. Issues surrounding spectrum allocation are virtually unknown by most sectors of the US population, yet this spectrum giveaway amounts to a huge financial windfall to the media monopolies and a great loss for the American people. Each time a repressive Internet bill arises with many implications for media corporations, it is incumbent upon social networks of grassroots activists to publicize and inform the public about the rights they stand to lose, because the mainstream media and entertainment industries will undoubtedly avoid the issue.

Currently the Internet Committee on Names and Numbers, the private entity that absorbed the public Internic, is auctioning off new, generic, top-level domain names (gTLD) to private corporations for millions of dollars, ensuring that the domain names system will generate only private profit, yet mention of this process is hard to find in corporate media. The once publicly accountable system of Internet names is now open to corporate bidding, driven by private entities' domain name squatting and monopolization. The price simply to apply for a new top-level domain is currently $185,000, with a $25,000 annual fee should the application prove successful.[92] This crude auctioning of such an important aspect of the Internet does not appear on the news agenda of mainstream media. Mainstream media rarely investigate the ethical problems of corporate concentration, but the foundation of any democracy rests upon an informed public. In our increasingly fragmented and alienated society, the role of the mass media to educate and inform, to expose and to investigate, is more important than ever. But courageous, strong, and independent institutions of mass media are increasingly rare.

Despite the rhetoric of the "free flow of information," corporate and governmental leaders are clearly uncomfortable with a more democratic system of communications and lobby extensively to corral the Internet into a business-friendly profit maker as a centralized system of consumerism and commodification. At the same time, they seek rhetorically to demonize or ridicule and legally to criminalize a system of grassroots, two-way communications. The regulators within the federal government, many with past histories working in the industries they are supposed to regulate, generally share this philosophy of a top-down control of information and media on the Internet, invoking the threat of terrorism or pornography to enforce the wisdom of censorship and the invasion of public privacy.

For many decades, public media advocates have urged those entrusted in government with the stewardship of a nation's natural resources to keep in mind its communications infrastructure—the airwaves and electrical conduits that connect the nation—belong to the people as a whole, as much as the mountains, waterways, plains, and forests. Failure to consider public owner-ship of these resources wastes valuable financial and material resources and fails to ensure citizens will have access to an unimpeded, fair, and democratic communications system, the lifeblood of any democracy. In 1961, then FCC Chairperson Newton Minow criticized commercial television in the United States for being a "vast wasteland." In 1991, thirty years later, he had this to say: "Today that 1961 speech is remembered for two words—but not the two I intended to be remembered. The words we tried to advance were 'public interest.' To me, the public interest meant, and still means, that we should con-stantly ask: What can television do for our country? For the common good?"[93]

Though our electronic delivery may have changed, the political economy of mass media is still relevant to understanding the extraction of money from the Internet. Media corporations are still in the business of counting view-ers and delivering audiences to advertisers, whether they are measured by Nielsen[94] and Arbitron[95] or by Adclick[96] on Web sites. The business interest sparked by the Internet and the World Wide Web, particularly after AOL connected its gated community to them in the 1990s, was driven by the vision that advertisers would be able to directly address individual consumers— the ideal goal of advertisers. This has been the direction of advertising since well before the Internet, with the explosion of demographic research in the 1960s and 1970s and the growth of cable television. Information for sale has become an integral part of the business model forecast for Internet profits.

While information has become an important commodity form in the Inter-net age, it is also important to recognize that information is much more than that. Information, media, "knowledge" products, and data are the means by which a community stays informed and communicates thoughts, ideas, and cultural values with each other. Western notions of democracy, from Thomas Paine to Alexis de Tocqueville, from John Locke to Jürgen Habermas, include a strong reliance on the freedom to communicate and on public access to information and the means of disseminating ideas. This freedom is increas-ingly weakened from the actions of corporate conglomerates that threaten to monetize, monopolize, and hegemonize the means of communication.

From the perspective of big business, the Internet is an efficient means to reach a mass audience, downplaying its potentially more valuable role as a conveyor of "horizontal" communication, and allowing for a quick flow of information between and among individuals, organizations, and member-ships. The original purpose of the Internet and the World Wide Web was to encourage these types of nonhierarchical collaborations not to become just another means of mass communication in the manner of radio or television. It would be naïve indeed to believe that the Internet will stay two-way and democratic without an enormous public effort to preserve it as such. We happen to be in a very unusual time when the technology has expanded faster than the corporate world can absorb it or governments restrict it. As many are aware, the Internet is useful for more than encouraging democracy, but antithetical to that purpose, it can also strengthen corporate monopolies, drive down working conditions by exploiting global divisions of labor, infringe on privacy rights, and threaten world peace by the long-distance command and control of missiles.

While these technologies can be used in ways harmful to public life, they are not monolithic. There are enough cracks and fissures in the technology and within their social and political contexts that can be exploited for public advocacy, civic engagement, and social justice. As we have seen in this book, an active public has been very adept at finding these cracks and fissures and at cultivating a wealth of innovative and effective practices to enhance media democracy. The history of communications democracy is full of such rich experiences, from the guerilla hijacking of mass media by Abbie Hoffman and the Yippies to the practitioners and advocates of public access television, community radio, community computing, microcinema, and all forms of DIY media. Today's drive to reclaim the community is rooted firmly in these movements of guerilla television, "free" radio, and underground media, movements that are finally reaping the harvest of decades of intervention and advocacy. The development of these alternative forms of communications has been given a tremendous boost with the proliferation of cheap and powerful new communications technologies, creating a new alternative electronic public sphere of discussion and debate. Many of these electronic conversations are based upon a locale, a community, or a neighborhood where there is often a critical mass of people who were previously not connected by mass media. New local initiatives—from low-power FM radio to the community wiki, from local Web sites and listservs to freecycle and activist networks—create new spheres of communication previously not possible. Wireless networking does not depend upon the street-to-home cabling infrastructure required by cable, cable-modem, or POTS/DSL. Increasingly, the services provided by wireless technology will extend and reinforce local content provided by both guerilla television and mini-FM because both of these components are increasingly online either by downloading, peer-to-peer networking, podcasting, or streaming. These new forms of local media can offer an important social bond for a new brand of local activism. The spirit of the public access movement is still alive in the many local initiatives to provide affordable Internet access to all members of a community. As telecommunications corporations squeeze consumers financially, local community organizers have taken initiatives to create citywide, public broadband networks, based on the model of rural electric cooperatives or community cable operations. Such co-ops are particularly beneficial in rural areas, which have mostly been abandoned by large corporations. According to a study of community broadband initiated by the New America Foundation, "[L]ocal communities are taking matters into their own hands and have created remarkable citywide, fiber-to-the-home broadband networks. Many offer services directly to residents, providing a much-needed alternative to the cable and telephone companies."[97] The report mentions that such initiatives result in lower prices and more employment, and they help to keep money circulating in the local economy.

The thorough integration of computer-based media has had startling and unpredictable effects on many areas of our personal lives and our work lives. It is increasingly clear that assumptions about invasion of privacy have been dramatically changed. It is no secret that a major aspect of social networking is the diarist, sometimes exhibitionist, uploading of the images, voice, and data of the subject him- or herself. Millions of people are clamoring to tell the world about themselves and to show the worlds they live in, the rooms they sleep in, and the shape of their hopes, fears, and dreams. For the most part, mainstream media has looked at this trend alarmingly, branding it as naïve, irresponsible, and dangerous. It is increasingly evident, though, that such practices are radically changing our notion of what privacy is and who gets to control it. Perhaps privacy is not as much a concern in our atomized, depersonalized world. Many people are using the new technologies as a way to reintegrate themselves into a more public life, discovering a new sense of community, relishing the loss of anonymity that sometimes accompanies opening oneself to public inspection.

When the tidal wave of dot-com startups swept through the so-called "Silicon Gulches" of the United States, an enormous amount of the workers were hired to create content. Interesting content drew audiences, whereas many other Web sites were simply click-throughs to other sites. Now much of the content is produced for free, generated from the raw materials of experiences, insights, photos, jokes, videos, and other personal items posted by users. This model is in fact an old model, one not unlike neocolonialism, where raw materials are extracted and shipped back to the economic centers where value is added and then sold back to where it came from. Lowering labor costs, even to zero, is as old as Adam Smith. Witness the *Huffington Post*, now owned by AOL, which sells the primarily free content generated by bloggers who want simply to be associated with the *Huffington Post*.

It has been observed that capitalism moves forward, colonizing what it can and commodifying what it can. The extension of communications technology and of work culture to the 24/7 week has resulted in arguably the greatest speed-up of information dispersal in world history. It has also expanded the commercial mentality into many spheres of life through simulations and entertainment, although the results of these incursions are still far from clear. Consumers' creative energies are being captured in many new, previously unthinkable ways. How many virtuoso guitar players sink their efforts into

Guitar Hero and Rock Band? How many urban farmers play Farmville in lieu of actually sinking seeds into real soil? Facebook, YouTube, Twitter, and other platforms are being used for righteous social ends, even as they stumble clumsily ahead, trying to turn their social capital into cash for their venture capitalists. These efforts are nothing new. When users of Facebook, YouTube, or Twitter protest online, do they carry their greater political interaction into the public sphere? Although many quantitative reports on the use of social media are available, the actual impact is still difficult to determine.

Communications tools are just that—tools—and nothing more. Technology will replace neither the importance of face-to-face communication nor the power of human bodies in physical space. Tools never replace the creativity, the determination, or the resourcefulness of human beings. But new communications tools can play a major role in rebuilding social discourse and in building movements for political change despite the current climate of media monopoly and corporate hegemony. New forms of expression and collaboration are emerging that will challenge the destruction of the local and deepen global understanding as well.

Still, new technologies have contributed greatly to a richer and faster culture of conversation and information sharing, be it trivial or profound. As an aspect of so many of our political and cultural lives, it is and will remain contested terrain, with many timeworn and familiar contradictions. The primary lesson of this trajectory is that human agency, not technological development, has been and will remain the driving force that leads to a more democratic system of communications. Many will be disappointed that humankind will not enter into an amazing new age by technological default. This is bad news for the many business endeavors and careers that depend on such an analysis. The good news, however, is that those who fight for communications democracy can know they stand within a long tradition of innovators, activists, inventors, labor organizers, and artists who share in the belief in public access to communications. The key to developing an analysis of communications democracy can be found within the many decades of innovators and activists who have always fought for the ability to speak. These projects, both big and small, facilitate communications from below that will change history.

Notes

NOTES TO THE INTRODUCTION

1. B. Bagdikian, *The New Media Monopoly* (Boston: Beacon Press, 2004).
2. J. Rosen, "Your Blog or Mine?" *New York Times Magazine,* December 14, 2004, http://www.nytimes.com/2004/12/19/magazine/19PHENOM.html (accessed October 30, 2012).
3. C. Atton, *Alternative Media* (London: Sage, 2000), 147.
4. This was the act sponsored by Al Gore and is the reason why he had claimed that he "invented the Internet."
5. George Stoney is a founder of the Alternate Media Center, a central player in the popularization of public access television.
6. Dee Dee Halleck is a founder of both Paper Tiger Television and Deep Dish Television.
7. M. Shamberg and Raindance, *Guerilla Television* (New York: Holt, 1971), 67.
8. C. Rodriguez, *Fissures in the Mediascape* (Cresskill, NJ: Hampton Press, 2001), 7.
9. B. Brecht, "The Radio as an Apparatus of Communication," in *Brecht on Theatre,* trans. and ed. John Willett (New York: Hill and Wang, 1964), 51–52.
10. H. M. Enzensberger, *The Consciousness Industry* (New York: Seabury Press, 1974), 98.
11. E. Herman and N. Chomsky, *Manufacturing Consent: The Political Economy of the Mass Media* (New York: Pantheon, 1988).
12. "Newspaper Public Attitudes," Project for Excellence in Journalism Annual Report, 2004. http://www.journalism.org/node/807 (accessed October 30, 2012).
13. *Chico News and Review,* "Gallup Poll," July 12, 2012.
14. J. Garofoli, "Social Media Leaves Spin Doctors in Dust," *SFGate,* October 4, 2012. http://www.sfgate.com/politics/joegarofoli/article/Social-media-leaves-spin-doctors-in-dust-3921046.php (accessed October 30, 2012).
15. D. Armstrong, *A Trumpet to Arms: Alternative Media in America* (Los Angeles: J. P. Tarcher, 1981).
16. S. Duncombe, *Notes from Underground: Zines and the Politics of Alternative Culture* (London: Verso, 1997).

NOTES TO CHAPTER 1

1. R. Nussbaum, *The World after Oil: The Shifting Axis of Power and Wealth* (New York: Simon and Shuster, 1983), 17.

2. D. Bell, *The Coming of Post-Industrial Society: A Venture in Social Forecasting* (New York: Basic Books, 1973).

3. T. B. Lee, "Qualifiers on Hypertext links . . .—alt.hypertext," August 2, 1991, http://groups.google.com/group/alt.hypertext/tree/browse_frm/thread/7824e490ea164c06/f61c1ef93d2a8398?rnum=1&hl=en&q=group%3Aalt.hypertext+author%3ATim+author%3ABerners-Lee&_done=%2Fgroup%2Falt.hypertext%2Fbrowse_frm%2Fthread%2F7824e490ea164c06%2Ff61c1ef93d2a8398%3Ftvc%3D1%26q%3Dgroup%3Aalt.hypertext+author%3ATim+author%3ABerners-Lee%26hl%3Den%26#doc_06dad279804cb3ba (accessed October 30, 2012).

4. T. Watson, Washington Apple Pi, 1943, http://ifaq.wap.org/computers/famousquotes.html (accessed October 30, 2012).

5. P. Starr, *The Creation of the Media: Political Origins of Modern Communications* (New York: Basic Books, 2004), 9.

6. "Acts against the education of slaves South Carolina, 1740 and Virginia, 1819," cited in William Goddell, The American Slave Code in Theory and Practice, pt. 2 (New York: American and Foreign Anti-Slavery Society, 1853). Dinsmore Documentation, Classoca on American Slavery, PBS.org, http://www.pbs.org/wnet/slavery/experience/education/docs1.html (accessed October 30, 2012).

7. E. Genovese, *Roll, Jordan, Roll: The World the Slaves Made* (New York: Vintage, 1970), 562.

8. Ibid.

9. V. I. Lenin, *What Is to Be Done?* (1907; reprint, Peking: Foreign Languages Press, 1975), 198.

10. E. M. Rogers, *A History of Communication Study* (Toronto: The Free Press, 1994), 491.

11. J. Carey, *Communication as Culture: Essays on Media and Society* (New York: Routledge, 2009), 95.

12. S. Douglas. *Inventing American Broadcasting: 1899–1922* (Baltimore: John Hopkins Press, 1987), 238.

13. R. W. McChesney, *Telecommunications, Mass Media, and Democracy: The Battle for the Control of US Broadcasting, 1928–1935* (New York: Oxford University Press, 1993), 14–15.

14. R. W. McChesney, "Free Speech and Democracy: Louis G. Caldwell, the American Bar Association and the Debate over the Free Speech Implications of Broadcast Regulation, 1928–1938," *The American Journal of Legal History* (October 1991): 351–392, 373.

15. *Chicago Tribune*, October 28, 1946.

16. *Exhibition of Ainu Pictures to Promote Human Rights* (Hokkaido, Japan: Asahi Shimbum Press, 1991).

17. A. Franken, *Lies (and the Lying Liars Who Tell Them): A Fair and Balanced Look at the Right* (New York: E. P. Dutton, 2003).

18. Rebellious Media Conference website, http://rebelliousmediaconference.org/ (accessed October 30, 2012).

19. K. McLeod, *Freedom of Expression: Overzealous Copyright Bozos and Other Enemies of Creativity* (New York: Doubleday, 2005), 8.

20. L. Lessig, *Free Culture: How Big Media Uses Technology and the Law to Lock Down Culture and Control Creativity* (New York: Penguin, 2004).

21. E. Herman and N. Chomsky, *Manufacturing Consent: The Political Economy of the Mass Media* (New York: Pantheon, 1988).

22. W. Lippman, *Public Opinion* (New York: Harcourt, Brace, and Co., 1922).

23. S. Ewen, *Captains of Consciousness: Advertising and the Social Roots of Consumer Culture* (New York: McGraw-Hill, 2001).

24. A. Huxley, *Brave New World Revisited* (New York: Harper Row, 1965).
25. H. Schiller, *Culture, Inc.: The Corporate Takeover of Public Expression* (New York: Oxford University Press, 1989).
26. L. Masterman, "A Rationale for Media Education" in *Media Literacy in the Information Age*, ed. R. Kubey (New Brunswick, NJ: Transaction, 1997), 60.
27. N. Chomsky, *Z-Space*, March 8, 1999, http://www.zcommunications.org/on-staying-informed-and-inteelectual-self-defense-by-noam-chomsky (accessed October 30, 2012).
28. E. Herman and N. Chomsky, *Manufacturing Consent: The Political Economy of the Mass Media* (New York: Knopf, 1988).
29. H. Schiller, *Culture, Inc.: The Corporate Takeover of Public Expression* (New York: Oxford, 1989).
30. R. K. L. Collins and T. Gitlin, *Introduction to Dictating Content: How Advertising Pressure Can Corrupt a Free Press* (Washington, DC: The Center for the Study of Commercialism, 1992).
31. I. de Sola Pool, *Technologies of Freedom* (Cambridge: Belknap Press, 1983).
32. T. B. Carter, M. A. Franklin, and J. B. Wright, eds., *The First Amendment and the Fifth Estate: Regulation of Electronic Mass Media* (Westbury, New York: The Foundation Press, 1989), 40.
33. J. Markoff, "Presidential Panel Urges More Flexible Use of Spectrum," *The New York Times*, May 26, 2012, B1.
34. B. Chen, "Q&A: Martin Cooper, Father of the Cellphone, on Spectrum Sharing," *The New York Times*, May 31, 2012, http://bits.blogs.nytimes.com/2012/05/31/qa-marty-cooper-spectrum-sharing/ (accessed October 30, 2012).
35. S. Douglas, *Inventing American Broadcasting: 1899–1922* (Baltimore: John Hopkins University Press, 1987), 218.
36. Ibid., 236.
37. R. W. McChesney, *Telecommunications, Mass Media, and Democracy: The Battle for the Control of US Broadcasting, 1928–1935* (New York: Oxford, 1993).
38. Ibid.
39. T. B. Carter, M. A. Franklin, and J. B. Wright, eds., *The First Amendment and the Fifth Estate: Regulation of Electronic Mass Media* (Westbury, New York: The Foundation Press, 1989), 72.
40. Telecommunications Act of 1996, Pub. LA. No. 104, 110 Stat. 56 (1996), http://www.fcc.gov/telecom.html (accessed October 30, 2012).
41. R. E. Summers and H. B. Summers, *Broadcasting and the Public* (Belmont, California: Wadsworth, 1966).
42. R. Somerset-Ward, *Quality Time? The Report of the Twentieth-Century Fund Task Force on Public Television* (New York: Twentieth Century Fund Press, 1993), 81–82.
43. E. Barnouw, *The Sponsor: Notes on a Modern Potentate* (Oxford: Oxford University Press, 1978), 64.
44. B. Bagdikian, *The Media Monopoly*, 6th ed. (New York: Beacon Press, 2000).
45. R. W. McChesney, *The Problem of the Media: US Communication Politics in the 21st Century* (New York: Monthly Review Press, 2004), 51.
46. R. Z. Hobbes, "Hobbes Internet Timeline" NIC 1.4 (1994), http://www.vtweb.com/swvis/timeline.html (accessed October 30, 2012).
47. J. V. St. Amand, *A Guide to Packet-Switched, Value-Added Networks* (New York: Macmillan, 1986).
48. V. Cerf, "How the Internet Came to Be," NIC (1993), http://www.netvalley.com/archives/mirrors/cerf-how-inet.html (accessed October 30, 2012).

49. J. Markoff, "Data Network Raises Monopoly Fear," *The New York Times*, December 19, 1991, D7.
50. R. W. McChesney, *Telecommunications, Mass Media, and Democracy: The Battle for the Control of US Broadcasting, 1928–1935* (New York: Oxford University Press, 1993).
51. J. J. Keller and G. Naik, "Merger Likely Signals Era of Bell Alliances," *Wall Street Journal*, repr. *Austin American Statesman* (April 4, 1996): D2.
52. "Fairness and Accuracy in Reporting," www.fair.org (accessed October 30, 2012).
53. "Freepress: Reform Media. Transform Democracy," www.freepress.net (accessed October 30, 2012).

NOTES TO CHAPTER 2

1. M. Tomasello, *Origins of Human Communication* (Cambridge: MIT Press, 2010).
2. E. Mandel, *Late Capitalism* (London: NLB, 1975).
3. T. Gitlin, *The Whole World Is Watching: Mass Media in the Making and Unmaking of the New Left* (Berkeley: University of California Press, 1980).
4. M. McLuhan, *Understanding Media: The Extensions of Man* (Cambridge: MIT Press, 1994).
5. Setting a date for new technology introduction can be difficult, as there can be a discrepancy between unveiling a prototype, releasing a limited introduction, and releasing it in different markets. While there were Portapaks as early as 1965, this model is considered to be the first standardized, marketable home video system. See, for example, B. Keen, "Play It Again Sony: The Double Life of Home Video Technology," in *Science as Culture* vol. 1 (London: Free Association Books, 1987).
6. K. Horsfield, "Busting the Tube: A Brief History of Video Art," in *Feedback: The Video Data Bank Catalog of Video Art and Artist Interviews,* eds. K. Horsfield and L. Hilderbrand (Philadelphia: Temple University Press, 2006), 9.
7. R. Houriet, *Getting Back Together* (New York: Putnam Publishing Group, 1971).
8. M. Rosler, "Video: Shedding the Utopian Moment," in *Illuminating Video: An Essential Guide to Video Art,* eds. D. Hall and S. J. Fifer (San Francisco: Bay Area Video Coalition/Aperture, 1990), 31.
9. M. Sturken, "Paradox in the Evolution of an Art Form," in ibid., 107.
10. D. Boyle, "A Brief History of American Documentary Video," in ibid., 59.
11. M. Rosler, "Video: Shedding the Utopian Moment," in ibid., 43.
12. Ibid., 39.
13. C. Leshne, "The Film and Photo League of San Francisco," *Film History* 18, no. 4 (2006): 361–373.
14. Ibid., 364.
15. M. Shamberg and Raindance, *Guerilla Television* (New York: Holt, Rinehart and Winston, 1971), 49.
16. R. Shuster, "A No-Budget Production," *Los Angeles Times*, September 2, 2001, http://articles.latimes.com/2001/sep/02/entertainment/ca-41150 (accessed October 30, 2012).
17. S. Anker, "A Haven for Radical Art and Experimental Film and Video," in *Radical Light: Alternative Film and Video in the San Francisco Bay Area, 1945–2000,* eds. S. Anker, K. Geritz, and S. Seid (Berkeley: University of California Press: 2012), 8.
18. L. Anderson, *Language Is a Virus (from Outer Space),* from an idea from William Burroughs, video, https://vimeo.com/14793787 (accessed October 30, 2012).

19. "Public Media: More Local, More Inclusive, More Interactive," Knight Foundation Report, http://www.knightcomm.org/rethinking-public-media/ (accessed October 30, 2012).
20. B. Bagdikian, *The New Media Monopoly* (Boston: Beacon Press, 2004), 121.
21. N. Minow, "Speech to the Federal Communications Commission," in *Radio and Television: Readings in the Mass Media,* eds. A. Kirschner and L. Kirschner (New York: Odyssey Press, 1971), 207–217.
22. Ibid.
23. C. Havighurst, *Air Castle of the South: WSM and the Making of Music City* (Chicago: University of Illinois Press, 2007).
24. R. W. McChesney, *The Problem of the Media: US Communications Politics in the 21st Century* (New York: Monthly Review, 2004), 43.
25. See http://www.vdb.org/titles/subject-change (accessed October 30, 2012).
26. S. Seid and M. Troy, 1999, *Back to the Future of Television: National Center for Experiments in Television Preservation Project Progress Report,* Video History Project website, http://www.experimentaltvcenter.org/back-future-television-national-center-experiments-television-preservation-project-progress-report (accessed October 30, 2012).
27. P. Aufderheide, *The Daily Planet: A Critic on the Capitalist Culture Beat* (Minneapolis: University of Minnesota Press, 2000), 129.
28. L. K. Fuller, "Public Access," in *Encyclopedia of Social Movement Media,* ed. J. Downing (London: Sage, 2011), 427.
29. J. Drew, "An Oasis in the Wasteland," *Video Networks* (San Francisco: Bay Area Video Coalition, 1992).
30. G. Braxton, "Racial Diversity Fades Out on Network Television: Nonwhite Families Rarely Seen on Prime-time Shows," *Sacramento Bee,* October 13, 2012, Section A, p. 1.
31. Ibid.
32. D. D. Halleck, *Hand-Held Visions: The Impossible Possibilities of Community Media* (New York: Fordham University, 2002), 108.
33. Ibid.
34. Paper Tiger tape 1, "Herb Schiller Reads the New York Times: The Steering Mechanism of the Ruling Class" (TRT: 28:00), 1981.
35. See http://dlib.nyu.edu/findingaids/html/fales/pttv/pttv.html (accessed October 30, 2012).
36. See http://papertiger.org/beingthemedia (accessed October 30, 2012).
37. J. Hubbard, "Fever in the Archive: AIDS Activist Video, " essay for exhibition, 2000, http://www.actupny.org/divatv/guggenheim.html (accessed October 30, 2012).
38. B. R. Rich, "The Authenticating Goldfish: Re-viewing Film and Video in the Nineties," published with the catalog of the 1993 Whitney Biennial, 91.
39. D. Bonetti, "Artists Ponder Clinton's Election," *San Francisco Examiner,* November 4, 1992, D1, D4.
40. *State of Emergency,* VHS, directed by L. Canner and J. Meltzer (Video Data Bank, 1993), http://www.vdb.org/titles/state-emergency
41. *Birth of a Nation: 4-29-92,* VHS, directed by M. McDaniel (Los Angeles: Guerilla Style Films, 1992).
42. J. Drew, "Newe Sogobia Is Not for Sale!," *Felix: A Journal of Media Arts and Communication* (New York, 1995).
43. *Newe Sogobia Is Not for Sale!,* VHS (Video Data Bank, 1992), http://www.vdb.org/artists/jesse-drew
44. Drawing the Line at Pittston, videotape (Paper Tiger Television, 1989), http://papertiger.org/node/728 (accessed October 30, 2012).

45. "FlashDance" (1986), videotape produced by Larry Evans and the Mill-hunk Herald, Pittsburgh, PA, broadcast on Deep Dish Television segment Labor Produces: Access to Solidarity. See http://www.deepdishtv.org/About/Default.aspx (accessed October 30, 2012).
46. *Desperately Sliming Salmon* (1986), videotape produced by Susanne Take-hara and Hobart Swan. Broadcast on Deep Dish Television segment Labor Produces: Access to Solidarity. See http://www.deepdishtv.org/About/Default.aspx (accessed October 30, 2012).
47. *Radio Today Annual Reports* (Arbitron). Other recent statistics show radio listening approximately doubling average time spent with print media, its dominance exceeded only by TV viewing. See R. A. Papper and M. E. Holmes, "Middletown Media Studies," *The International Digital Media and Arts Association Journal* (1998; Spring 2004).
48. For an excellent history of the beginnings of radio in the United States, see R. W. McChesney, *Telecommunications, Mass Media, and Democracy* (New York, Oxford, 1993).
49. Government regulatory agencies are sometimes referred to as "revolving doors" because the people selected for them frequently come from or return to the very industries they are supposedly regulating.
50. L. Soley, *Free Radio: Electronic Civil Disobedience* (Boulder, Colorado: Westview Press, 1999), 55.
51. Ibid., 58.
52. S. Dunnifer, "Micropower Broadcasting: A Technical Primer," in *Seizing the Airwaves: A Free Radio Handbook,* eds. R. Sakolsky and S. Dunnifer (Edinburgh, Scotland; San Francisco, CA: AK Press, 1998), 185–205.
53. L. Soley, *Free Radio: Electronic Civil Disobedience.* (Boulder, CO: Westview Press, 1999).
54. J. Drew, "Pirate Radio," *San Francisco Bay Guardian,* May 13, 1992, 13.
55. Brief by Committee on Democratic Communications and National Lawyers Guild on behalf of *Stephen Dunnifer v. FCC.*
56. J. Drew, "Free Radio Takes to the Airwaves," *(sub)TEX* 6 (April 1995), http://www.utwatch.org/archives/subtex/drew_issue6.html (accessed October 30, 2012).
57. J. Bekken, "Community Radio at the Crossroads: Federal Policy and the Professionalization of a Grassroots Medium, " in *Seizing the Airwaves: A Free Radio Handbook,* eds. R. B. Sakolsky and S. Dunnifer (Edinburgh, Scotland; San Francisco, CA: AK Press, 1998), 29–46.
58. *Low Power Empowerment: Neighborhood Radio in Ireland and the United States,* VHS (Paper Tiger Television, 1992), www.papertiger.org (accessed October 30, 2012).
59. See http://www.prometheusradio.org/ (accessed October 30, 2012).
60. "We Won! Senate Joins House in Passing the Local Community Radio Act!" Prometheus Radio.org, par. 3, http://prometheusradio.org/we_won (accessed October 30, 2012).
61. D. A. Ross, "*Radical Software* Redux," par. 6, http://www.radicalsoftware.org/e/ross.html (accessed October 30, 2012).
62. See http://www.radicalsoftware.org/e/index.html (accessed October 30, 2012).
63. T. Athanasiou, "High Tech Alternativism: The Case of the Community Memory Project," in *Making Waves: The Politics of Communications*, Radical Science Collective 16 (London: Free Association Books, 1985), 38.
64. From "An Introduction to Community Memory," reprinted in ibid., 38–39.
65. J. Curran, "Rethinking Internet History," in *Misunderstanding the Internet* eds. J. Curran, N. Fenton, and D. Freedman (New York: Routledge, 2012), 39.
66. T. M. Grundner, "Freenets," *Global Networking Newsletter* (1993): 11.

NOTES TO CHAPTER 3

1. *Paper Tiger TV Catalog, 1997–98* (New York: Paper Tiger TV, 1997).
2. "Paper Tiger Television Re-presents the Media," Catalog (Mahwah, NJ: Ramapo College, 1987), 7.
3. *Deep Dish Directory: A Resource Guide for Grassroots Television Producers, Programmers, Activists, and Cultural Workers* (New York: Paper Tiger TV, 1986).
4. Ibid., 14.
5. *Deep Dish Directory: A Resource Guide for Grassroots Television Producers, Programmers, Activists, and Cultural Workers* (New York: Paper Tiger TV, 1988).
6. Ibid., 4.
7. D. Brooks, "Free Delivery, the Newsletter of Deep Dish TV," *Media Active* 1, no. 4 (1987): 6.
8. A. Horowitz, "Domestic Communications Satellites," *Radical Software* 36–40 (1972).
9. M. Miner, "Careful, It's the 90s/Artistic License," *Chicago Reader* (October 1, 1992), http://www.chicagoreader.com/chicago/careful-its-the-90sartistic-license/Content?oid=880560 (accessed October 30, 2012).
10. R. Feder, "Chicago's Media Burn Archive Receives 'America's Treasures' Federal Grant," *Time Out Chicago* (February 7, 2011), http://timeoutchicago.com/arts-culture/chicago-media-blog/190943/chicago%E2%80%99s-media-burn-archive-honored-as-%E2%80%98american-treasure%E2%80%99?page = 0,0 (accessed October 30, 2012).
11. "A History of Free Speech," *Free Speech TV*, http://www.freespeech.org/history-future (accessed October 30, 2012).
12. "About ITVS," *Independent Television Service*, http://www.itvs.org/about (accessed October 30, 2012).
13. A. DiMaggio, *When Media Goes to War* (New York: Monthly Review Press, 2009), 43.
14. Ibid.
15. D. D. Halleck, S. Farkondeh, C. Scott, and M. Lucas, "Making Outrage Contagious: Chronology of the Gulf Crisis TV Project with Texts and Testimonies," http://www.papertiger.org/index.php?name = outrage, and reprinted in D. D. Halleck, *Hand Held Visions: The Impossible Impossibilities of Community Media* (New York: Fordham University Press, 2002). Special thanks to Martha Wallner, Dee Dee Halleck, and Simone Farkondeh for their comments.
16. J. Drew, "Instant Access: Paper Tiger TV-West Covers the San Francisco Anti-war Movement," in *ROAR: The Paper Tiger Television Guide to Media Activism* (New York City: Paper Tiger Television), 37–38.
17. This was a weekly series aired on numerous Bay Area public access stations called "Finally Got the News." There is a compilation film of this material in a program called "Just Say No . . . to the New World Order," which played in numerous theatres and public spaces. The material is available from Paper Tiger Television in New York City at www.papertiger.org.
18. "SF Says No . . . to the New World Order," VHS (Paper Tiger Television-West, 1991).
19. R. Mader, "Globo Village: Television in Brazil," in *Channels of Resistance: Global Television and Local Empowerment*, ed. T. Downmunt (London: BFI Publishing, 1993), 86.
20. W. Currie and M. Markovitz, "The People Shall Broadcast: The Struggle for a Post-apartheid National Television Culture in South Africa," in *Channels*

of Resistance: Global Television and Local Empowerment, ed. T. Downmunt (London: BFI Publishing, 1993), 95.

21. "1993 Biennial Exhibition," Catalog (New York: Whitney Museum of American Art, 1993).
22. D. D. Halleck, *Hand Held Visions: The Impossible Impossibilities of Community Media* (New York: Fordham University Press, 2002), 425.
23. J. D. H. Downing, *Radical Media: Rebellious Communication and Social Movements* (London: Sage Publications, 2001), 43.
24. R. W. McChesney, "The Internet and the Future of Democracy," in *Media and Democracy,* eds. D. Hazen and L. Smith (San Francisco: Institute for Alternative Journalism, 1996), 22.
25. G. Gerbner, "Culture Wars and the Liberating Alternative," in *Media and Democracy,* eds. D. Hazen and L. Smith (San Francisco: Institute for Alternative Journalism), 91.
26. R. W. McChesney, *The Problem of the Media: US Communication Politics in the 21st Century* (New York: Monthly Review Press, 2004).
27. "Interactive Plaza, What Is It? Joseph Goldin and the Origin of the 'Interactive Plaza,'" *Brian Webster and Associates,* par. 5–6, http://www.brianwebster.com/interactiveplaza.html (accessed October 30, 2012).
28. D. D. Halleck, *Hand Held Visions: The Impossible Impossibilities of Community Media* (New York: Fordham University Press, 2002), 333.
29. Subcomandante Marcos, "Address to the Free the Media Conference" (New York City, February, 1997); compact disc (Seven Stories Press, 2005).
30. Subcomandante Marcos, "Speech to the Mexico City March" (Mexico City, March 11, 2001, EZLN Archives).
31. A. Goodman, *The Exception to the Rulers* (New York: Hyperion Publishing, 2004), 311.
32. J. Perlstein (Director of the Independent Media Center, Seattle, Washington), in discussion with the author, 2008.
33. C. Atton, *Alternative Internet: Radical Media, Politics and Creativity* (Edinburgh: Edinburgh University Press, 2004), 31.
34. R. Kahn and D. Kellner, "Technopolitics, Blogs, and Emergent Media Ecologies," in *Tech: The Culture of Digital Tools*, ed. B. Hawk, D. Rieder, and O. Oviedo (Minneapolis: University of Minnesota Press, 2008), 24.
35. T. V. Ford and G. Gil, "Radical Internet Use," in *Radical Media: Rebellious Communication and Social Movements,* ed. J. D. H. Downing (London: Sage Publications, 2001), 212.
36. "FreeNets," *Global Networking Newsletter* no. 3 (1993): 34.
37. FidoNet Policy Document, version 4.07 (FidoNet Archive, June 9, 1989), par. 6–7, http://www.fidonet.org/policy4.txt (accessed October 30, 2012).
38. "FreeNets," *Global Networking Newsletter* no. 3 (1993): 34.
39. Ibid., 10.
40. Subcomandante Marcos, "Speech to the Free the Media Conference" (New York City, February, 1997); compact disc (Seven Stories Press, 2005).
41. J. D. H. Downing, "The Independent Media Center Movement and the Anarchist Socialist Tradition," in *Contesting Media Power: Alternative Media in a Networked World,* ed. N. Couldry and J. Curran (Lanham, MD: Rowman and Littlefield, 2003), 243–258.
42. A. Mattleart, *Networking the World: 1794–2000.* (Minneapolis: University of Minnesota Press, 2000), 111.
43. D. Kidd, *Making our Media: Global Initiatives Toward a Democratic Public Sphere,* eds. C. Rodriguez, D. Kidd, and L. Stein (Cresskill, NJ: Hampton Press, 2010), 90.

44. C. Roach, "The Movement for a New World Information and Communication Order: A Second Wave?," in *Media, Culture and Society* 12, no. 3 (1990): 302–303.
45. A. B. Durning, "People Power and Development," *Foreign Policy* no. 76 (1989): 66–67.
46. B. Mody, *Designing Messages for Development Communication: An Audience Participation-based Approach.* (Newbury Park, CA: Sage Publications, 1991), 29.
47. P. Waterman, "Reconceptualizing the Democratization of International Communication," *International Social Science Journal* 123 (1990): 77.
48. Ibid., 77–91.
49. P. Aufderheide, "Latin American Grassroots Video: Beyond Television," *Public Culture* 5 (1993): 579–592.
50. F. Ginsburg, "Aboriginal Media and the Australian Imaginary," *Public Culture* 5 (1993): 557–578.
51. J. A. Lent and G. Sussman, G., eds., *Transnational Communications: Wiring the Third World* (Newbury Park, CA: Sage Publications, 1991).
52. *Video Documents from Asia,* VHS (New York: Deep Dish TV, 1990).
53. A. Goodman, *The Exception to the Rulers* (New York: Hyperion Publishing, 2004), 7.
54. "History and Highlights" Democracy Now! http://www.democracynow.org/about/history (accessed October 30, 2012).
55. A. Goodman, *The Exception to the Rulers* (New York: Hyperion Publishing, 2004), 7.
56. On January 3, 2013, it was announced that *Al-Jazeera* was buying Current TV. A version of this article appeared January 2, 2013, on page B1 in the US edition of the *Wall Street Journal* with the headline "Al-Jazeera Acquires Al Gore's Network," written by K. Hagey and J. Jannarone.

NOTES TO CHAPTER 4

1. A. Mattelart, *The Invention of Communication* (Minneapolis: University of Minnesota Press, 1996), 7.
2. A. Smith, *The Wealth of Nations* (Middlesex, UK: Penguin Press, 1971), 109.
3. M. Chevalier, "System de la Mediterranee," *Le Globe*, February 12, 1832, p. 38, quoted in Mattelart, *The Invention of Communication* (Minneapolis: University of Minnesota Press, 1996), 105.
4. L. Mumford, *Technics and Civilization* (New York: Harcourt, Brace and Co., 1934), 225.
5. Ibid., 226.
6. J. W. Carey, *Communication as Culture: Essays on Media and Society* (Boston: Unwin Hyman, 1988).
7. Ibid., 212.
8. C. Tolouse, "Political Economy after Reagan," in *Trade Union Politics: American Unions and Economic Change*, eds. G. Perusek and K. Worcester (Atlantic Highlands, NJ: Humanities Press, 1995), 29.
9. L. K. Mytelka, "Knowledge-intensive Production and the Changing Internationalization Strategies of Multinational Firms," in *A Changing International Division of Labor*, ed. J. Caporaso (London: Pinter Publishers, 1987), 48.
10. J. D. Blackburn, *Time-based Competition: The Next Battleground in American Manufacturing* (Homewood, IL: Business One Irwin, 1991).

11. J. Lent, "The Global Cartooning Labour Force, Its Problems and Coping Mechanisms: The Travails of the Marginalized Cartoonist," *Work, Organization, Labour, and Globalization* 4, no. 2 (Autumn 2010): 160–172.
12. P. Costantini, "Mexican and US Unions Lose Opening Round," *Interpress Third World News Agency* (December 15, 1994), http://www.ipsnews.net/1994/12/trade-nafta-mexican-and-us-unions-lose-opening-round/ (accessed October 30, 2012).
13. M. Belanger, "SoliNet: A Computer Conferencing System Designed for Trade Unions" (August 1993), http://www.net4dem.org/cyrev/archive/issue1/articles/SoliNet/SoliNet.PDF (accessed October 30, 2012).
14. M. Belanger, "SoliNet: Canada's Solidarity Network" (paper for the conference: Information Technology, Electronic Communications, and the Labour Movement. April 14–16, 1992, GMB College, Manchester, Britain), http://www.angelfire.com/poetry/stevewalker/labtel92/Belanger-SoliNet.htm (accessed October 30, 2012).
15. H. H. Frederick, "Computer Communications in Cross-border Coalition Building: North American NGO Networking Against NAFTA," *Gazette* 50 (1992): 229.
16. J. E. Brenner, "Internationalist Labor Communication by Computer Network: The United States, Mexico, and NAFTA," (lecture for the course International and Comparative Communication Policy, American University, Washington, D.C., 1994).
17. M. McGinn, "After NAFTA: Worker Rights," *Multinational Monitor* (January/February 1994): 9–10.
18. "Mexican Organizer Helps UE Win in Milwaukee," *Labor Notes* 2 (March 1995).
19. Associated organizers and activists, in discussion with the author. (Fall 1995)
20. Associated organizers and activists, in discussion with the author, fall 1995.
21. N. Snyder, "For a Solidarity Built on Organizing," *Crossroads* (1994): 22.
22. J. Brecher and T. Costello, "Taking on the Multinationals," *The Nation* (December 19, 1994): 759.
23. Ibid., 757–760.
24. Director of the Holt Labor Library, interviewed by author, San Francisco, California. (September 1997).
25. T. Dowmunt, *Channels of Resistance: Global Television and Local Empowerment* (London: BFI, 1993).
26. *Dirty Business*, VHS (Migrant Media Productions: Watsonville, CA, 1992).
27. *$4.00 a Day, No Way!* VHS (individual members of the United Automobile Workers: personal videotape collection).
28. J. Mayer, "Television That Works," *Socialist Review* 23, no. 2 (1993): 78.
29. A. Dean, "Why Are Working People Invisible in the Mainstream Media?" in *Truthout* (July 20, 2012), par. 4, http://truth-out.org/opinion/item/10375-why-are-working-people-invisible-in-the-mainstream-media (accessed October 30, 2012).
30. B. Sim, *Workers of the World Undermined: American Labor's Role in US Foreign Policy* (Boston: South End Press, 1992), 4–6.
31. Ibid.
32. C. R. Martin, *Framed! Labor and the Corporate Media* (Ithaca, New York: Cornel University Press, 2004).
33. H. Kelberk, "LaborTalk: AFL-CIO Shocked by Survey It Commissioned," December 18, 1994, par. 8, http://www.mail-archive.com/pen-l@galaxy.csuchico.edu/msg08392.html (accessed October 30, 2012).
34. R. Milkman, "New Workers, New Labor, and the New Los Angeles" in *Unions in a Globalized Environment: Changing Borders, Organization Boundaries, and Social Roles*, ed. B. Nissen (New York: M.E. Sharpe, 2002), 103.

35. D. Bacon, *Illegal People: How Globalization Creates Migration and Criminalizes Immigrants* (New York: Beacon, 2008), 132.
36. Migration Policy Institute, "Immigrant Union Members: Numbers and Trends," *Immigration Fact*, no. 7 (May 2004): 4.
37. I. Ness, *Immigrants, Unions, and the New US Labor Market* (Philadelphia: Temple University Press, 2005), 150–161.
38. R. Shaw, *Beyond the Fields: Cesar Chavez, the UFW, and the Struggle for Justice in the 21st Century* (Berkeley: University of California Press, 2008), 213.
39. M. Dubofsky and F. R. Dulles, *Labor in America: A History* (Wheeling, IL: Harlan Davidson, 2004).
40. Teresa Watanabe and Joe Mathews, "Unions Helped to Organize 'Day Without Immigrants,'" *Los Angeles Times* (May 3, 2006), http://articles.latimes.com/2006/may/03/local/me-organizers3 (accessed October 30, 2012).
41. M. Zweig, *The Working Class Majority: America's Best Kept Secret* (Ithaca, NY: Cornell University Press, 2012), 189.
42. See http://www.excludedworkerscongress.org/index.php (accessed October 3, 2012).
43. S. Woodman, "Labor Takes Aim at Walmart—Again," *The Nation*, January 4, 2012, http://www.thenation.com/article/165437/labor-takes-aim-walmart-again (accessed October 30, 2012).
44. M. Manilov, "Innovations in Base Building," *Web of Change*, August 31, 2012, par. 4, http://webofchange.com/blog/innovations-in-base-building (accessed October 30, 2012).
45. W. A. Gamson, "Political Discourse and Collective Action," *International Social Movement Research* 1 (1989): 255.
46. A. Gill, "Social Media Acts as Megaphone and Sword in CTU Strike," *The Bez* (Chicago: Chicago Public Media, September 14, 2012), http://www.wbez.org/blogs/bez/2012–09/social-media-acts-megaphone-and-sword-ctu-strike-102437 (accessed October 30, 2012).

NOTES TO CHAPTER 5

1. See W. Benjamin, "The Work of Art in the Age of Mechanical Reproduction." Originally published in *Zeitschrift für Sozialforschung*, 1936, http://www.marxists.org/reference/subject/philosophy/works/ge/benjamin.htm (accessed October 30, 2012).
2. US Congress, *Digital Millennium Copyright Act of 1998*, http://www.copyright.gov/title17/92appb.pdf (accessed October 30, 2012).
3. "Digital Millennium Copyright Act," Electronic Frontier Foundation, par. 2, https://www.eff.org/issues/dmca (accessed October 30, 2012).
4. L. Lessig, "Let the Stories go," par. 3, http://www.nytimes.com/2001/04/30/opinion/let-the-stories-go.html (accessed October 30, 2012).
5. D. Mitchell, "Is Comcast Violating Net-Neutrality Rules?" *CNNMoney*, May 16, 2012, http://tech.fortune.cnn.com/2012/05/16/comcast/ (accessed October 30, 2012).
6. E. Wyatt, "US Court Curbs F uthority on Web Traffic," *The New York Times*, April 6, 2012, http://www.   imes.com/2010/04/07/technology/07net.html?pagewanted = all (accessed October 30, 2012).
7. T. Lee, "Verizon: Net Neutrality Violates Our Free Speech Rights," *arstechnica*, July 3, 2012, http://arstechnica.com/tech-policy/2012/07/verizon-net-neutrality-violates-our-free-speech-rights/ (accessed October 30, 2012).
8. M. Welsh, "Net Neutrality: World War Web," *newsreview.com*, April 10, 2008.

9. P. Higgins and P. Eckersley, "An Open Letter from Internet Engineers to the US Congress," Electronic Frontier Foundation, December 15, 2011, https://www.eff.org/deeplinks/2011/12/internet-inventors-warn-against-sopa-and-pipa (accessed October 30, 2012).
10. D. O'Neill, interview by A. Haden-Guest, *Down the Programmed Rabbit Hole* (London: Hart-Davis, MacGibbon, 1972), 268.
11. *Sonic Outlaws,* film, directed by C. Baldwin (San Francisco: Other Cinema, 1995), http://www.othercinemadvd.com/sonic.html (accessed October 30, 2012).
12. J. Lowensteinm, *The Author's Due: Printing and the Prehistory of Copyright* (Chicago: University of Chicago, 2002), 18.
13. K. B. LeFevre, *Invention as a Social Act* (Carbondale, IL: Southern Illinois University Press, 1987), 19.
14. Ibid., 41–42.
15. J. Thomas, "The Myth of the 'Information Age,'" *Intertek: Special Issue on Economic, Social and Technical Aspects of Information* (San Carlos, California: Intertek, 1993), 7.
16. J. Berger, *Ways of Seeing* (New York: Penguin, 1990).
17. D. Corn and S. Munger, "Anti-liberal Limbaugh Is a Rockin' Radio Pirate," *Metro Santa Cruz,* August 27–September 3, 1997.
18. J. C. McKinley, "GOP Candidates Are Told, Don't Use the Verses, It's Not Your Song," *Rolling Stone Magazine*, February 3, 2012.
19. "Stop Using My Songs, Republicans! A Guide to Disgruntled Rockers," *Rolling Stone Magazine*, October, 10, 2010, http://www.rollingstone.com/music/news/stop-using-my-song-republicans-a-guide-to-disgruntled-rockers-20081010?print = true (accessed October 30, 2012).
20. M. Perpetua, "Cee Lo Green Outrages John Lennon Fans by Changing Lyrics to 'Imagine,'" *Rolling Stone Magazine*, January 2, 2012, http://www.rollingstone.com/music/news/cee-lo-green-outrages-john-lennon-fans-by-changing-lyrics-to-imagine-20120102 (accessed October 30, 2012).
21. P. C. Spehr, *The Movies Begin: Making Movies in New Jersey, 1887–1920* (Newark, NJ: Newark Museum, 1977), 64.
22. A. Dorfman and A. Mattelart, *How to Read Donald Duck: Imperialist Ideology in the Disney Comic* (New York: International General Editions, 1971), 19.
23. D. Bollier, *Brand Name Bullies* (Hoboken, NJ: Wiley and Sons, 2005), 106–107.
24. T. Waits, Letter to the Editor, *The Nation,* October 7, 2002, http://www.thenation.com/article/perception-doors (accessed October 30, 2012).
25. C. Hays, "John Densmore Speaks Out on the Legacy of the Doors," *Examiner.com*, April 8, 2012, http://www.examiner.com/article/john-densmore-speaks-out-on-the-legacy-of-the-doors (accessed October 30, 2012).
26. F. Contreras, "Family of 'Lion Sleeps Tonight' Writer Gets Millions," *All Things Considered*, National Public Radio, March 24, 2006, http://www.npr.org/templates/story/story.php?storyId=5300359 (accessed October 30, 2012).
27. "Bob Dylan: 'Wussies' Complain about Plagiarism," *Huffington Post*, September 13, 2012, par. 6, http://www.huffingtonpost.com/2012/09/13/bob-dylan-wussies-pussies-plagiarism_n_1880?tml (accessed October 30, 2012).
28. E. S. Sklar and D. L. Hoffman, eiing *Arthur Is Popular Culture* (London: McFarland and Company, 5.
29. L. Lessig, *Free Culture: How Big Media Uses Technology and the Law to Lock Down Culture and Control Creativity* (New York: Penguin Press, 2004), 8.
30. See *Bert Is Evil: The Only Official Evil Portal*, http://www.bertisevil.tv/ (accessed October 30, 2012).

31. See *Pepper Spraying Cop*, http://peppersprayingcop.tumblr.com/ (accessed October 30, 2012).

32. See "Non-exhaustive List of Amazon Trademarks," http://www.amazon.com/gp/help/customer/display.html/?nodeId=200738910 (accessed October 15, 2012).

33. D. Sullivan, "Now, Mitt Romney Has a Santorum-like Bing and Google Problem," *Search Engine Land*, February 10, 2012, par. 13, http://searchengineland.com/now-mitt-romney-has-a-santorum-like-bing-google-problem-111061 (accessed October 30, 2012).

34. See "Let's Go! Arctic," http://arcticready.com/ (accessed October 30, 2012).

35. J. Cash, "One Piece at a Time," *One Piece at a Time*, compact disc, Columbia Records, 1976.

36. C. Carlsson, ed., *Bad Attitude: The Processed World Anthology* (London: Verso Press, 1990).

37. J. Drew, "Technopranks," *Processed World Magazine*, 2004.

38. A. M. Cole, "ICE Domain Name Seizures Threaten Due Process and First Amendment Rights," *Free Future: Protecting Civil Liberties in the Digital Age*, June 20, 2012, par. 3, http://www.aclu.org/blog/free-speech-national-security-technology-and-liberty/ice-domain-name-seizures-threaten-due (accessed October 30, 2012).

39. "Internet Rights Organizations Strongly Denounce Attack on Anonymous Online Speech by US Government," Association for Progressive Communications, April 20, 2012, par. 6, http://www.apc.org/en/news/apc-statement-progressive-internet-rights-organisa (accessed October 30, 2012).

40. T. Claburn, "Google Joins Copyright Police Force," *Information Week*, August 13, 2012, par. 9, http://www.informationweek.com/internet/google/google-joins-copyright-police-force/240005329 (accessed October 30, 2012).

NOTES TO CHAPTER 6

1. H. G. Wells, *The Sleeper Awakes*, Project Gutenberg, 2004, http://www.gutenberg.org/ebooks/12163, originally published serially in *The Graphic*, 1898–1903.

2. J. Verne and M. Verne, *In the Year 2889* Project Gutenberg, http://www.gutenberg.org/ebooks/19362, originally in *Forum*, February 1889: 262.

3. N. Singer, "Do Not Track? Advertisers Say 'Don't Tread on Us,'" *The New York Times*, October 13, 2012, par. 12, http://www.nytimes.com/2012/10/14/technology/do-not-track-movement-is-drawing-advertisers-fire.html (accessed October 30, 2012).

4. K. Bachman, "Do Not Track Browser Angers Online Ad Industry," *Adweek*, June 1, 2012, http://www.adweek.com/news/technology/microsofts-do-not-track-browser-angers-online-ad-industry-140863 (accessed October 30, 2012).

5. M. Musgrove, "Sleuths Crack Tracking Code Discovered in Color Printers," *Washington Post*, October 19, 2005, http://www.washingtonpost.com/wp-dyn/content/article/2005/10/18/AR2005101801663.html (accessed October 30, 2012).

6. *Olmstead v. US*, 277 U.S. 438 (1928), http://scholar.google.com/scholar_case?case=5577544660194763070&hl=en&as_sdt=2&as_vis=1&oi=scholarr (accessed October 30, 2012).

7. N. Chomsky and E. Herman, *Manufacturing Consent: The Political Economy of Mass Media* (New York: Pantheon, 1988).

8. C. Duhigg, "Campaigns Mine Personal Lives to Get Out Vote," *The New York Times*, October 13, 2012, par. 3, http://www.nytimes.com/2012/10/14/us/

politics/campaigns-mine-personal-lives-to-get-out-vote.html?ref = charlesduhigg (accessed October 30, 2012).

9. S. Sengupta, "Facebook Delivers a Confident Sales Pitch to Advertisers," *The New York Times*, October 2, 2012, par. 14, http://www.nytimes. com/2012/10/03/technology/facebook-delivers-confident-pitch-to-advertisers. html?ref = technology (accessed October 30, 2012).

10. C. Arthur, "iPhone Keeps Record of Everywhere You Go," *Guardian*, April 20, 2011, http://www.guardian.co.uk/technology/2011/apr/20/iphone-tracking-prompts-privacy-fears (accessed October 30, 2012).

11. J. Oates, "Channel Islanders Attack Street View Car," *Register*, September 24, 2010, http://www.theregister.co.uk/2010/09/24/street_view_guernsey_vandal/ (accessed October 30, 2012).

12. J. Brodkin, "Facebook Bends to Europe's Will, Disables Facial Recognition (For Now)," *Arstechnica*, September 21, 2012, http://arstechnica.com/tech-policy/2012/09/facebook-bends-to-europes-will-disables-facial-recognition-for-now/ (accessed October 30, 2012).

13. G. W. Domhoff, *Who Rules America?* (Engleside Cliffs, NJ: Prentice-Hall, 1967).

14. See L. Steffens, "The Shame of the Cities," *Wikisource*, http://en.wikisource. org/wiki/The_Shame_of_the_Cities (accessed October 26, 2012).

15. See "The Power Elite," *Wikipedia*, http://en.wikipedia.org/wiki/The_Power_ Elite (accessed October 26, 2012).

16. G. W. Domhoff, "Social Cohesion and the Bohemian Grove: The Power Elite at Summer Camp," *Who Rules America?* April 2005, http://www2.ucsc.edu/ whorulesamerica/power/bohemian_grove.html (accessed October 30, 2012).

17. B. Bagdikian, *The Effete Conspiracy and Other Crimes of the Press* (New York: Harper and Row, 1972).

18. B. Bagdikian, *The Media Monopoly* (Boston: Beacon Press, 1992).

19. *Bay Area Dailies,* VHS (New York: Paper Tiger Television, 1985).

20. *Murray Bookchin Reads Time Magazine: History as a Television Series*, VHS (New York: Paper Tiger Television, 1982).

21. *Martha Rosler Reads Vogue: Wishing, Dreaming, Winning, Spending*, VHS (New York: Paper Tiger Television, 1982).

22. *Mutiny on the Corporate Sponsorship*, VHS (New York: Paper Tiger Television, 1991).

23. J. Drew, ed., *Paper Tiger Guide to TV Repair* (San Francisco: San Francisco Art Institute, 1992).

24. H. Schiller, *The Culture Industry* (New York: Oxford University Press, 1989).

25. J. On, *They Rule*, http://www.theyrule.net/ (accessed October 26, 2012).

26. B. Seale, *Seize the Time: The Story of the Black Panther Party and Huey P. Newton* (New York: Random House, 1970).

27. *Video Witnesses 3: Networking in the 90s.* Catalog. (Buffalo, NY: Hallwalls Contemporary Arts Center, October 10, 1992).

28. J. Drew, *Newe Sogobia Is Not for Sale!* VHS (Chicago: Video Data Bank, 1992), http://www.vdb.org/ (accessed October 30, 2012).

29. J. Drew, "Newe Sogobia Is Not for Sale!" *Felix: A Journal of Arts and Communication* 2, No. 1, 1995: 123–129.

30. See Tobacco Control Archives, University of California, San Francisco, Libraries, http://www.library.ucsf.edu/tobacco (accessed October 26, 2012).

31. J. Schwartz, "File Sharing Pits Copyright Against Free Speech," *The New York Times*, November 3, 2003, par. 2, http://www.nytimes.com/2003/11/03/ business/media/03secure.html (accessed October 30, 2012).

32. J. C. Smyth, "Voting Machine Controversy," *Cleveland Plain Dealer*, August 28, 2003, http://www.commondreams.org/headlines03/0828–08.htm (accessed October 30, 2012).

33. S. Gaudin, "Facebook Moves to Remedy Mobile Revenue Woes," *Computer-World*, August 8, 2012, http://www.computerworld.com/s/article/9230097/ Facebook_moves_to_remedy_mobile_revenue_woes (accessed October 30, 2012).

34. G. Tinti, "Allen and the 'Macaca' Incident," *Outside the Beltway*, August 15, 2006, http://www.outsidethebeltway.com/allen_and_the_macaca_incident_ video/ (accessed October 30, 2012).

35. "Alleged LAPD Brutality Video Sparks Probe," CBS/AP, February 11, 2009, http://www.cbsnews.com/2100–201_162–2170342.html (accessed October 30, 2012).

36. R. Bhattacharjee, "UC Students Protest Taser Gun Incident at UCLA Library," *Berkeley Daily Planet*, November 24, 2006, http://www.berkeleydailyplanet. com/issue/2006–11–24/article/25701?headline=UC-Students-Protest-Taser-Gun-Incident-at-UCLA-Library (accessed October 30, 2012).

37. TheDirtyNews, "Police Shooting at BART Station—Oscar Grant," You-Tube, January 5, 2009, http://www.youtube.com/watch?v=bmJukcFzEX4 (accessed October 30, 2012).

38. B. Weiser and R. Leonard, "Video of Police Encounter May Play Key Role in Lawsuit," *The New York Times*, September 11, 2012, par. 6, http://www.nytimes. com/2012/09/11/nyregion/video-of-police-altercation-may-take-key-role-in-civil-rights-suit.html?r=1&hpw&pagewanted=print (accessed October 30, 2012).

39. "No Shooting at Protest? Police May Block Mobile Devices via Apple," *RT*, September 5, 2012, par. 10, http://rt.com/news/apple-patent-transmission-block-408/ (accessed October 30, 2012).

40. D. Corn, "WATCH: Full Secret Video of Private Romney Fundraiser," *Mother Jones*, September 18, 2012, http://www.motherjones.com/politics/2012/09/ watch-full-secret-video-private-romney-fundraiser (accessed October 30, 2012).

41. "BPI Announces Defamation Lawsuit over 'Pink Slime,'" *ABC News*, September 13, 2012, http://abcnews.go.com/Health/bpi-announces-defamation-lawsuit-pink-slime/story?id=17222933#.UI12cRylhwc (accessed October 30, 2012).

42. P. Kornbluh, "WikiLeaks: The Latin America Files," *The Nation*, August 13/20, 2012, p. 14.

43. "The Freedom of Information Act," National Security Archive, http://www. gwu.edu/~nsarchiv/nsa/foia.html (accessed October 28, 2012).

44. See "CovertAction Quarterly: Back Issues," *[Redacted]news*, http://redactednews. blogspot.com/p/covertaction-quarterly-back-issues.html (accessed October 28, 2012).

45. J. Walker, "Agee's Revenge: It's Past Time to Kill the Intelligence Identities Protection Act," *Reason*, July 14, 2005, par. 3, http://reason.com/archives/2005/07/14/ agees-revenge (accessed October 30, 2012).

46. J. Stein, "CIA Renegade Agee's Files Surface at NYU," *Washington Post Online*, October 25, 2010, par. 1, http://voices.washingtonpost.com/spy-talk/2010/10/ cia_renegade_agees_files_surfa.html (accessed October 30, 2012).

47. "The Complete Collection of Political Documents Ripped-off from the FBI Office in Media, PA, March 8, 1971," WIN, 1972, http://www.scribd.com/ doc/46984771/The-Complete-Collection-of-Political-Documents-Ripped-off-from-the-FBI-Office-in-Media-Pa-March-8–1971-WIN-March-1972 (accessed October 28, 2012).

48. "Anonymous: The Secret Group's Five Biggest Hacks," *The Week*, March 7, 2011, http://theweek.com/article/index/212846/anonymous-the-secret-groups-5-biggest-hacks (accessed October 30, 2012).

49. J. Surowiecki, *The Wisdom of Crowds: Why the Many are Smarter than the Few and How Collective Wisdom Shapes Business, Economies, Societies, and Nations* (New York: Doubleday, 2004), 70.

50. "What Is Free Software?" Gnu Project, July 1, 2012, par. 4, http://www.gnu.org/philosophy/free-sw.html (accessed October 30, 2012).

51. "Wikipedia: About," *Wikipedia,* http://en.wikipedia.org/wiki/Wikipedia:About (accessed October 28, 2012).

52. J. M. Reagle, Jr., *Good Faith Collaboration: The Culture of Wikipedia* (Cambridge, MA: MIT Press, 2010), 3–4.

53. "About the Internet Archive," *Internet Archive*, par. 4, http://archive.org/about/ (accessed October 28, 2012).

54. B. Carter, "All the TV News Since 2009, on One Web Site," *The New York Times*, September 18, 2012, http://www.nytimes.com/2012/09/18/business/media/internet-archive-amasses-all-tv-news-since-2009.html (accessed October 30, 2012).

55. "The History and Philosophy of Project Gutenberg by Michael Hart," Project Gutenberg, August 1992, par. 3, http://www.gutenberg.org/wiki/Gutenberg:The_History_and_Philosophy_of_Project_Gutenberg_by_Michael_Hart (accessed October 30, 2012).

56. B. Evangelista, "Brewster Kahle's Internet Archive," *SF Gate*, October 15, 2012, para. 25, http://www.sfgate.com/news/article/Brewster-Kahle-s-Internet-Archive-3946898.php (accessed October 30, 2012).

57. S. Johnson, "The Internet? We Built That," *New York Times Magazine*, September 23, 2012, par. 10, http://www.nytimes.com/2012/09/23/magazine/the-internet-we-built-that.html?pagewanted=all (accessed October 30, 2012).

58. R. Mackey, "Video That Set off Tunisia's Uprising," *The New York Times*, January 22, 2011, http://thelede.blogs.nytimes.com/2011/01/22/video-that-triggered-tunisias-uprising/ (accessed October 30, 2012).

59. I. Black, "Tunisia's Protests Spark Suicide in Algeria and Fears Through Arab World," *Guardian*, February 16, 2011, http://www.guardian.co.uk/world/2011/jan/16/tunisia-protests-suicide-algeria-arab (accessed October 30, 2012).

60. S. A. Kouddous, "Uprising in Egypt," *Democracy Now!* February 5, 2011, video, http://www.democracynow.org/2011/2/5/uprising_in_egypt_a_two_hour (accessed October 30, 2012).

61. A. Kamat, "Uprising in Egypt," *Democracy Now!* February 5, 2011, video, http://www.democracynow.org/2011/2/5/uprising_in_egypt_a_two_hour (accessed October 30, 2012).

62. "Asmaa Mafouz and the YouTube Video That Helped Spark the Egyptian Uprising," *Democracy Now!* February 8, 2011, video, http://www.democracynow.org/2011/2/8/asmaa_mahfouz_the_youtube_video_that (accessed October 30, 2012).

63. D. Kirkpatrick, "Mubarek Orders Crackdown with Revolt Sweeping Egypt," *The New York Times*, January 29, 2011, par. 9, http://www.nytimes.com/2011/01/29/world/middleeast/29unrest.html?r=2&hp (accessed October 30, 2012).

64. @twittercomms, Twitter, January 25, 2011, https://twitter.com/twittercomms/status/30063209247408128 (accessed October 30, 2012).

65. D. Kirkpatrick, "Mubarek Orders Crackdown with Revolt Sweeping Egypt," *The New York Times*, January 29, 2011, par. 9, http://www.nytimes.com/2011/01/29/world/middleeast/29unrest.html?r=2&hp (accessed October 30, 2012).

66. W. Saletan, "Springtime for Twitter: Is the Internet Driving the Revolutions of the Arab Spring?" *Slate.com*, July 18, 2011, par. 9, http://www.slate.com/articles/technology/future_tense/2011/07/springtime_for_twitter.html (accessed October 30, 2012).

67. Social Capital Blog, "Twitter, Facebook, and YouTube's Role in Arab Spring (Middle East Uprisings)," January 26, 2011, updated October 12, 2012,

par. 14, http://socialcapital.wordpress.com/2011/01/26/twitter-facebook-and-youtubes-role-in-tunisia-uprising/ (accessed October 30, 2012).

68. S. Reardon, "Was the Arab Spring Really a Facebook Revolution?" *New Scientist*, April 13, 2012, par. 1, http://www.newscientist.com/article/mg21428596.400-was-the-arab-spring-really-a-facebook-revolution.html (accessed October 30, 2012).

69. Ibid.

70. C. Crittenden, "The Internet and Global Justice 2.0," *The Berkeley Blog*, July 23, 2012, http://blogs.berkeley.edu/2012/07/23/the-internet-and-global-justice-2-0/ (accessed October 30, 2012).

71. M. White, "What Is Clicktivism? Rejecting Clicktivism" http://www.clicktivism.org/, par. 2 (accessed October 28, 2012).

72. M. Hardt and A. Negri, *Multitude: War and Democracy in the Age of Empire* (New York: Penguin, 2004), 262–263.

73. M. Lim qtd. in W. Saletan, "Springtime for Twitter: Is the Internet Driving the Revolutions of the Arab Spring?" *Slate.com*, July 18, 2011, par. 5, http://www.slate.com/articles/technology/future_tense/2011/07/springtime_for_twitter.html (accessed October 30, 2012).

74. Z. Fox, "How the Arab World Uses Facebook and Twitter," *Mashable*, June 8, 2012, par. 1, http://mashable.com/2012/06/08/arab-world-facebook-twitter/ (accessed October 30, 2012).

75. S. Kassim, "Twitter Revolution: How the Arab Spring Was Helped by Social Media," *PolicyMic*, July 2012, par. 3, http://www.policymic.com/articles/10642/twitter-revolution-how-the-arab-spring-was-helped-by-social-media (accessed October 30, 2012).

76. W. Ghonim, *Revolution 2.0: The Power of the People is Greater Than the People in Power* (Boston, MA: Houghton-Mifflin-Harcourt, 2012), 143.

77. J. Beinin, "The Rise of Egypt's Workers," *Carnegie Paper*, June 2012, par. 3, http://carnegieendowment.org/2012/06/28/rise-of-egypt-s-workers/coh8 (accessed October 30, 2012).

78. AFL-CIO, "Arab-Spring-Leaders-Receive-2012-George-Meany-Lane-Kirkland-Human-Rights-Award," para. 2, http://www.aflcio.org/Press-Room/Press-Releases/Arab-Spring-Leaders-Receive-2012-George-Meany-Lane-Kirkland-Human-Rights-Award (accessed October 30, 2012).

79. P. Walker, "Amnesty International Hails WikiLeaks and *Guardian* as Arab Spring 'Catalysts,'" *Guardian*, May 12, 2011, par. 10, http://www.guardian.co.uk/world/2011/may/13/amnesty-international-wikileaks-arab-spring (accessed October 30, 2012).

80. R. Mackey, "A Green Revolution for Iran?" *The New York Times*, June 10, 2009, http://thelede.blogs.nytimes.com/2009/06/10/a-green-revolution-for-iran/ (accessed October 30, 2012).

81. B. Berkowitz, "From a Single Hashtag, a Protest Circled the World," *Reuters*, October 17, 2011, par. 12, http://www.reuters.com/article/2011/10/17/us-wallstreet-protests-social-idUSTRE79G6E420111017 (accessed October 30, 2012).

82. "Twitter Gives Occupy Wall Street Tweets to New York Judge," AP, September 14, 2012, http://www.huffingtonpost.com/2012/09/14/twitter-occupy-wall-street-tweets_n_1882973.html (accessed October 30, 2012).

83. P. Barron and K. Ryan, "OccuPoetry, Issue 2," *OccuPoetry: Poets Supporting Economic Justice*, July 23, 2012, http://occupypoetry.org/occupoetry-issue-2/ (accessed October 30, 2012).

84. See http://www.2600.com/.

85. US Department of Hopeland Security, *Hackers on Planet Earth* catalog, 2012, p. 12.

86. A. O'Leary, "Worries over Defense Department Money for 'Hackerspaces,'" *The New York Times*, October 5, 2012, par. 8, http://www.nytimes.com/2012/10/06/us/worries-over-defense-dept-money-for-hackerspaces.html?r=1&ref=technology &pagewanted=print (accessed October 30, 2012).

87. D. Coldewey, "German Parliament Bans Laptops; Members Bring a Typewriter," *NBC News Digital*, September 29, 2012, par. 3, http://www.nbcnews.com/technology/gadgetbox/german-parliament-bans-laptops-members-bring-typewriter-6124837 (accessed October 30, 2012).

88. B. Barber, *Strong Democracy: Participatory Politics for a New Age* (Berkeley, CA: University of California Press, 1984).

89. B. Evangelista, "Social Networks Growing as News Sources," *SF Gate*, September 27, 2012, http://www.sfgate.com/technology/article/Social-networks-growing-as-news-sources-3900341.php (accessed October 30, 2012).

90. M. Hindman, *The Myth of Digital Democracy* (Princeton, NJ: Princeton University Press, 2009), 128.

91. "Project Censored Story Index: 1995 Flyer—Stories of 1995," Project Censored, http://ringnebula.com/project-censored/1976–1992/1995/proj_cens_1995.htm (accessed October 28, 2012).

92. V., "New Top-Level Domain Names and the Future of the Internet," *New York City Marketing*, August 1, 2012, http://themainstreetanalyst.com/2012/08/01/new-top-level-domain-names-and-the-future-of-the-internet-infographic/ (accessed October 30, 2012).

93. R. Somerset-Ward, *Quality Time? The Report of the Twentieth-Century Fund Task Force on Public Television* (New York: Twentieth Century Fund Press, 1993), 40.

94. See "What People Watch, What People Buy," *Nielson*, http://www.nielsen.com/content/corporate/us/en.html (accessed October 28, 2012).

95. See "Arbitron Radio Ratings and Media Research," *Arbitron*, http://www.arbitron.com/home/content.stm (accessed October 28, 2012).

96. See "AdClickMedia: Pay-per-Click Ad Network," *AdClickMedia*, http://adclickmedia.com/ (accessed October 28, 2012).

97. C. Mitchell and S. Meinrath, "Want to Pay Less and Get More? How Communities Are Banding Together to Create High-Speed, Affordable Broadband Access," *Slate.com*, August 1, 2012, par. 6, http://www.slate.com/articles/technology/future_tense/2012/08/community_based_projects_make_broadband_internet_access_high_speed_and_affordable_.html (accessed October 30, 2012).

Index

For Product Safety Concerns and Information please contact our EU
representative GPSR@taylorandfrancis.com
Taylor & Francis Verlag GmbH, Kaufingerstraße 24, 80331 München, Germany

www.ingramcontent.com/pod-product-compliance
Lightning Source LLC
Chambersburg PA
CBHW071421050326
40689CB00010B/1926

* 9 7 8 1 1 3 8 8 8 8 2 5 8 *